Intellectual Property Law in the European Community: A Country-by-Country Review

Published by:

WORLD TRADE Executive

International Business Advisories™
Law • Finance • Tax • Energy

Publisher, Gary A. Brown
WorldTrade Executive, Inc.

Executive Editor, Angus Phang
Assistant Editor, Alexandra Wenderoth
Willoughby & Partners (U.K.)
in association with Rouse & Co. International

Associate Editor
Kathryn Rosenblum
WorldTrade Executive, Inc.

The editors wish to thank Jill Clarke at Rouse & Co. International for her outstanding contribution to the task of compiling this report.

It is important to apply information in this report in the context of any recent amendments to the laws and regulations they discuss. This report is intended to provide guidance in understanding legal and practical conditions, but it does not constitute legal advice.

©2004 WorldTrade Executive, Inc. The contributing firms also assert their copyright in the chapters they have contributed as well as all related rights including the right to be identified as author of the work. All rights reserved. No part of this publication may be reproduced or transmitted in any form or by any means, electronic or mechanical, including photocopying, without permission from WorldTrade Executive, Inc. and the author.

Order inquiries should be addressed to the publisher:
WorldTrade Executive, Inc. P.O. Box 761, Concord, MA 01742, USA.
Phone (978) 287-0301; Fax: (978) 287-0302; E-Mail: info@wtexec.com
Website: http://www.wtexec.com
ISBN 1-893323-53-6

Contributors

AUSTRIA
Barbara Kuchar
Gassauer-Fleissner Rechtsanwälte
Wallnerstraße 4
1010 Vienna
Tel: +43 1 205 206 100
Email: b.kuchar@gassauer.at

BELGIUM
Florence Verhoestraete
NautaDutilh
Chaussee de la Hulpe 177/6
1170 Brussels
Tel: +32 2673 0007
Email: florence.verhoestraete@nautadutilh.com

CYPRUS
Dr. Eleni Chrysostomides
Dr. K. Chrysostomides and Co.
1 Lambousa St., P.O. Box 22119
Nicosia 1095
Tel: +357 22 777 000
Email: kchrysos@logos.cy.net

CZECH REPUBLIC
Barbora Rovenska
Horák & Chvosta
Melnicka 13
Prague 5
Tel: +420 257 313 434
Email: brovenska@hcak.cz

DENMARK
Martin Sick Nielsen
Zacco Hofman Bang
Hans Bekkevolds Alle 7
Hellerup, Copenhagen DK 2900
Tel: +45 394 88000
Email: msn@zacco.dk

ESTONIA
Viive Näslund
Lepik Ja Luhaäär AS
Dunkri Street 7
Tallinn 10123
Tel: +372 6 306 460
Email: naslund@abll.ee

FINLAND
Leif Nordin
Berggren Oy Ab
P.O. Box 16
FIN-00101 Helsinki
Tel: +358 9693 70221
Email: leif.nordin@berggren.fi

FRANCE
Jacques Beaumont
Deprez Dian Guignot
21 rue Clement-Marot
Paris 75008
Tel: +33 1 5323 8000
Email: beaumont@ddg.fr

GERMANY
Christian Meister
Jones Day
Prinzregentenstr 11
80538 Munich
Tel: +49 89 20 60 42 200
Email: cwmeister@jonesday.com

GREECE
Nicolas K. Dontas
Dontas Law Offices
14 Voulis Street
Athens 10563
Tel: +302 10 32 35 525
Email: dontas@compulink.gr

HUNGARY
Dr. Tamás Éless
Réti Szegheo & Partners
Zugligeti ut 41
H-1121 Budapest
Tel: +361 275 2785
Email: tamas.eless@ars.hu

IRELAND
Cliff Kennedy
MacLachlan & Donaldson
47 Merrion Square
Dublin 2
Tel: +353 1 676 3465
Email: kennedyc@maclachlan.ie

ITALY
Donatella Prandin
Bugnion S.p.A.
Viale Lancetti 17
Milan 20158
Tel: +39 02 693 031
Email: prandin@bugnion.it

Contributors

LATVIA
Gatis Merzvinskis
Petersona Patents
2 Ausekla Street, Suite 2
LV-1010 Riga
Tel: +371 732 4695
Email: gatis@petpat.lv

LITHUANIA
Marius Jakulis Jason
AAA Legal Services
Rudninku 18/2
2001 Vilnius
Tel: +370 5 212 0482
Email: info@aaa.lt

LUXEMBOURG
Sophie Wagner-Charles
Arendt & Medernach
14 rue Erasme
BP 39, L-2010
Tel: +352 40 7878 253
Eamil: sophie.wagner@arendt-medernach.lu

MALTA
Austin Sammut
Gando Sammut
35-36 Archbishop Street
Valletta VLT 08
Tel: +356 2124 7109
Email: asammut@gandosammut.com

NETHERLANDS
Albert Ploeger
Houthoff Buruma
Postbus 75505
Amsterdam 1070AM
Tel: +312 0577 2361
Email: aploeger@houthoff.nl

POLAND
Jaroslaw Kulikowska
Kulikowska & Kulikowski
00-975 Warszawa 12
P.O. Box 130
Warsaw
Tel: +482 2621 5202
Email: ahordejuk@kulikowska.pl
(Agnieszka Hordejuck)

PORTUGAL
Isabel Franco
J. E. Dias Costa, Lda.
Rua do Salitre, 195
1269-063 Lisbon
Tel: +351 2138 41300
Email: diascosta@jediascosta.pt

SLOVAK REPUBLIC
Marta Majlingová
Majlingová Fajnorová Bachratá
PO Box 56
850 07 Bratislava 57
Tel: +421 2 6381 1420
Email: patmark@internet.sk

SLOVENIA
Tomaz Ilesic
Colja, Rojs & Partnerji
Tivolska 48
1000 Ljubljana
Tel: +386 1 23 06 750
Email: ilesic@colja-rojs-partnerji.si

SPAIN
Kaisor Basar
Ecija Abogados
Jorge Juan, 9
28001 Madrid
Tel: +34 91 781 61 60
Email: kbasar@ecija.com

SWEDEN
Bengt Eliasson
Zacco Sweden AB
Sveavagen 170
Box 23 101
104 35 Stockholm
Tel: +46 8 729 9500
Email: bengt@zacco.se

UNITED KINGDOM
Angus Phang
Willoughby & Partners
in association with Rouse & Co. International
Pembroke House, Pembroke Street
Oxford OX1 1BP
Tel: +44 1 865 791990
Email: aphang@iprights.com

Table of Contents

Chapter 1: Introduction
By Angus Phang and Alexandra Wenderoth (Willoughby & Partners in association with Rouse & Co. International) .... page 7

Chapter 2: Basic Intellectual Property Concepts
By Angus Phang and Alexandra Wenderoth (Willoughby & Partners in association with Rouse & Co. International) .... page 13

Chapter 3: The European Community
By Angus Phang and Alexandra Wenderoth (Willoughby & Partners in association with Rouse & Co. International) .... page 21

Chapter 4: Austria
By Barbara Kuchar (Gassauer-Fleissner Rechtsanwälte) .... page 39

Chapter 5: Belgium
By Florence Verhoestraete (NautaDutilh) .... page 57

Chapter 6: Cyprus
By Dr. Eleni Chrysostomides (Dr. K. Chrysostomides & Co.) .... page 77

Chapter 7: Czech Republic
By Barbora Rovenska (Horák & Chvosta) .... page 85

Chapter 8: Denmark
By Martin Sick Nielsen (Zacco Hofman Bang) .... page 97

Chapter 9: Estonia
By Pirkko-Liis Harkmaa and Viive Näslund (Lepik Ja Luhaäär AS) .... page 109

Chapter 10: Finland
By Leif Nordin (Berggren Oy Ab) .... page 125

Chapter 11: France
By Jacques Beaumont, Isabelle Brenn and Frédéric Dumont (Deprez Dian Guignot) .... page 131

Chapter 12: Germany
By Alexandra Barth, Christian Meister, Mathias Ricker, Richard Schloetter and Monica Warchhold (Jones Day) .... page 173

Chapter 13: Greece
By Nicolas K. Dontas (Dontas Law Offices) .... page 187

Chapter 14: Hungary
By Dr. Tamás Éless and Dr. Zita Tamás (Réti Szegheo & Partners) .... page 195

Chapter 15: Ireland
By Cliff Kennedy (Maclachlan & Donaldson) .... page 207

Chapter 16: Italy
By Donatella Prandin (Bugnion S.p.A.) .... page 219

Chapter 17: Latvia
By Gatis Merzvinskis (Petersona Patents) .... page 231

Chapter 18: Lithuania
By Marius Jakulis Jason (AAA Legal Services) .... page 239

Chapter 19: Luxembourg
By Sophie Wagner-Charles and Heloise Bock (Arendt & Medernach) .... page 249

Chapter 20: Malta
By Austin Sammut (Gando Sammut) .... page 267

Chapter 21: The Netherlands
By Albert P. Ploeger (Houthoff Buruma) .... page 279

Chapter 22: Poland
By Monika Chimiak (Kulikowska & Kulikowski) .... page 297

Chapter 23: Portugal
By Isabel Franco (J.E. Dias Costa, Lda.) .... page 311

Chapter 24: Slovak Republic
*By Marta Majlingová, Mária Fajnorová, Magdaléna Bachratá, Katarína Sepeláková, Baya Nikolajová
and Katarína Majlingová (Majlingová Fajnorová Bachratá)* .... page 317

Chapter 25: Slovenia
By Tomaz Ilesic (Colja, Rojs & Partnerji) .... page 339

Chapter 26: Spain
By Hugo Ecija Bernal and Emilio Hurtado (Ecija Abogados) .... page 347

Chapter 27: Sweden
By Bengt Eliasson and Helena Östblom (Zacco Sweden AB) .... page 373

Chapter 28: United Kingdom
*By Angus Phang and Alexandra Wenderoth (Willoughby & Partners
in association with Rouse & Co. International)* .... page 385

Chapter 29: Afterword
*By Angus Phang and Alexandra Wenderoth (Willoughby & Partners
in association with Rouse & Co. International)* .... page 403

Chapter 1: Introduction

Introduction

Introduction

By Angus Phang and Alexandra Wenderoth
(Willoughby & Partners in association with Rouse & Co. International)

Businesses that are highly profitable or grow quickly tend to have something in common. Nearly always this is an idea, process or talent—so-called intellectual property which is unique and which gives their businesses the technological and competitive edge. However, those intellectual property assets are of little value if they are not legally protected. In other words, it does not matter how brilliant or groundbreaking the idea is, if competitors can easily replicate it. This report provides a brief guide to the various intellectual property rights the law protects.

Topics Considered

Intellectual property is a wide and diverse area and it would be impossible within the parameters of this report to treat in detail all the rights which arise in this field. This report covers patents, designs, copyright, trade marks and confidential information. However, the report does not deal with the topographies of semiconductor products, utility models, data protection legislation or rights in plant varieties.

Glossary

The following expressions used in this report have the meanings below.

Community	The European Community
EC or EU	The European Community (also known as the European Union)
EC Treaty	The Treaty Establishing the European Community (Treaty of Rome) 1957
European Community	The community of Member States which is introduced in chapter 3. Also known as the European Union
European Union	See 'European Community'
OHIM	Office for the Harmonisation of the Internal Market
Member State	Member state of the European Community. The 15 current Member States and the 10 future Member States which will join on May 1, 2004 are set out in chapter 3.
WIPO	World Intellectual Property Organisation

Angus Phang and Alexandra Wenderoth are attorneys at Willoughby & Partners in London and Oxford, the local legal practice of Rouse & Co. International. Rouse & Co. is an intellectual property consultancy, providing a full range of IP services. Mr. Phang specialises in all aspects of IP and IT law, with a particular emphasis on brand protection, technology transfer, e-commerce law and data protection, and intellectual asset management. Ms. Wenderoth specialises in non-contentious IP, including IPR registration and portfolio management, and licensing and commercial agreements.

Introduction

TYPES OF INTELLECTUAL PROPERTY RIGHTS

The following table shows some of the more common intellectual property rights the law provides for the protection of business assets. These may vary from country to country.

Parts of your business	Example	Patents	Registered Designs	Unregistered Designs	Trade Marks	Copyright	Database Right	Confidential Information
Company Logo	HARLEY-DAVIDSON MOTOR	✗	✓	✗	✓	✓	✗	✗
Company Name	BP p.l.c.	✗	✗	✗	✓	✗	✗	✗
Brand Name	NIKE®	✗	✗	✗	✓	✗	✗	✗
Invention		✓	sometimes	sometimes	✗	✗	✗	✓

© 2004 WorldTrade Executive, Inc. and Willoughby & Partners in association with Rouse & Co. International

Introduction

Shape or appearance of products / packaging	✗	✓		sometimes	sometimes	✗	✗
Business Information	✗	✗	✗		✓	✓	✓
Databases	✗	✗	✗		✓	✓	✓
Trade Secrets	✗	✗	✗		✓	✓	✓

© Willoughby & Partners 2003

The HARLEY-DAVIDSON MOTORCYCLES Bar & Shield Logo is a registered trademark of H-D Michigan Inc, and is used with permission.
BP p.l.c. is a company name, and BP® is a registered trade mark of BP p.l.c. in the United Kingdom, the United States and many other countries, used with permission.
NIKE is a registered trade mark of Nike International Limited, used with permission.

Intellectual Property Law in the European Community

Chapter 2:
Basic Intellectual Property Concepts

Basic Intellectual Property Concepts

By Angus Phang and Alexandra Wenderoth
(Willoughby & Partners in association with Rouse & Co. International)

Patents

What is a patent?

A patent is a monopoly right conferred by law in respect of inventions. This gives the owner or patentee the exclusive right for the life of the patent (usually 20 years) to prevent others from exploiting the invention. However, details of the invention must be published. This means that, although the grant of a patent rewards the inventors, technological development is promoted generally as details of the patent are made public and may be exploited by anyone after the patent has expired.

What can be patented?

Only certain types of innovation can be patented, namely inventions (including products, methods and processes) which are new, contain an inventive step, (i.e. are non-obvious) and which could have an industrial application. 'Non obvious' in this context means the invention must not be obvious to a person skilled in the art (the technology to which the patent relates). It is not possible to patent what is known already. Thus in relation to technology developed for an ordinary hi-fi system, it would be difficult to argue that applying this same technology to a car hi-fi system was a new application and therefore deserving of a separate patent.

Competition

Applicants or patentees considering granting licenses of their rights in applications, patents and/or know-how should be aware of national and European

---

Angus Phang and Alexandra Wenderoth are attorneys at Willougby & Partners in London and Oxford, the local legal practice of Rouse & Co. International. Rouse & Co. is an intellectual property consultancy, providing a full range of IP services. Mr. Phang specialises in all aspects of IP and IT law, with a particular emphasis on brand protection, technology transfer, e-commerce law and data protection, and intellectual asset management. Ms. Wenderoth specialises in non-contentious IP, including IPR registration and portfolio management, brand and product clearance, licensing and commercial agreements, IPR acquisition & due diligence.

Basic Intellectual Property Concepts

Community competition laws which may have an impact on the provisions and restrictions which can be included in the license agreement. European Community competition law is dealt with further in chapter 3.

Geographical scope of protection

A patent granted under the national laws of one country will only afford protection throughout that country. Most countries in the world grant their own patents and so the owner of the rights of a patentable invention may decide to make a series of applications in each country in which the invention is to be exploited; for example in the European Community (the members of which are part of a European central filing system), the United States and Japan. If protection in a large number of countries is required, then filing applications in each country can be a financial and administrative burden. Systems for streamlining this process are dealt with in chapter 3.

Related intellectual property rights

It should not be forgotten that associated with a patentable invention there may well be know-how and/or other non-patentable technology, which a party may wish to keep confidential, and which can be exploited alongside the patent. Often such non-registered rights can continue to be exploited after the associated patent has expired (see for example Confidential Information in the United Kingdom chapter).

Designs

Registered Designs
What are registered designs?

Registered designs are monopoly rights which protect the appearance of the whole, or part, of a product resulting from the features (in particular, the lines, contours, colours, shape, texture or materials) of the product or its ornamentation. A registered design does not protect any features which are dictated only by the technical function of the product. Nor does a registered design protect any features which are for parts of complex products not visible in normal use.

What do registered design rights protect?

Registered design protection may be sought for any product which is an industrial or handicraft item other than a computer program. Packaging, get-up, graphic symbols, typographic type-faces, and parts intended to be assembled into a complex product are all examples of articles which have been specified as being able to be protected by a registered design.

Basic Intellectual Property Concepts

What are the criteria for registration?

In order to qualify for registration a design must:

- be new (it must not be the same as any design which has already been made available to the public);
- have individual character (the overall impression produced by the design must differ from the overall impression produced by a design which is already available to the public); and
- not have been disclosed to the public before the filing date except under obligations of confidentiality. Users of the registered design system benefit from a 12 month grace period, whereby disclosures to the public in a 12 month period prior to the date of application will not preclude the design from registration. However, if a third party independently creates a design which creates the same overall impression within the grace period, this will preclude registration of the design.

Scope

The rights afforded by the registered design protect the appearance of the product, and not the article to which it is applied. Therefore a registered design for a get-up used on a soft drink container will provide the proprietor with rights to bring infringement proceedings against a third party who, without authorisation, applies the design to, say, a clock-radio.

Unregistered Design Right

There is also a European Community right of unregistered design, and some countries have their own national unregistered design rights. These are discussed more fully in the relevant chapters.

Trade Marks

What is a trade mark?

A trade mark is a sign or indication applied by a trader to his or her goods or services which enables consumers to differentiate the goods and services of that trader from those of another. In other words, a trade mark is a badge, indicating origin and quality.

Unregistered trade marks may also be protected under national laws relating to passing off and unfair competition. The laws relating to unregistered trade marks are dealt with under each country chapter.

What can be registered?

Any mark can be registered if it can be represented graphically and is capable of distinguishing goods or services of one trader from those of another. This is a

Basic Intellectual Property Concepts

very broad definition and today all kinds of things can be registered, including:
- words ('Kodak')
- slogans ('I can't believe it's not butter')
- designs (the Guinness harp)
- letters (IBM)
- numerals (501 jeans)
- three-dimensional shapes of goods and their packaging (Coca-Cola bottle; Toblerone)
- smells ('fresh cut grass')
- colour (turquoise for Heinz baked beans)

Classes of goods and services

The trade marks register is divided into 45 internationally recognized classes representing different categories of commercial activity. Applicants can apply for a mark in more than one class in the same application. For example, a mark for a computer software product will often be registered in class 9 (computer software) and class 16 (program documentation and manuals.) These are known as multi-class applications and the number of classes for which registration is sought will determine the cost of securing registration.

Trade marks must be suitable for protection abroad

Where a business has overseas operations and is intending to market a new product or service, care should be taken to select a mark which can be registered and is free for use in each country where the goods or services are to be traded. It is not uncommon for a trade mark to be registrable in some countries and not in others (due to the existence of prior conflicting registrations in some countries and national differences in criteria.) It is therefore worth instructing foreign trade mark agents to conduct searches in the countries of interest before deciding on a mark for a new product.

It should also be borne in mind that some marks which are successful trade marks in one country can be unacceptable in others. For example, PSHITT soft drinks are not sold in the United Kingdom, for obvious reasons, despite their popularity on the continent.

Copyright

What is copyright?

The law of copyright protects a wide variety of original works including those embodied in books, photographs, paintings, sculpture, music, records, films, software and broadcasts.

Basic Intellectual Property Concepts

Do I need to register copyright?

Unlike designs, patents and trade marks, copyright is generally not required to be registered in order to exist; it comes into existence immediately upon creation of the work. In some countries, registration is still useful for enforcing copyright.

What rights does copyright give?

Copyright does not protect against independent development of the same ideas, but principally acts as a bar to the actual copying or adaptation of another's work. It can also however prevent unauthorised use of copies of a work.

Database right

Rights similar but distinct from copyright also apply to protect databases, where there has been a substantial investment of financial, human or technical resources in obtaining, verifying or presenting the material constituting the database.

Confidential Information

It is also possible to protect confidential information, such as trade secrets and know-how. Whilst the preceding discussion has focused on intellectual property rights which are conceptually relatively easy to grasp–patents, designs, trade marks and copyright–the area of confidential information, the particular expertise which gives a business a competitive advantage, is far more difficult to conceptualise. The laws relating to the protection of confidential information are dealt with separately in the relevant country chapters.

Chapter 3:
The European Community

The European Community

By Angus Phang and Alexandra Wenderoth
(Willoughby & Partners in association with Rouse & Co. International)

Introduction

European Community law is the main source of development in intellectual property laws in the Member States. Given its importance, it will be considered in some detail detail below.

Overview of the European Community

History of the European Community

The European Community was set up after World War II under the *Treaty Establishing the European Community (Treaty of Rome) 1957 (the 'EC Treaty')*. It was founded to enhance political, economic and social co-operation. The process was launched on 9 May 1950 when France officially proposed to create 'the first concrete foundation of a European federation'. Six countries (Belgium, Germany, France, Italy, Luxembourg and the Netherlands) acceded initially. Today, the EC has 15 Member States and is preparing for 10 more eastern and southern European countries to join on 1 May 2004.

The principal objectives of the EC are to establish European citizenship; ensure freedom, security and justice; promote economic and social progress; and assert Europe's role in the world.

The Member States

As at February 2004, the 15 Member States of the European Community are:

Austria	Germany	Netherlands
Belgium	Greece	Portugal
Denmark	Ireland	Spain
Finland	Italy	Sweden
France	Luxembourg	United Kingdom

Angus Phang and Alexandra Wenderoth are attorneys at Willougby & Partners in London and Oxford, the local legal practice of Rouse & Co. International. Rouse & Co. is an intellectual property consultancy, providing a full range of IP services. Mr. Phang specialises in all aspects of IP and IT law, with a particular emphasis on brand protection, technology transfer, e-commerce law and data protection, and intellectual asset management. Ms. Wenderoth specialises in non-contentious IP, including IPR registration and portfolio management, brand and product clearance, licensing and commercial agreements, IPR acquisition & due diligence.

European Community

However, in 2004, the European Community will welcome the following 10 new Member States:

Cyprus	Latvia	Poland
Czech Republic	Lithuania	Slovak Republic
Estonia	Malta	Slovenia
Hungary		

Structure of the European Community

The Member States delegate sovereignty (or 'rule') to common institutions representing the interests of the EC as a whole on questions of joint interest. All decisions and procedures are derived from the basic treaties ratified by the Member States. The EC is not a new State replacing existing ones. It is based on the principles of democracy.

The EC is run by five institutions, each playing a specific role:
- The European Commission (the executive body and driving force);
- The European Parliament (elected by the peoples of the Member States);
- The Council of the EC (made up of the governments of the Member States);
- The Court of Justice (charged with ensuring compliance with the law);
- The Court of Auditors (management of the EC budget).

Sources of European Community law

The Council and the Parliament have power to make 'regulations' having general application and to issue 'directives' to the Member States. A regulation is automatically directly applicable in all Member States and may be enforced by individuals against the Member States in their national courts. A directive binds the Member States but gives them a choice as to the implementation (and occasionally the extent) of the directive. It may be relied on against a State which has failed to enact legislation to implement it adequately. The European Commission also makes decisions, recommendations and opinions.

Treaties and agreements

Many Member States are also members of or signatories to the key international treaties and agreements relating to intellectual property. These treaties and agreements attempt to narrow the gaps in the way intellectual property rights are protected around the world, and to bring them under common international rules. When there are trade disputes over intellectual property rights, in some cases dispute settlement systems are now available.

All current and future Member States are members of the World Trade Organisation

(WTO). All WTO agreements (including the Agreement on Trade-Related Aspects of Intellectual Property Rights or 'TRIPS Agreement') apply to all WTO members upon joining.

All current and future Member States are also signatories to the Paris Convention for the Protection of Industrial Property 1883 and the Berne Convention for the Protection of Literary and Artistic Works 1971.

Table A on the following page shows the current and future Member States which are members of or signatories to other important treaties and agreements relating to intellectual property.

Intellectual property in the European Community: The Free Movement of Goods

The EC Treaty aims to create a single market with free movement of goods and services throughout the EC.

Harmonisation

To achieve this, the EC has embarked upon a gradual process of harmonizing the laws relating to intellectual property in the EC. This has been a slow and piecemeal approach given the significant differences between the laws regulating intellectual property in each Member State. However, the EC has achieved the implementation of a number of Community-wide laws, based on the efficiencies of having Community-wide rights or the need to remove differences of national law which may restrict the free flow of goods within the internal market. The Community-wide laws which have been achieved to date are discussed later in this chapter.

Competition

Also in furtherance of the ideal of the free movement of goods, the Treaty contains rules to guard against the distortion or restriction of competition within the EC. These rules have a significant impact on the exploitation of intellectual property rights, which by their nature create monopolies and confer market power. These issues are also discussed in further detail below.

Unfair competition

Intellectual property also impinges on non-statutory liability, such as breach of confidence or the tort of 'passing off' in the United Kingdom, or the European doctrine of 'unfair competition'. Adjudicating on the disparities between such laws in various Member States, where they give rise to conflicts which affect the ideal of the free movement of goods, requires a balancing of factors.

European Community

Table A

The following table shows key treaties, agreements and conventions to which the current and future Member States are party at the time of writing.

	WIPO Copyright Treaty (Geneva, 1996)	Patent Cooperation Treaty (Washington 1970)	Protocol Relating to the Madrid Agreement Concerning the International Registration of Marks (1989)	Trademark Law Treaty (Geneva, 1994)	European Patent Convention (1973)
Austria		√	√		√
Belgium		√	√		√
Cyprus		√		√	√
Czech Rep.	√	√	√	√	√
Denmark		√	√	√	√
Estonia		√	√	√	√
Finland		√	√		√
France		√	√		√
Germany		√	√		√
Greece		√	√		√
Hungary	√	√	√	√	√
Ireland		√	√	√	√
Italy		√	√		√
Latvia	√	√	√	√	
Lithuania	√	√	√	√	
Luxembourg		√	√		√
Malta					
Netherlands		√	√	√	√
Poland		√	√		
Portugal		√	√		√
Slovak Rep.	√	√	√	√	√
Slovenia	√	√	√	√	√
Spain		√	√	√	√
Sweden		√	√		√
United Kingdom	√	√	√	√	

The approach of the European Court of Justice has been to accept inconsistencies in the national laws of member states which impede the free movement of goods in the EC to the extent that:

- the laws can be justified as being necessary to satisfy compulsory requirements relating to fairness in commercial practices and consumer protection;
- the laws apply equally to both local and imported products; and
- there are no overriding common rules relating to the production and marketing of the goods or services in question.

Patents

In an attempt to consolidate the processes of applying for patents across numerous countries, two systems for filing international applications have been adopted by Member States of the European Community. In addition, the European Community has proposed the introduction of a 'Community Patent'. These three systems are dealt with below.

The Patent Co-operation Treaty

The first system came into being as a result of The Patent Co-operation Treaty (PCT) of 1978. Under this system an applicant may file a single international application for patent protection in a number of designated countries. When choosing which countries to designate, the applicant may only select from those countries which are party to the Treaty (these include most major countries, including the United States of America and the 15 existing and 10 future Member States, with the exception of Malta). The application is forwarded from the applicant's local Patent Office to the WIPO in Geneva which acts as a central processing office. WIPO conducts a simple preliminary examination to ensure all formalities have been complied with, after which the application is passed on to the patent offices of each of the designated countries for examination and ultimately registration. The substantial cost and work in obtaining a patent occurs after the PCT application has been passed to local patent offices. This is referred to as the 'national phase'. The result of a successful PCT application will be a series of national patents being granted from the single application.

European Patent Convention

The second system is governed by the European Patent Convention (EPC) under which an applicant may file a single application either to a local Patent Office or to the European Patent Office in Munich. A PCT application may also designate the European Patent Office (EPO) so the EPO will process the application as part of the national phase. The application designates those European coun-

European Community

tries which are signatories to the Convention in which the applicant is seeking patent cover. The 15 existing and 10 future Member States are all signatories of the European Patent Convention, except Latvia, Lithuania, Malta and Poland. Latvia and Lithuania are expected to join shortly.

A successful application will eventually result in the grant of a European Patent. Once granted, this becomes a bundle of national patent rights as the subsequent administration and enforcement of the patent is handled in the courts and patent offices of the individual countries concerned.

Applicants should bear in mind that a European Patent may be opposed by any third party up to nine months after grant.

Community patent

The European Council has now agreed to introduce a 'Community Patent', which will offer an alternative route for patent protection in Europe alongside the existing national and consolidated systems outlined above. The Community Patent will give inventors the option of obtaining, with just one application, a single patent legally valid throughout the European Community at a fraction of the existing cost of doing so. Currently, patent protection in just eight European countries costs some €50,000 (approximately USD 53,500). The Community Patent across 25 Member States would cost around €25,000 (approximately USD 27,000).

A Community patent would be valid across all Member States. However, if the patent were successfully challenged, it would also fall across all Member States.

The European Council has reached agreement on a "common political approach" concerning the proposed Community Patent, including the main outlines of the system of jurisdiction, the language regimes, costs, the role of national patent offices and the distribution of fees.

However, unanimous agreement as to the details is proving very difficult, particularly with regard to the establishment of a centralised community court at first as well as at second instance. At present, negotiations continue.

It is difficult to predict when all the various measures will be completed and Community patent applications can begin, but it seems unlikely to be before 2007/2008. The current European and national patent systems will continue in force.

Supplementary protection certificates

Supplementary protection certificates have been introduced under EC Regulations to extend the life of patents, once expired, for up to 5 years for medicinal products and plant protection products. The rationale for the certificates is to compensate patent owners for the time lost while carrying out testing to obtain the requisite marketing approval, which can be an extensive period of time for these types of products. These Regulations have direct effect in all Member States.

Biotechnology

The patenting of biological inventions is governed by the provisions of Articles 1 to 11 of European Directive (98/44/EC) on the legal protection of biotechnological inventions. The purpose of the Directive is to harmonise the national patent laws of the Member States of the European Community which concern biotechnological inventions.

The Directive covers issues such as the patentability of certain biotechnological inventions and the scope of patent protection, and makes it clear that certain processes and things cannot be patented on the grounds that their commercial exploitation would be contrary to morality. For example, processes for cloning human beings, modifying the germ line genetic identity of human beings and commercial or industrial uses of human embryos will not be afforded patent protection. Patents will also not be obtainable for genetic modifications of animals which are likely to cause them suffering unless there is substantial medical benefit to man or animal. In addition, certain farming practices are exempt from patent infringement.

Under the Directive, human genes as they exist in the cells in our bodies cannot be patented as they are not of themselves an invention. However, inventions concerning isolated genes which are identical to those found in nature may obtain patent rights, provided they meet the general conditions for patentability outlined in chapter 2.

Design Rights

The European Community has implemented several measures to harmonize design law across the Community. In particular, it has introduced the Registered Community Design Right ('Community Design') and the Unregistered Community Design Right.[1] It has also directed Member States to harmonize their national laws relating to registered designs.[2]

Registered Design Right
Community designs

As of 1 April 2003, design owners can seek registered design protection throughout the European Community with a Community Design. Community Designs are registered at OHIM in Alicante Spain.

European Community

Duration

Community Designs remain in force for a maximum of 25 years (provided renewal fees are paid every 5 years).

Territory

At present the Community Design offers design owners protection in the 15 Member States of the European Community. However, in 2004 when the European Community extends to the 10 new Member States, existing Community applications and registrations at the date of expansion will automatically extend to the new Member States with an effective date in these countries of the expansion date (May 1, 2004).

Ownership

The rights to first ownership of the Community Design rest with the designer, or if the design was created in the course of employment, with the employer. There is no provision for the design to be owned by a person who commissioned the design: a formal assignment from the designer to the commissioner would be required.

Qualification

Any 'legal person' can hold a Community Design. Therefore there is no territorial restriction on a United States corporation or resident owning a Community Design.

Exploitation

Community Designs can only be licenced or assigned as a whole and for the whole area of the European Community.

The Community Design offers a viable alternative form of protection to 3D and logo trademarks.

Unregistered Design Right

Community unregistered design right took effect on March 5, 2001.[3] This right is not a monopoly right but only a right to prevent copying. It arises throughout the European Community automatically upon publication of the design.

Community unregistered design right provides a three year term of protection for a design from the date on which it was first made available to the public within the European Community. Novelty and individual character are also assessed as at this date.

European Community

Trade Marks and Geographical Indications

This chapter deals with registered trade marks which apply throughout the European Community, and geographical indications of agricultural products and foodstuffs.

Community trade marks

The Community Trade Mark came into being on 1 January 1996 and is regulated by a series of European Community Regulations. A Community Trade Mark is a single trade mark registration which gives the proprietor uniform protection throughout the European Community. Application is made to OHIM in Alicante.

OHIM will only reject a mark based on absolute grounds (for example the mark is not sufficiently distinctive), not on relative grounds: OHIM will not refuse to register a mark simply because it is similar or identical to a prior mark. OHIM will conduct a search of the Community Trade Mark Registry and the national registries in 12 of the 15 current Member States, but the results it obtains are for the applicant's information only and OHIM will not prevent an application from proceeding to advertisement based on the results. It is up to the owner of the prior mark to file an opposition to prevent registration. It is good practice to set up watch services which notify trade mark owners of new applications which may infringe their mark.

The Community Trade Mark currently offers owners protection in the 15 Member States of the European Community. As with Community Designs, Community Trade Marks will also benefit from the enlargement of the European Community in 2004 when the 10 new Member States join.

In the event of a Community Trade Mark application being refused, it is possible to convert such an application into a series of national applications which will benefit from the date of the Community Trade Mark application. Such applications will then proceed under the registration processes of the relevant country's national procedures and laws.

How long does community trade mark registration last?

Community trade marks can be registered for an initial period of 10 years and are renewable thereafter in perpetuity for further 10 year periods upon payment of renewal fees. Registrations can however be revoked, in full or in part, upon application by a third party if the mark has not been used after registration for a continuous period of 5 years.

Advantages of community trade marks

There has been considerable debate since its introduction as to the benefit of such a unitary registration as distinct from separate national registrations. In ad-

European Community

dition to the maintenance and cost benefits, however, a further advantage must be that use of Community Trade Mark in any one Member State constitutes use for the purposes of the whole European Community.

The Madrid Protocol

The Madrid Agreement of 1891 afforded nationals of contracting states the opportunity of making a single application to register a trade mark in all or some of the other contracting states. In 1989, a new international system, the Madrid Protocol, was adopted. This retains the basic elements of its older sibling (simplicity, efficiency and economy) but introduces certain new features. All existing and incoming Member States have ratified the Protocol other than Cyprus and Malta.

An application is filed at the national trade mark office of the home application or registration in the contracting state, which then forwards the application to the International Bureau of WIPO in Geneva. WIPO then forwards the application to the various national offices.

Geographical indications and designations of origin

Traditionally it has been difficult to register indications of origin of products as trade marks. The courts are reluctant to grant property in a geographical name which other traders may legitimately wish to use in the course of trade.

However, under the law of passing off, the courts have seen fit in certain cases to restrain traders from misleading use of certain geographic indicators, such as 'Champagne', 'Swiss' cheese and chocolate, 'Parma' ham and 'Scotch' whiskey.

There is now a European Community system for the protection through registration of geographic indications and designations of origin in relation to agricultural products and foodstuffs.[4] Registration confers on the registrant the right to restrain other parties from using the geographical indication on 'comparable' goods. Registration can be sought by following the application procedure in the Member State in which the geographical location is situated.

Wine products and spirit beverages are covered by separate legislation.

Copyright and Related Rights

Harmonisation

The European Commission is in the throes of harmonizing copyright law throughout the European Community. This is a gradual and technical process due to the difficulties in harmonizing both civil and common law systems of copyright protection. Outlined below are some of the key implications of European Community directives which affect copyright law throughout the European Community.

Term of protection

The European Community has harmonized the term of protection as follows:[5]

- The copyright in artistic works and original photographs will run for the life of the author and for 70 years after his or her death.
- The copyright in an audio-visual work will run for 70 years after the death of the last of the following persons to survive: the principal director, the author of the screenplay, the author of the dialogue and the composer of music specifically created for use in the audio visual work.
- The rights of producers of the first fixation of an audio-visual work will expire 50 years after the fixation is made or 50 years after the first lawful publication or communication to the public, whichever is earlier.
- Where the country of origin (as defined under the Berne Convention) is a third country and the author is not a European Community national, copyright will expire on the date of expiry of protection granted in the country of origin provided it is less than 70 years after the death of the author.

This applies to all works and subject matter which were protected under copyright law, in at least one Member State, on 1 July 1995. The Community does not regulate the duration of protection of moral rights, which are regulated by individual Member States.

Computer programs

The European Commission has also issued a Directive harmonizing aspects of the protection of software.[6] The concept of 'originality' with respect to computer programs under the Directive is defined as 'the author's own intellectual creation'. The Directive also contains provisions allowing back up copies and decompilation of programs in certain circumstances.

Database right

Database right arises from a European Commission Directive[7] protecting databases where there has been a substantial investment of financial, human or technical resources in obtaining, verifying or presenting the material constituting the database. What is being protected is the investment that the compiler has made in physically gathering, checking or presenting the information.

Database right arises automatically, and gives the owner the right to prevent anyone from extracting or re-utilising all or a substantial part of the contents of the database. The duration of database right is 15 years from creation. This term recommences upon any substantial modification being made to the database which results in a 'new' database being created.

European Community

New economic rights

Under the most recent Directive relating to copyright,[8] all copyright owners are to be granted the following economic rights:

- The right to prohibit direct or indirect, temporary or permanent reproduction by any means and in any form, in whole or in part;
- The right to authorize or prohibit any communication to the public of their works, by wire or wireless means, including the making available to the public of their works in such a way that members of the public may access them from a place and at a time individually chosen by them;
- The right to authorize or prohibit any form of distribution to the public by sale or otherwise, in respect of the original or copies of their works. The distribution right is not exhausted within the European Community in respect of the original or copies of the work, except where the first sale of other transfer of ownership on the European Community of that object is made by the right holder or with his or her consent.

The Directive also deals with the legal protection of technical measures used by rights owners to protect their works against unauthorized reproduction and other infringement. Member States must protect against devices and services which illegally circumvent these measures.

The Directive also sets out a regime of compulsory and permitted defences to allegations of copyright infringement.

Other directives

The European Commission has also issued directives dealing with rental and lending rights,[9] and with satellite broadcasting and cable retransmission.[10]

Protection abroad

International conventions, such as the Berne Convention, greatly assist in the recognition of the rights of foreign copyright owners, but, subject to the above, the rights pertaining to copyright still vary considerably from country to country. Copyright is a complex area of the law, and expert advice on the rights involved should always be taken if investments are being made in reliance on such rights.

Competition

Dealing with intellectual property

All forms of intellectual property can be licensed or sold. Indeed, many research and development companies operate by developing a product up to prototype stage and then selling on all the intellectual property rights associated with that product to a trade buyer, usually a major company in the field. Licensing can present an excellent opportunity for a company that lacks production facilities to see a major launch of its product by the licensee - often in more than one market at once. In addition, the licensee can bring valuable marketing expertise and resources to the launch of the product.

However, because by their very nature license agreements frequently contain certain restrictions, such as exclusivity within a territory, such agreements must be considered in the light of competition laws.

Competition throughout the European Community

The EC Treaty renders unenforceable terms included in agreements which have as their object or effect the prevention, restriction or distortion of competition within the European Community and which may affect trade between the Member States of the European Community. Such terms are automatically void and the European Commission can impose fines for infringement.

However, the Commission has the power to exempt agreements under the Treaty, and to reduce the need for individual applications for exemption. The Commission can issue block exemptions which exempt whole categories of agreements. Apart from patents and know how, the Commission has issued block exemptions for agreements such as exclusive purchasing and distribution agreements, research and development and franchise agreements.

Provisions to avoid in licenses of intellectual property, to ensure that they will not fall foul of the EC Treaty, include the following:

- resale price maintenance
- absolute bans on exporting outside the European Economic Area (which currently comprises the Member States plus Norway, Iceland and Liechtenstein). However, export restrictions may be individually exempted provided only active selling (that is, soliciting custom) is banned, so that the licensee is permitted to take unsolicited orders from outside the EEA
- restrictions on maximum quantities to be supplied.

The EC Treaty also prohibits companies which are dominant in their particular market from abusing that dominant position by engaging in anti-competitive practices.

Parallel importation and exhaustion of rights

The free movement of goods principle under the EC Treaty (discussed earlier in this chapter) requires that goods which are placed on the market in one Member State can be freely exported by third parties and sold in other Member States. This is known as parallel importation. The owner of any trade marks, copyright or designs in such goods may only enforce those trade marks, copyright or design

European Community

rights in the Member State into which the goods are being parallel imported in certain limited circumstances. The owner's rights to oppose import on the grounds of infringement is said to be 'exhausted'.

Conclusion

This chapter has introduced the European Community and outlined its history, structure and policies. It has also summarised the laws relating to intellectual property which regulate the European Community as a whole, providing a précis of the areas of patents, designs, trade marks, copyright and competition to the extent that they are consistent across the European Community.

The following chapters are country by country reviews of the laws governing the protection and exploitation of intellectual property in each Member State to the extent that they differ from the position outlined above.

Footnotes
[1] Council Regulation (EC) No. 6 2002 of December 12 2001 on Community Designs.
[2] EC Directive 98/71/EC of the European Parliament and of the Council of October 13, 1998 on the legal protection of designs (L289//28 – October 28, 1998).
[3] Council Regulation (EC) No. 6 2002 of December 12 2001 on Community Designs.
[4] Regulation [1992] 208/92 on the Protection of Geographical Indications and Designations of Origin for Agricultural Products and Foodstuffs.
[5] Council Directive harmonizing the term of protection (October 29, 1993; 93/98/EEC).
[6] Council Directive on the legal protection of computer programs (May 14, 1991: 91/250/EEC.)
[7] Directive of the European Parliament and of the Council 96/9/EC on the legal protection of databases
[8] Directive 2001/29/EC of the European Parliament and of the Council of May 22, 2001 on the harmonisation of certain aspects of copyright and related rights in the information society.
[9] Council Directive 92/100/EEC on rental right and lending right and on certain rights related to copyright in the field of intellectual property.
[10] Council Directive 93/83/EEC on the co-ordination of certain rules concerning copyright and rights related to copyright applicable to satellite broadcasting and cable retransmission.

European Community

Chapter 4:
Austria

Austria

By Barbara Kuchar
(Gassauer-Fleissner Rechtsanwälte)

Introduction

Major issues affecting intellectual property

The protection of intellectual property in Austria is, in large part, already harmonised with the EU Legislation. Patent and design rights may be enforced at special court senates competent to hear patent and design infringement matters (part of the Commercial Court in Vienna), at which cases are heard by a panel of judges, including a patent attorney. Trademark and copyright cases are heard before the general commercial courts by single judges. Intellectual property rights may also be enforced under criminal law.

Treaties and conventions

Austria is, *inter alia*, a party to the following multinational conventions protecting intellectual property rights:

- Agreement on Trade-Related Aspects of Intellectual Property Rights (TRIPs) of April 15, 1994;
- Berne Convention for the Protection of Literary and Artistic Works, Paris Act of July 24, 1971;
- Budapest Treaty on the International Recognition of the Deposit of Micro organisms for the Purposes of Patent Procedure of April 28, 1977;
- Convention Establishing the World Intellectual Property Organization of July 14, 1967;
- Convention for the Protection of Producers of Phonograms Against Unauthorized Duplication of Their Phonograms of October 29, 1971;
- Convention on the Grant of European Patents of 5 October 1973;
- Convention Relating to the Distribution of Programme-Carrying Signals Transmitted by Satellite of May 21, 1974;
- Locarno Agreement Establishing an International Classification for Industrial Designs Signed at Locarno on October 8, 1968;

Barbara Kuchar is a partner wtih Gassauer-Fleissner Rechtsanwälte in Vienna. Ms. Kuchar works primarily in the fields of intellectual property law and unfair competition law, including trade libel. She publishes frequently on IP subjects. Gassauer-Fleissner Rechtsanwälte specializes in commercial law matters. The firm has one of the biggest IP departments in Austria.

Austria

- Madrid Agreement Concerning the International Registration of Marks of April 14, 1891 (Stockholm version);
- Nice Agreement Concerning the International Classification of Goods and Services for the Purposes of the Registration of Marks of June 15, 1957 (Geneva version);
- Paris Convention for the Protection of Industrial Property of March 20, 1883 (Stockholm version);
- Protocol of June 28, 1989 Relating to the Madrid Agreement Concerning the International Registration of Marks;
- Patent Cooperation Treaty (PCT) of June 19, 1970;
- Rome Convention for the Protection of Performers, Producers of Phonograms and Broadcasting Organisations of October 26, 1961;
- Strasbourg Agreement Concerning the International Patent Classification of March 24, 1971;
- Treaty on the International Registration of Audiovisual Works of 1989 – application suspended;
- Universal Copyright Convention of July 24, 1971;
- WIPO Copyright Treaty of December 20, 1996 – not yet in force;
- WIPO Performances and Phonograms Treaty of December 20, 1996 – not yet in force.

Additionally, Austria has entered into numerous bilateral agreements on the protection of intellectual property rights.

Current legislative climate

In the course of 2003, the Copyright Act and the Model Protection Act were amended due to necessary implementations of EC Regulations. A significant amendment to the Patent Act was called off due to new elections in the previous year. Currently under discussion is a small amendment dealing with the implementation of the Biotechnology EC Directive.

Patents

What is the application procedure?

Patent Law in Austria is regulated by the Patent Act 1970 as amended. A patent application in Austria has to be filed before the Austrian Patent Office and has to include a description of the invention, as well as an abstract and claims, accompanied by necessary drawings and examples. The Patent Office scrutinises novelty, inventiveness and industrial applicability, which are conditions that are necessary to obtain a patent.

Austria

Discoveries, scientific theories, mathematical methods, aesthetic forms, schemes, rules, procedures concerning mental activities, games or commercial activities, and computer programs are not regarded as inventions by law. Some inventions may not be protected by patent rights, such as surgical or therapeutic procedures for treatment of persons (products for the use in such treatments, however, may be patented) and all kinds of plants and animals as well as biological methods for the breeding of animals and the cultivation of plants. Methods concerning micro-organisms, however, may be patented.

An invention is considered new, if it is not part of the state of the art. The state of the art represents everything available to the public before the date of the application. The content of older patent applications which are published after the application will also defeat novelty. The Austrian Patent Office offers an official prior art research for a fee. An invention may be patented if it does not obviously (to an expert) result from the state of the art. Upon request, the Austrian Patent Office will render its opinion about whether an invention is sufficiently inventive to be registered as a patent, taking into account the prior art. This non-binding opinion enables potential applicants to evaluate the likelihood of obtaining a patent before filing a costly application.

Within four months after publication of the patent application, an opposition may be filed. The opposition is decided in writing, without an oral hearing. An appeal can be filed within two months of the decision.

A patented invention is protected from the moment of the registration, i.e. four months after publication of the invention if no opposition was filed and up to 4-5 years in the event an opposition was filed.

How long does a patent last?

Austrian patents are granted for a period of 20 years from the date of filing, as long as the annual fees are paid.

To whom can a patent be granted?

A patent is granted either to the inventor(s) or under certain conditions to the employer against adequate consideration to be paid to the employee for an employee's invention.

Once granted, is the patent safe?

A granted patent may be revoked if the invention was not new, inventive or patentable at all or if the patent does not reveal the invention with the accuracy and completeness necessary for an expert to put it into effect. A patent may be revoked if the invention or its main contents belong to another person. A patent may also be revoked if the patent owner has not sufficiently granted compulsory licenses for the use of a patent.

Austria

What rights does a patent give?

A patent entitles the owner to exclusively produce, trade and use the invention and to prevent others from exploiting and infringing his patent.

Exploitation

Patents may be exploited either by the owner of the patent or by an exclusive or single licensee. Under certain statutory requirements, compulsory licenses can be imposed on the owner of the patent.

Infringement

The owner of a patent can pursue an infringer with a cease and desist claim, a claim for removal, for rendering of accounts, appropriate consideration, damages, restitution of the profit and a claim for publication of the judgment.

Streamlined Court procedure

The only competent court for all Austrian patent infringements is the Commercial Court of Vienna, which has specialized panels of two professional judges and one lay-judge.

The main proceedings of a patent litigation have to be stayed if the defendant claims that the plaintiff's patent is null, unless it is obvious that the patent is not null. Therefore, plaintiffs generally combine the complaint with an application for a provisional injunction. As regards the provisional injunction, the judge, with the help of the patent attorney in the court senate, has to deal with the nullity claim of the defendant and may not stay the proceedings until the Patent Office has decided upon the defendant's claim.

Intentional patent infringement can constitute a criminal offense.

Designs

Registered Designs

Legislation

Registered designs in Austria are regulated by the Model Protection Act 1990, as last amended on August 26, 2003 in order to implement the EC Directive 98/71/EC on the legal protection of designs, as mentioned in the European Community chapter.

What is a design?

The definition of a design is the same for both Austria and the European Community forms of protection (as defined in the Council Regulation (EC) No. 6 of December 12, 2001 on Community Designs), as mentioned in the European Community chapter.

Austria

Registered designs and trade marks compared

Trademarks can also be registered for three-dimensional designs. In contrast to design protection, no industrial applicability or novelty are required to register a trademark, but the trademark must be distinctive. A sign which consists exclusively of the shape which results from the nature of the good itself is excluded from trademark protection. A design right does not subsist in features of appearance of a product which aresolely dictated by their technical function. Trademark protection also has the advantage of an unlimited period of protection of the trademark provided the renewal fees are paid.

Registration process

A design application has to be filed with the Austrian Patent Office in writing. The application must either comprise a sample of the design itself, together with pictures for publication and registration, or simply a picture of the design together with a list of goods the design shall be protected for. A description of the design may be attached for explanatory purposes. The Model Protection Act enables applicants to file all documents in a sealed envelope and to register a model without disclosing it for a maximum period of 18 months.

The Patent Office does not conduct a novelty search but carries out a simple examination of the legal requirements. Like European Community designs, an Austrian design model may remain in force for a maximum of 25 years, provided that the renewal fees are paid.

Prior disclosure - 12 month grace period

Austrian designs benefit from the 12-month grace period in respect of prior disclosure provided by the EC-Directive 98/71/EC on the legal protection of designs.

Commissioned designs

If the design of an employee falls within the scope of business of the employer and the development of the design was part of the duties of the employer, or if otherwise outside of an employment agreement a design was created upon commission, the employer or commissioner or its successor in title are entitled to claim ownership in the design if nothing different was agreed between the parties.

Infringement

The owner of an Austrian design model has the exclusive right to use it and to prevent any third party from using it which includes in particular the making, offering, putting on the market, importing, exporting or using of a product in

Austria

which the design is incorporated or to which it is applied, or stocking such a product for those purposes. The scope of protection of a design is extended to any design which does not trigger a different overall impression by the informed user.

The design owner has a cease and desist claim, a claim for removal, rendering of accounts, appropriate consideration, damages, restitution of the profit and publication of the court's decision. The cease and desist order may be made subject to a provisional infringement.

Intentional infringement of designs may also be pursued under criminal law upon application of the owner of the design.

Nullification

Nullification of a design may be requested by anyone (a) if the design does not fulfill the legal requirements or (b) if the design infringes the prohibition of double protection or (c) if the design is not a design within the legal definition. Upon application of the legitimate person, nullification of a design can be requested if the owner of the design is not the legitimate owner.

Unregistered Design Right

The Austrian Model Protection Act 1990 does not provide any national unregistered design model but grants protection for unregistered EU-design models as mentioned in the European Community chapter.

Trade Marks

Registered trade marks

Trade marks in Austria are regulated under the Trade Marks Act 1970 as amended by the Trade Marks Right amending law 1999.

Registrability and the application procedure

The types of marks that can be registered in Austria are all signs capable of being represented graphically, provided that they are capable of distinguishing the goods or services of one undertaking from those of other undertakings.

The Austrian Trade Marks Registry will examine each application and, broadly, will reject any mark which:

- is not sufficiently distinctive or is merely descriptive, unless the sign has acquired distinctiveness in Austria through use before filing the application; or
- which is contrary to public policy or likely to deceive or confuse the public.

Although the Austrian Trade Marks Registry does search the Register for any conflicting prior registrations, the Austrian Trade Marks Registry does not object to the application if any of the earlier marks are too similar. An older identical or similar trade mark does not prevent registration. The owners of the older conflicting trade marks are not notified about a new trade mark application. The monitoring of the Registry is incumbent on the trade mark owners. There is no opportunity by third parties to oppose a trade mark application.

If the mark is registered it will be advertised in the Journal "Markenanzeiger". Thereafter, third parties have the opportunity to file a cancellation application against the trade mark.

A straightforward trade mark application should be registered within 3-6 months of filing.

How long does trade mark registration last?

Trade marks can currently be registered for an initial period of 10 years and are renewable thereafter in perpetuity for further 10 year periods upon payment of renewal fees. Trade marks can be cancelled, in full or in part, if the mark has not been used for a continuous period of 5 years (it is up to a third party to bring such a challenge).

What rights does it give?

A registered trade mark gives the registrant exclusive rights to prevent others in the course of business from:

1. using a sign identical to the registrant's trade mark in relation to identical goods or services;
2. using a sign identical or similar to the registrant's trade mark in relation to identical or similar goods or services and there exists a likelihood of confusion on the part of the public including the likelihood of association between the sign and the trade mark;
3. using a sign identical or similar to the registrant's trade mark in relation to dissimilar goods or services if the trade mark has a reputation in Austria and its use takes unfair advantage of or is detrimental to the distinctive character or the repute of the trade mark. The reputation of the trade mark in Austria has to be given on the application date of the younger trade mark at the latest, if applicable also on the priority date of the younger trade mark.

Advantages of registration

A registered trade mark firstly enjoys the advantage of a clear priority date – all trade marks and signs which are identical or similar and registered or used later than this date can be pursued by the registrant of the trade mark. Secondly, during the first five years after registration, the registrant of the trade mark can

Austria

pursue infringements of the trade mark without the requirement of evidencing any kind of use of his trade mark. After that five year period, the registrant only has to demonstrate serious use of the trade mark: it is not necessary to have obtained a reputation of the trade mark in Austria.

Unregistered trade marks

Unregistered signs can also enjoy legal protection in Austria provided they are distinctive and have a reputation. The owner of such a sign basically can claim the cancellation of a younger identical trade mark registered for identical or similar goods and services and can pursue infringers of his reputable sign on the basis of the Unfair Competition Act. The owner of the unregistered sign has to prove that, as at the application date of the contested trade mark, the unregistered sign had been considered within the trade circles concerned as designation of his undertaking's goods or services. Such reputation usually is evidenced by opinion polls among the trade circles concerned. His claim will be unlikely to succeed if the contested sign, before its trade mark registration, has also been used for at least the same duration of time as the unregistered sign has been used by its owner.

In conclusion, a trade mark registration provides a huge advantage for pursuing infringers compared to an unregistered sign, in particular due to the much less costly evidence procedure.

Domain names and brand protection on the internet

Domain names in Austria are registered without examination of conflicting prior rights on the basis of first come first served.

Domain names are protected by law, provided the domain name is distinctive or has the character of a name. Infringements of a domain therefore can be pursued in the same way as the infringement of the denomination of a business or a name.

Domain–grabbing (i.e. 'cybersquatting') is considered the acquisition of a domain name in particular for the purpose of obstructing a competitor or exploiting a competitor's reputation. The use of a domain name by other technical means (i.e. as a metatag) can also be trade mark infringing or otherwise obstructing of a competitor's business or misleading and thus a breach of the Unfair Competition Act.

Copyright and Related Rights

What is copyright?

Copyright in Austria is regulated by the Copyright Act 1936 as last amended in 2003.

The law of copyright protects works which are original intellectual creations in the area of literature, music, fine arts and cinematography. Also computer programs are protected by the Copyright Act as explicitly being subsumed under "linguistic" works.

Do I need to register copyright?

It is not necessary or possible to register copyright in Austria. Therefore, proving ownership of copyright and date of creation can be difficult unless proper written records are kept. It is recommended to deposit the work in a sealed envelope with an attorney of law or a notary public – to evidence the date of creation the envelope should be sent by registered mail and kept unopened – in order to have evidence for the date of creation and ownership of the work in case the work is copied in an unauthorized manner.

Copyright notice

It is advisable to attach a copyright notice to the work, setting out the © symbol followed by the year of publication and the author's or owner's name. Although it is not essential in Austria to prove ownership, it can help in infringement proceedings, it may be needed to show copyright in certain foreign jurisdictions, and it can serve as a warning notice to others against copying.

What rights does copyright give?

Copyright generally only protects the expression of an idea and not the idea itself. Copyright does not protect against independent development of the same ideas, only against the actual copying of another's work. The moral and economic interests of the author of a work are protected by copyright.

The author has the exclusive right to commercially exploit his work, which mainly includes any kind of copying, distribution, broadcasting and performing of the work. The author also has the right to grant third parties exploitation rights or permits to use the work in the scope agreed between the parties. The author has the exclusive right to edit his work. As regards moral rights the author may claim authorship to the work, the author can determine if and to which extent the nomination of the author shall be attached to the work, and the author can object to any infringements of his above described rights.

The Copyright Act provides for certain statutory limitations of the copyright such as the free use of a work, for example for private purposes, in libraries and schools. These limitations are set out in much detail in the Copyright Act and were amended by the 2003 amendment implementing the European Directive on copyright on new economic rights into Austrian law.

Term

The term of copyright in Austria is in accordance with the European Community directive discussed in the European Community chapter.

Austria

What else does copyright protect?

The Copyright Act also regulates rights related to copyright which are granting protection and commercial rights to the work of performers, in particular regarding the fixations of the performance on films and phonograms, to photos, phonograms, broadcastings, and posthumous works, databases, letters, diaries and similar confidential notes, protection of images of human beings, news and titles of works (also of works of art and literature not falling under the scope of the Copyright Act) as well as the appearance of a work.

Status of latest European Community directive on copyright

The recent European Directive on copyright on new economic rights discussed in the European Community chapter[1] already was implemented into Austrian Copyright law, which amendment came into force on July 1, 2003.

Confidential Information

Confidential information, or trade secrets, are facts of commercial or technical nature related to a business known to a certain and limited number of people, which are inaccessible or difficult to access, and which further according to the intention of the authorized person shall be kept within the circle of the informed persons. And finally, the owner of the business must have an economic interest in the non-disclosure of these secrets.

Commercial secrets therefore are:
- Facts related to the business
- Which are not evident
- With the intention to keep them secret
- With the interest to keep them secret

The responsible persons therefore should mark trade secrets as secret in order to show their intention to keep this information actually secret.

Trade secrets and know-how compared

In Austria there exists no statutory definition of "know-how." According to Cartel Law, know-how must be secret, substantial and identified (EC Regulation 240/96). According to Austrian court practice of the Supreme Court, trade secrets are not identified and do not have to be substantial. Although trade secrets are IP rights, they cannot be licensed.

Protection of confidential information

The main way to protect confidential information is by contract. Usually a monetary damage of disclosure of a trade secret is difficult to determine, therefore it often is provided in contracts that in case of disclosure of a business secret a monetary fine independent from the actual damage has to be paid. If the amount is high enough, this serves also as a certain threat for the infringement of the contract.

There is no legal remedy for disclosure of a trade secret which was discovered independently by a third party and subsequently made known to the public.

Patents and designs

Contractual protection of confidential information is critical in the area of patents and designs, in particular to prevent third parties from claiming to having made the invention by themselves by registering such rights. Until the decision of such a dispute, which can take a considerable amount of time, the use of the patents or designs can be prevented by the prima facie legitimate owner.

Exploitation

As mentioned, trade secrets can be licensed as valuable know-how under certain statutory restrictions.

Employer/employee relationship

During the term of an employment contract, the duty of confidence of the employee is comprised by the duty of loyalty. A betrayal of business secrets by the employee gives the employer the right to immediate termination of the employment contract.

After the termination of the employment contract, the duty of loyalty is not given any more. There are, however, certain statutory provisions which impose a duty to keep commercial information secret even after termination of the employment contract, for example, obligations with regard to employee's inventions. It is not fully clear yet if a general duty to discreetness with regard to commercial secrets also exists after termination of the employment contract. The Austrian Supreme court, however, has ruled that a limited duty to loyalty and discreetness continue to have a certain effect thereafter, but its scope and kind are not decided yet.

Anti-compete clauses are permitted for a maximum of one year after termination of the employment agreement. The Austrian Supreme Court has ruled that the duration of a confidentiality agreement for a period of five years after termination of an employment agreement is not inadequate.

Remedies

Remedies for breach of confidence include cease and desist orders, account of profits, damages, and publication of the court's decision. The cease and desist order may be subject to a provisional injunction.

Austria

Competition

In Austria, competition law is governed by the regime outlined in the European Community chapter.

This regime co-exists with the national Cartel Act 1988 as amended, which prohibits anti-competitive agreements (agreements which have the effect of preventing, restricting or distorting competition) unless they have received an individual exemption from the Director General of Fair Trading, or are the subject of a block exemption which exempts whole categories of agreements.

Practical Tips for Protection of Intellectual Property

The reader is referred to the detailed and comprehensive advice given in the United Kingdom chapter.

Footnotes
[1] 2001/29/EC of the European Parliament and of the Council of May 22, 2001 on the harmonisation of certain aspects of copyright and related rights in the information society

Useful Industry Contacts

Österreichisches Patentamt
1200 Wien, Dresdner Straße 87
Tel.: 43/1/534 24 – 0/Fax: 43/1/534 24 110
e-mail: info@patent.bmvit.gv.at
http://www.patent.bmwa.gv.at

AKM Staatlich genehmigte Gesellschaft der Autoren, Komponisten und Musikverleger, reg. GenmbH
1030 Wien, Baumannstraße 8-10, PF 259
Tel.: 43/1/717140/Fax.: 43/1/71714107
e-mail: mailto:direktion@akm.co.at
homepage: http://www.akm.co.at

Austro Mechana Gesellschaft zur Verwaltung und Auswertung mechanisch musikalischer Urheberrechte, GesmbH
1030 Wien, Baumannstr 10
Tel.: 43/1/717 87-0; 712 35 75-0/Fax.: 43/1/712 71 36
e-mail: office@aume.at

Literar-Mechana
Wahrnehmungsgesellschaft für Urheberrechte GesmbH
1060 Wien, Linke Wienzeile 18
Tel.: 43/1/587 21 61-0/Fax.: 43/1/587 21 61-9
e-mail:literar.mechana@netway.at

Austria

LVG Staatlich genehmigte Literarische Verwertungsgesellschaft reg.Gen.m.b.H.
1060 Wien, Linke Wienzeile 18
Tel.: 43/1/587 21 61-0/Fax.: 43/1/587 21 61-9

VGR Verwertungsgesellschaft Rundfunk
1136 Wien, Würzburggasse 30
Tel.: 43/1/87878/2300/Fax.: 43/1/87878/2302
e-mail: bettina.cerny-veits@orf.at

LSG Wahrnehmung von Leistungsschutzrechten GesmbH
1010 Wien, Schreyvogelgasse 2/5
Tel.: 43/1/5356035/Fax.: 43/1/5355191
e-mail: ifpi@ifpi.at

ÖSTIG Österreichische Interpretengesellschaft
1060 Wien, Bienengasse 5
Tel.: 43/1/5877974/Fax.: 43/1/5872194

VAM Verwertungsgesellschaft für audiovisuelle Medien
1070 Wien, Neubaug 25/Stg 1
Tel.: 43/1/526 43 01...-0;/Fax.: 43/1/526 43 01-13

VDFS Verwertungsgesellschaft Dachverband Filmschaffender GenmbH
1010 Wien, Bösendorferstraße 4
Tel.: 43/1/504 76 20/Fax.: 43/1/504 79 71
e-mail: office@vdfs.at
http://www.vdfs.at

VBK Verwertungsgesellschaft bildender Künstler
1120 Wien, Tivolig 67/8
Tel.: 43/1/815 26 91/Fax.: 43/1/813 78 35
e-mail: vbk@nextra.at
http://www.vbk.at/vbk

VBT Verwertungsgesellschaft für Bild und Ton
1010 Wien, Schreyvogelgasse 2/5
Tel.: 43/1/5356035/Fax.: 43/1/5355191
e-mail: ifpi@ifpi.at

Musik Edition Gesellschaft zur Wahrnehmung von Rechten und Ansprüchen aus Musikeditionen reg. GenmbH
1010 Wien, Karlsplatz 6,1010 Wien
Tel.: ++43/1/33723 0/Fax.: ++43/1/33723500
e-mail: office@universaledition.com
http://www.uemusic.at

Österreichischer Patentinhaber- und Erfinderverband
1020 Wien, Wexstraße 19,23
Tel.: ++43/1/6038271
http://www.erfinderverband.at

Austria

Österreichische Computer Gesellschaft
1010 Wien, Wollzeile 1-3
Tel.: ++43/1/5120235/Fax: ++41/1/5120235-9
e-mail: ocg@ocg.at
http://www.ocg.at

Nic.at – Internet Verwaltungs- und Betriebsgesellschaft m.b.H.
5020 Salzburg, Jakob-Haringer Straße 8
Tel.: ++43/662/4669-0/Fax: ++43/662/4669 – 29
e-mail: service@nic.at
http://www.nic.at

Austria

Chapter 5:
Belgium

Belgium

By Florence Verhoestraete
(NautaDutilh)

Introduction

The value of a company may be partly or even largely determined by its intellectual property rights and their management. It is therefore crucial to be aware of the various intellectual property rights, their conditions for protection, the rules governing ownership and their scope of protection. Furthermore, a good housekeeping of the intellectual property rights portfolio is required.

Explicit reference is made to the chapters on the European Community and the United Kingdom.

The next sections provide some basic information under Belgian law on the two major categories of IP rights: registered rights (patents, registered designs, trademarks and applications for the same) and unregistered rights (copyright, database rights, unregistered design rights, know-how and trade secrets). They address the following key issues, with emphasis on differences, if any, with the law applicable in the United Kingdom, as set out in Chapter 28:

- applicable legislation;
- definition;
- conditions of protection;
- ownership;
- term of protection;
- scope of protection;
- useful addresses and/or links.

Patents

Applicable legislation

Patent Law in Belgium is regulated by the Patent Act of 28 March 1984 (BPA). One of the most important purposes of the BPA was to transpose into Belgian law the major international conventions, namely TRIPs and the European Patent Convention (EPC), which aim at harmonising patent law at the global and Community levels.

Florence Verhoestraete joined NautaDutilh in 1994. Her practice focuses on trade marks, patents, designs and unfair competition law. She is also a member of NautaDutilh's multidisciplinary Life Sciences group. NautaDutilh's Intellectual Property Group includes over thirty lawyers based in Amsterdam, Brussels and Rotterdam, making it the largest such group in the Benelux.

Belgium

It is worth mentioning that Belgium has not yet transposed Directive 98/44/EC of the European Parliament and of the Council of July 6, 1998 on the legal protection of biotechnological inventions, although it should have done so by July 30, 2000. Controversy continues to surround the transposition of this Directive. In the meantime, the European Commission has referred Belgium and seven other of the 15 European Union (EU) member states before the European Court of Justice for non implementation of legislation to allow the patenting of biotechnological inventions.

Definition

The definition of a patent set forth in the EPC was adopted in Article 2 of the BPA, where "patent for invention" is defined as the *"exclusive and temporary right[s] of exploitation of the invention which is new, which involves an inventive step and which is capable of industrial application"*.

Neither the BPA nor the EPC define the term "invention". Rather they only set forth the material requirements that the invention must meet in order to be patentable, i.e. novelty, use of an inventive step and capability of industrial application (Articles 5, 6 and 7 of the BPA).

The BPA contains what can be considered a negative definition of the term "invention". It refers expressly to items that do not constitute inventions, such as discoveries, scientific theories, mathematical methods, aesthetic creations, schemes, rules and methods (for performing mental acts, playing games or doing business), computer programs and presentations of information. Aside from these creations, the BPA also excludes from patent protection plant varieties protected by the Act of May 20, 1975. Some creations, not expressly excluded by the BPA, will nevertheless be denied patent protection if their exploitation is deemed contrary to public policy or morality, provided that the exploitation is not deemed contrary thereto merely because it is prohibited by national law. This provision was modified by the Law of January 28, 1997 in order to meet the requirements of TRIPs. The primary change is that the main publication of an invention deemed contrary to public policy or morality is no longer excluded from patent protection.

Conditions of protections

One of the basic requirements for patentability is novelty in that nothing can be patented if it is not new. Accordingly, particular care ought to be granted to the confidentiality of information. Publications or exhibitions during fairs, etc. may destroy the novelty of the invention, if they take place before the filing of the patent application.

The other main requirement is that the invention must be <u>inventive</u>. The question of what constitutes an inventive step has given rise to a great number of decisions and analysis. It is a difficult question which to some extent involves a subjective assessment.

The third requirement for patentability is that an invention should be <u>capable of industrial application</u>. Industrial application is defined broadly and includes the making or using of an invention in any kind of industry. The threshold tends to be low.

Finally, the person skilled in the art <u>must be able to carry out the invention</u> on the basis of the description, the drawings and the claims without any inventive activity of his or her own. This requirement applies to the whole patent rather than to any particular claim.

Ownership

The BPA contains a presumption of ownership in favour of the patent applicant. The applicant can be the inventor or a party to whom the inventor has assigned its rights. It is worth mentioning that the inventor is entitled to claim that he be mentioned in the patent as the inventor. He is likewise entitled to object thereto. This "paternity right", which is a moral right, cannot be assigned but may be waived by contract.

If a patent application is filed by a party who is not entitled to the invention (i.e. a party who filed the application either in bad faith or in breach of a legal or contractual obligation), the rightful owner may bring revocation proceedings and require that the patent be registered in its name.

The BPA does not contain any provision concerning the ownership of rights in inventions created by employees. Hence, parties are free to make contractual arrangements in this respect. Under Belgian law, a distinction is made between the following situations, in the absence of contractual arrangements:

- It is generally accepted that rights over inventions created in the course of and within the scope of an employment agreement belong to the employer. No compensation is due to the employee for such inventions; the compensation is actually deemed comprised in the employee's wages.
- The ownership of rights in inventions which are created with means and know-how belonging to the employer but outside the scope of the employee's employment agreement, is not clear-cut. Nor is the question of whether compensation is due for such inventions, assuming that the employer is considered as the owner.

Belgium

- Inventions created with the employee's own means and outside the scope of his/her employment agreement are deemed to belong to the employee.

Also important is the fact that any employee is under a legal obligation of secrecy, which means that he cannot disclose any inventions, trade secrets or confidential information he would have access to as a result of his/her employment.

Term of protection

In Belgium patents are granted, after a limited formal examination, for a period of 6 years or, after a search carried out by the Search Division of the European Patent Office, for a period of 20 years.

Scope of protection

A patent does not grant a positive right to do something but the means to prevent others from exploiting the patented subject matter. Pursuant to Article 27 of the BPA, the patent bestows on its holder the right to forbid any of the following acts by a third party:

- the fabrication, the offering, the marketing, the use, the importation or the possession for such purposes of the patented product or of any product that is directly obtained from the patented process;
- the use of the patented process or the offer to use such patented process, provided that the third party knew or, according to the circumstances, was deemed to know that the use of the patented process was forbidden without the prior consent of the patentee;
- the provision, or the offering to provide, on the Belgian territory to any unauthorised person means allowing the application of the invention in this territory regarding an essential element of the invention, provided that the third party knows that those means can be used for such application, or when the circumstances render that conclusion obvious.

This is an exhaustive enumeration, so all acts not listed under this provision should theoretically be allowed.

The BPA recognises some exceptions to the exclusive right of the patentee. These are listed under Article 28 of the BPA. The two main exceptions are acts performed privately and for non-commercial purposes and acts performed for experimental purposes relating to the subject matter of the patented invention. Article 28 of the BPA emphasizes, however, that all acts undertaken for commercial purposes are forbidden, even private acts. The case law clarifies that whenever a party examines, for example, a patented system so as to identify its advantages or to try to find possible improvements, use of the patented system is not restricted to mere experimentation and thus constitutes an infringement.

Another important exception to the rights of the patentee is set forth in Article 30 of the BPA, which recognises a prior user right. Any person who uses in good faith the subject matter of the patented invention on Belgian territory before the filing or priority date of the patent is entitled to use the invention. Belgian Supreme Court has held that it is sufficient that a prior user had a practical and complete knowledge of the invention so that s/he would have been able to commence exploitation of the invention at the time of the filing of the patent (or the priority date).

Finally it is worth mentioning that good or bad faith are generally irrelevant in establishing infringement. The fact that the infringing party did not know that the act was prohibited does not preclude a finding of liability vis-á-vis the owner of the patent.

Useful addresses and/or links
Intellectual Property Office
Patents division
Boulevard du Roi Albert II, 16
1000 Brussels
Tel. +32 2 206 41 11
Fax +32 2 206 57 50

Designs

Applicable legislation

Designs in Belgium are regulated under the Uniform Benelux Designs Act (BDA) of 25 October 1965. The BDA entered into force on 1 January 1975.

The BDA will soon be amended in order to implement Directive 98/71/EC of the European Parliament and of the Council of 13 October 1998 on the legal protection of designs.

Definition

The BDA provides that the new appearance of a product having a utilitarian function may be protected. Registered Benelux designs (like trademarks – see below) are unitary rights for the entire Benelux, i.e. the Netherlands, Belgium and Luxembourg.

The BDA makes a distinction between designs and models. A design is a two-dimensional form, e.g. the pattern or design on wallpaper, textiles, tiles, etc., which can be applied by printing or in another way, e.g. by means of embroidery. A model is a utilitarian article with a three-dimensional form. Some designs consist in a combination of two-dimensional and three-dimensional forms, e.g. a decorated vase.

Belgium

While the BDA is focused on registered designs, it provides that designs with a "clear artistic character" are protected under the BDA and under the national Copyright Acts, if the protection criteria of both acts are being met. In practice, this means that unregistered designs with a "clear artistic character" are protected by copyright. The "clear artistic character" criterion has been interpreted in exactly the same manner as the "originality" criterion for copyright protection. This requirement will moreover be dropped in the amended version of the BDA implementing the Designs Directive.

Conditions of protection

A design must be new and it may not be contrary to public order or morality in one of the Benelux countries. Upon implementation of the Designs Directive, there will be a supplementary requirement of "individual character."

The novelty requirement in the BDA is limited in time and territory. The BDA provides indeed that a design is not new if an identical or similar design has enjoyed de facto notoriety in the Benelux territory within the interested circles in a period of 50 years prior to the date of filing or if there are prior registrations for an identical or similar design in the Benelux Design Register. In the near future, the novelty requirement will be extended to all designs known within the Community by the interested circles.

Design protection is excluded when a design is contrary to public order or morality in one of the Benelux countries. In such case, the BDO may postpone or refuse to grant registration until a decision is rendered in this respect.

The BDA provides that an object without any utilitarian function is not susceptible to design protection. After the implementation of the Designs Directive, the "utilitarian function" will no longer be a requirement.

Designs which are solely dictated by their technical function are excluded from design protection.

Further exceptions (in particular for spare parts) will be introduced in the BDA in order to implement the Designs Directive.

Ownership

The holder of a design registration will be deemed the "owner" of the design and will benefit from the exclusive rights. It is worth mentioning that the designer is entitled to claim that s/he be mentioned in the patent as the designer.

If a design application is filed by a party who has no rights over the design, the rightful owner may bring revocation proceedings and require that the design be registered in its name.

Insofar as designs created by employees are concerned, the BDA provides that the employer is deemed to own the design rights if the designs were created in the course of and within the scope of the employee's employment agreement, irrespective of whether the design is registered or not, unless provided otherwise. This rule is also applicable to the copyright in registered designs. There is, however, no unanimous support in legal doctrine about who owns the copyright in unregistered designs with a "clear artistic character."

Term of protection

Under the BDA a design is protected for an initial period of five years, renewable for two successive terms of five years. Upon implementation of the Designs Directive, the number of renewals will be increased to four. As a matter of fact, the BDO already applies this rule.

Scope of protection

The BDA provides that the holder of a design may prohibit third parties from manufacturing, importing, selling, offering for sale, hiring, offering for hire, displaying, supplying or using, or keeping stock, for any of the aforementioned purposes, of products identical or similar in appearance with the registered design.

It is worth mentioning that the BDA provides for an exception of prior use. A right of personal possession shall be recognised in favour of any third party who, prior to the date of filing of a design application (or the date of priority), has manufactured an identical or similar design within the Benelux territory. Although the Designs Directive does not provide for this exception, it will be maintained after implementation.

Useful addresses and/or links
The Benelux Designs Office
Bordewijklaan 15
NL-2591 XR The Hague
Tel. : +31 70 349 11 11
Fax : +31 70 347 57 08
E-mail : info@bbtm-bbdm.org
Web site : www.bbtm-bbdm.org

Trademarks

Applicable legislation

Trademarks in Belgium are regulated under the Uniform Benelux Trademark Act (BTMA) of 19 March 1962. The BTMA entered into force on 1 January 1971 and has been amended by three subsequent Protocols.

Belgium

The BTMA will soon be amended again further to the adoption of a fourth Protocol. The amendments are expected to enter into force in the course of 2004.

Definition

Article 1 of the BTMA provides a non-exhaustive list of signs that are capable of distinguishing goods and/or services and that can be protected as trademarks. Put briefly, a trademark must be capable of being represented graphically and must have a distinctive character relating to the goods or services for which it is registered.

A Benelux trademark is a single title granting protection in the three Benelux countries. It is as such comparable to the community trademark which covers all Member States of the European Union, be it on a much smaller scale.

Conditions of protection

Trademarks must be deposited to confer rights to legal protection to their owners. Unlike in the United Kingdom, there are no unregistered trademark rights in Belgium (and the Benelux).

The exclusive right to a mark is acquired by the first deposit thereof with either the Benelux Trademark Office (BTMO) or the Office of the World Intellectual Property Organisation (WIPO) in Geneva. However, the fourth Protocol amending the BTMA provides, in line with the Trademarks Directive 89/104/EEC, that the rights to a trademark are only acquired by registration. This amendment is expected to come into force in the course of 2004.

The BTMO may refuse to proceed to registration if the trademark applied for:
- lacks distinctiveness;
- is contrary to the Public Order or Principles of Morality;
- is deceptive;
- infringes upon a geographical indication for wine or spirit;
- consists exclusively of a three-dimensional shape resulting from the nature of the goods themselves or which is necessary to obtain a technical result or which gives substantial value to the goods.

These are the so-called "absolute grounds of refusal."

The BTMA does currently not provide for "relative grounds of refusal" on the basis of earlier marks. An opposition procedure will, however, be introduced further to the adoption of the fourth Protocol amending the BTMA. It is expected that this will take place in 2004. Holders of earlier rights (including earlier trademarks, earlier trade names, earlier copyrights, etc.) are, however, entitled to challenge the registration and/or the use of the later trademark.

Belgium

Ownership

The holder of a trademark registration will be deemed the "owner" of the trademark and will benefit from the exclusive rights.

In the event of bad faith registration (for example, deposit of a principal's mark by a local agent), the application registration may be subject to cancellation action and/or a claim to recover the trademark.

Term of protection

A trademark is registered for a duration of ten years and can be renewed indefinitely for successive periods of ten years. The trademark must, however, be used normally without interruption during periods of five years or more. Otherwise, it may become vulnerable to a cancellation action for lapse of rights.

Scope of protection

The trademark confers some sort of monopoly right to the owner to oppose:

- any use in the course of trade made of the mark in relation to goods or services for which the mark is registered;
- any use in the course of trade made any sign that is identical or similar to the trademark in relation to goods or services which are identical or similar to those for which the mark is registered, provided there is a likelihood of confusion;
- any use in the course of trade of any sign that is identical or similar to the trademark in relation to goods or services that are not similar to those for which the mark is registered, where the mark enjoys a reputation and where use of that sign takes unfair advantage of, or is detrimental to, the distinctive character or the repute of the mark;
- any use in the course of trade of any sign that is identical or similar to the trademark, otherwise than for the purpose of distinguishing goods or services (e.g. use in comparative advertising where the mark is not used to distinguish the products of the user, use as a trade name, use as or in a slogan, etc.), where such use takes without due cause an unfair advantage of, or is detrimental to, the distinctive character or the reputation of the trademark.

The three first situations are also provided by the Community Trademark Regulation. The latter, however, is an additional remedy granted under Benelux Trademark law.

Belgium

Useful addresses and/or links
The Benelux Trademarks Office
Bordewijklaan 15
NL-2591 XR The Hague
Tel. : +31 70 349 11 11
Fax : +31 70 347 57 08
E-mail : info@bmb-bbm.org
Web site : www.bmb-bbm.org

Copyright

Applicable legislation

Copyright in Belgium is regulated by the Act of 30 June 1994 on copyright and neighbouring rights (BCA).

Reference must also be made to the Computer Programs Act of 30 June 1994, implementing Council Directive 91/250/EEC of 14 May 1991 on the legal protection of computer programs, and to the Database Act of 31 August 1998, implementing Directive 96/9/EC of the European Parliament and of the Council of 11 March 1996 on the legal protection of databases.

Definition

The BCA provides that "literary and artistic works" can be protected by copyright. The term "literary and artistic works" does not only cover "literary and artistic" works in the traditional sense (i.e. books, paintings and sculptures, musical compositions, photographic works, dramatic works, audio-visual works, etc.) but also functional and factual works, such as any element of corporate identity (logo, letterhead, etc.), pamphlets, catalogues, web sites and so on. It is a very broad concept including every production in the literary, scientific and artistic domain, regardless of the mode or form of expression.

It is important to know that copyright does not protect the underlying information or ideas contained in work. Copyright protects the particular expression in which this information or these ideas are imbedded.

Conditions of protection

Since Belgium is a member of the Bern Convention, copyright protection is not subject to any formalities.

Copyright originates by the mere creation of a work if the work meets the sole criterion for copyright protection, namely originality. The consequence thereof is that there is no system of copyright registration in Belgium and thus no method for verifying whether a certain work is protected by copyright. "Originality" is defined as one's "own intellectual creation" or one reflecting the "imprint of the personality" of its author. Originality must be distinguished from "novelty", because any adaptation of a pre-existing work can be protected by copyright as an original work, without prejudice to the copyright of the pre-existing work.

Ideas are not protected (nor are methods, or mere data). Copyright protection applies only to the expression of the work in its finished form.

Computer programs are considered to be (binary) literary works and can thus be protected by copyright, if deemed original.

Databases can be protected by copyright if they are original by reason of the selection or arrangement of their contents and/or by a *sui generis* right, if it is shown that there has been a substantial investment in either the obtaining, verification or presentation of the contents of the database.

Ownership

The natural person who creates the literary or artistic work is the author and thus the initial owner of the copyright. However, it is important to know that the BCA provides for a rebuttable presumption of ownership in favour of the person or company whose name or identification sign is mentioned on the work.

The economic aspects of copyright protection can be transferred, assigned or licensed by contract. When such contracts are concluded by the author, i.e. the initial owner of the copyright, they must comply with stringent mandatory rules provided for in the BCA. Under Belgian law, the assignment of copyright in a work is indeed always interpreted restrictively in favour of the author.

One of the consequences of this principle is that there is no automatic transfer of the employee's copyright to the employer. The copyright must be assigned on an individual basis and the assignment must be explicitly provided for in the employment agreement or in another agreement executed between the employee and the employer. The same rule applies to works made for hire.

The situation is different insofar as computer programs are concerned. The copyright in computer programs created by an employee in the execution of his or her duties or pursuant to instructions given by the employer are deemed to vest in the employer, unless otherwise provided by contract.

A similar rule applies to databases protected by copyright insofar as the database was created in a "non-cultural" industry. The *sui generis* right for databases is granted to the party who bears the investment risk.

Term of protection

In general, the duration of copyright protection is the life of the author plus seventy (70) years.

Belgium

Scope of protection

Copyright law offers dual protection, i.e., it protects both "moral" and "economic" rights. The term "moral rights" refers to the artistic interests of the author; the term "economic rights" obviously refers to the economic aspects of the copyright.

The moral rights of the author include the right of disclosure, the right to claim authorship and the right to the integrity of the work. These moral rights are inherent in the author and cannot be transferred or assigned to a third party.

The economic (and assignable) rights can be divided into two main groups: the right of reproduction (i.e. the exclusive right to carry out or authorise any reproduction, adaptation or distribution to the public by sale, rental or otherwise of the material) and the right of communication to the public (i.e. the exclusive right to carry out or to authorise any broadcasting, publication on the Internet, etc.). Whenever the act of a user can be considered as the reproduction or the communication to the public of a protected work, the prior authorisation of the author or copyright holder is required. However, copyright law provides for some exceptions to the prior authorisation requirement for the exploitation of economic rights, e.g. reproduction for private use, teaching purposes, scientific research, quotations, use by the press, etc.

Infringement of Belgian copyright law or of the *sui generis* right for databases may result in the imposition of both civil and criminal sanctions.

Useful addresses and/or links

Hereunder are the addresses of some of the most important collecting societies in Belgium :
SABAM (music industry) www.sabam.be
SOFAM (visual arts) www.sofam.be
SACD (literary works) www.sacd.be

Know-How, Trade Secrets and Confidential Information

Under Belgian law, there is no specific Act dealing with confidential information. However, it is worth mentioning that various sections from acts of a totally different nature intend to protect confidential information against misappropriation:

- article 309 of the Criminal Code (criminal law)
- article 17, 3°, a of the Employment Agreements Act of July 3, 1978 (employment law)
- article 93 of the Fair Trade Practices Act of July 14, 1991 (unfair competition law)

Each of the above provisions has proper criteria in respect of the exact nature of the confidential information covered, the scope of misappropriation which it intends to sanction, and the category of persons which fall under its scope of application.

It should be borne in mind that these provisions may, however, never restrict fundamental principles of Belgian law which are free competition and freedom of trade embodied in the Decree of March 2-17("*Décret d'Allarde*") and the freedom of work consecrated in article 1780 of the Civil Code and article 7 of the Employment Agreements Act of July 3, 1978.

Criminal law

Article 309 of the Criminal Code prohibits the misappropriation of "trade secrets." The person who maliciously and fraudulently communicates secrets of the company where he worked or where he is still working, will be punished with imprisonment and/or a fine.

The meaning of the word *"trade secrets"* has been defined *sensu stricto* by the Supreme Court in a decision of September 27, 1943:

A technical fact contributing to the realisation of a company's operations in order to obtain a determined product, which provides the company with technical advantages and a superiority over its competitors, and hence an economic advantage to keep that fact confidential from its competitors.

Because of the narrow meaning of trade secrets and because of the requirement of malicious and fraudulent intent of the person divulging the information to a third party—which is obviously difficult to establish—there are very few applications of art. 309 of the Criminal Code in case law.

Employment law

Even if no particular clauses are provided for in his employment agreement, an employee must respect the secrecy of certain information, during and after termination of his employment agreement.

Article 17, 3° of the Employment Agreements Act provides indeed the following:

Whether in the course or after termination of his contract, an employee must refrain from :

a. disclosing trade or business secrets, as well as the secrecy of any confidential or personal matters that he would have become aware of in the exercise of his professional activity;

b. to commit or participate to any unfair competition activities.

It is important to observe that this provision is limited *ratione personae*, since it only applies to (ex-)employees. However, the scope of the information covered by the employee's confidentiality obligation is broader than trade secrets *sensu stricto* within the meaning of the criminal code, since business secrets and all information or knowledge of financial or commercial nature are covered as well, provided they are original.

Here follow a few practical examples. Some case law provided that a customers list would only be regarded as a business secret if it contains names which are not well-known by anyone. In another case, it was decided that a blue collar employee who had disclosed company restructuring plans, had breached his confidentially obligation. Also prices in vigour in a company or the preferential price applied to some suppliers may be confidential information that may not be disclosed by an employee.

In a nutshell, any employee is under a legal obligation of secrecy under Belgian law. This means that s/he cannot disclose any inventions, trade secrets or confidential information s/he would have access to as a result of his/her employment. However, an employee may not be prevented from using the skills and knowledge s/he has acquired during his/her employment. In other words, there is a grey zone between acquired skills and confidential information.

It is therefore appropriate to make contractual arrangements to safeguard know-how and trade secrets. Non compete clauses may be an option too, provided they are in accordance with all legal requirements. Otherwise they may be considered null and void.

Unfair competition law

Employment law is seldom relied upon independently. In most cases, reference is also made to article 93 of the Fair Trade Practices Act, which provides for the following general prohibition :

> *Any act contrary to the fair trade practices by which a vendor undermines or may undermine the professional interests of one or several traders is prohibited.*

Using trade secrets which should have been kept confidential is generally considered to be an unfair trade practice.

It is impossible to give a general definition for what information must be kept confidential. Each particular case needs to be examined separately.

However, several general guidelines concerning the scope and limits of protection under the Fair Trade Practices Act can be drawn from the case-law:

- It is generally admitted that an ex-employee is entitled to refer to her/his experience and education with her/his ex-employer, if this reference does not entail any confusion or disparaging practices.

  A distinction must be drawn between the experience, the knowledge which cannot be separated for the employee's person, and knowledge of secrets on the basis of confidential documents, know-how, etc. to which the employee would not have had access, had s/he worked in the same field though with a different employer. The line between both is very thin and must be assessed in each case separately.

- Documents belonging to a former employer and copies thereof should be returned on termination date of the employment agreement (article 17, 5∞ of the Employment Agreements Act). If the employer fails to do so, he is in breach of contract. If those documents are moreover used to compete with his former employer, the employee is moreover guilty of unfair trade practices; the plaintiff (former employer) will have to establish that documents which are not in the public domain have been kept by the employee on an illegal basis and that the employee has used the same to compete with him.
- It is generally admitted that an ex-employee can make use of the contacts s/he has had with clients, suppliers, etc. under her/his former employer, if doing so does not entail any confusion or disparaging practices.

The fact that the employee would her/himself have had contacts with those clients, suppliers, etc. seems to be irrelevant.

Practical Tips

Insofar as the protection of IP rights is concerned, it is equally important to be aware of the proceedings available under Belgian law.

A first distinction should be made between civil and criminal proceedings.

In most cases of infringement of intellectual property rights, legal proceedings are brought before the Belgian civil courts. However, it is possible to bring criminal proceedings in cases of trademark or copyright infringement which amount to a criminal offence. A trademark or copyright infringement will amount to a criminal offence, mainly in cases of piracy or slavish counterfeit, if it is established that the perpetrator knew or should have known that he was infringing the proprietor's rights.

Before the Belgian civil courts, parties can bring either summary proceedings (*référé / kort geding*) in order to obtain interim relief (e.g., a temporary injunction, seizure of counterfeit goods, expert investigations, etc.) or proceedings on the merits (*procédure au fond / bodemprocedure*) to obtain permanent relief (e.g., a permanent injunction, damages, nullification of IP rights, etc.).

Two conditions must normally be met in summary proceedings: the matter must be urgent and the relief sought must be of a provisional nature. Summary proceedings are usually *inter partes* proceedings, which means that the proceedings are held in the presence of all parties concerned. However, there are ways to obtain interim relief on an *ex parte* or *inaudita altera parte* basis, which means that the respondent is not involved and not heard. This is generally only possible in cases of particular urgency and "absolute necessity", a concept which, in principle, covers two scenarios :

- either the situation is exceptionally urgent and, no delay (not even a few hours) is possible; or
- in view of the nature of the measure, recourse to an *inter partes* procedure would render the action completely ineffective; which means, in other words, where the necessity of an *ex parte* procedure is inherent in the nature of the measures requested.

The alleged infringer may oppose *ex parte* measures by a procedure known as a "third party opposition" (*tièrce opposition / derdenverzet*), within one month of notification of the order. A third party opposition is initiated by a writ, issued to all parties, and is heard by the judge who initially ordered the *ex parte* relief.

Finally, there is a very effective *ex parte* summary procedure, the "descriptive seizure" (*saisie-description / beslag inzake namaak*), which, unlike the other summary proceedings, does not necessarily require a finding of particular urgency. This procedure is available to the holders of copyrights, patent rights or breeders' rights. Unfortunately, and oddly enough, the Belgian legislature has not allowed this procedure in cases of trademark infringement. The Supreme Court has recently held that a descriptive seizure can also be requested on the basis of a foreign IP right, if the purpose of the procedure is to establish the infringement of this foreign right.

The descriptive seizure allows the right holder, if his or her application is granted by the judge, to have certain items (such as the allegedly infringing goods and any instruments pertaining directly to such goods, as well as all plans, documents, calculations, writings, etc., which serve as evidence of the alleged infringement) and account details examined and searched on the premises of the allegedly infringing party by a court appointed expert, with a view to establishing the existence, the origin and the extent of the infringement. The right holder may also obtain an injunction to prevent the infringing party from disposing of the alleged counterfeit goods under penalty. To maintain the effects of the descriptive seizure and to be able to rely on the expert's findings, proceedings on the merits must be initiated within one month from the date of filing of the expert's report.

Belgium

The advantages of this procedure are that it is swift and effective since the other party is not aware of the requested measures (the element of surprise). The descriptive seizure grants an important advantage to the right holder and can be a major inconvenience to the alleged infringer. If an action of this type is feared, it is recommended to establish internal guidelines so as to be prepared to respond appropriately when the time comes.

Chapter 6: Cyprus

Cyprus

By Dr. Eleni Chrysostomides
(Dr. K. Chrysostomides & Co.)

Trademarks

Legislation

The Cyprus Trade Marks Law Cap. 268 as amended by Laws Nos. 63/1962, 69/1971, 206/1990 and Law No. 176(I)/2000. Law No. 176(I)/2000 has brought the basic Law in line with European Trade Marks legislation.

The Law defines "trade mark", as *"a mark which comprises of any sign capable of being represented graphically, which can inherently distinguish the goods or services of one undertaking from those of other undertakings, provided the mark is used or is intended to be used for the purpose of such distinction."*

Signs which may operate as trade marks include the shape of goods or their packaging. Certification and Collective marks can also be registered on the Cyprus Trade Mark Register and there are specific rules governing the procedure for registration of such marks.

An application for the registration of a trade mark must be accompanied by the following documentation:

- An Authorisation of Agent.
- Eight representations of the mark if this is in colour. If the mark is to be in black and white then one representation of the mark will suffice.
- A detailed description of the goods or services to be covered by the proposed trade mark and their class.

The Law provides for specific absolute and relative grounds for refusal of registration of a trade mark. Once accepted, a trade mark is published in the Official Gazette of the Republic and opposition proceedings may be filed by a third party within two months from the date of publication.

A trade mark is registered initially for 7 years, followed by renewable periods of 14 years.

Dr. Eleni Chrysostomides is Senior Partner in the law firm of Dr. K. Chrysostomides & Co. in Nicosia, Cyprus. Dr. Chrysostomides specialises in intellectual property law, and has published legal works both in Cyprus and in international legal journals. The law firm of Dr. K. Chrysostomides & Co., one of the largest law offices in Nicosia, also has offices in Larnaca and a presence in Brussels.

Cyprus

Revocation proceedings may be brought in cases where, inter alia, the proprietor fails to make genuine use of his mark for a continuous period of 5 years and there is no reasonable excuse for the non-use.

Designs

Legislation

The Law on the Protection of Designs and Models No. 4(I)/2002. This Law, adopts the provisions of EU Directive 98/71 of 13.10.1998.

The Law sets up a system for the recording of designs which are novel and have an individual character.

"Design" or "model" is defined as the appearance of the whole or part of a product which results from its features and in particular, the line, contours, colours, shape, texture and/or materials of the product itself and/or its ornamentation.

"Product" is defined as any industrial or handicraft item including, inter alia, parts intended to be assembled into a complex product, the packaging, the get-up, graphic symbols and typographical typefaces, but excluding computer programs.

Applications for the recording of designs can be filed by nationals of EU member states, or individuals domiciled in Cyprus or EU member states, companies with real or effective commercial establishment in Cyprus or one of the EU member states.

The proprietor of a recorded design has an exclusive right of use of his design and can prevent any unauthorised third party user.

Protection is afforded for an initial period of five years which is renewable every five years up to a maximum duration of twenty-five years.

Copyright

Legislation

The Right of Intellectual Property Law No.18(I)/93 as recently amended by Law No.128 (I)/2002. Law No. 128(I)/2002 has harmonised the basic Law with EU Directives Nos. 91/250, 92/100, 93/83, 93/98 and 96/9. Cyprus has also ratified the Berne Convention for the Protection of Literary and Artistic Works.

The Law does not provide for a procedure for the registration of copyrights. Copyright is automatically afforded to works which are original and have been put down in writing or have been presented in some material form.

The owner of copyright has the exclusive right to control his work's reproduction, advertisement, sale, licensing, distribution, lending, exhibition, transmission, adaptation, translation and transmission through cable.

Cyprus

Protection extends to:

Type of work	Duration (years)
Scientific works	70
Literary works, including computer programs	70
Musical works	70
Artistic works, including photographs of every nature	70
Movies	70
Original Databases	70
Non-Original Databases	15
Recordings	50
Broadcasts	50
Publication of previously unpublished works	25
Performances and readings by artists	50

The event triggering the commencement of the above mentioned periods of protection varies from work to work.

Patents

Legislation

The Patents Law No. 16(I)/1998 as amended by Law No. 21(I)/1999, 153(I)/2000 and Law No. 163(I)/2002. Law No. 163(1)/2002 harmonised the basic Law with EU Directive 98/44 on the protection of biotechnological inventions.

Cyprus is a member of the European Patent Convention (EPC) and the Patent Cooperation Treaty (PCT).

This Law sets up a new system on the basis of which patent applications are examined according to specific criteria of patentability viz. novelty, inventiveness and industrial applicability.

A patent is granted for a period of twenty years from the date of filing of the application, provided that the due annuity fees are paid. Supplementary Protection Certificates may be obtained in connection with medicinal products and plant protection products.

The Law also provides the legal framework for validation in Cyprus of European Patents designating Cyprus. An application for the validation of a granted EP designating Cyprus are the following:

(a) A copy of the granted patent (B1).
(b) A translation into Greek of the granted patent. The translation must be filed in the Cyprus Patent Registry within 3 months from the date of pub-

lication of the European Patent Bulletin of the notice of grant or of the decision to maintain it in an amended form following the hearing of an opposition.

(c) A copy of the drawings as well as a copy of the abstract of the invention, duly translated into Greek.

(d) An Authorisation of Agent.

The Law also provides for a procedure for provisional protection of EP applications designating Cyprus.

Other IP Laws

- Law providing for the registration and protection of Applications of origin and geographical indications for agricultural products or foodstuffs and other related matters No. 7(I)/2002. This Law adopts the provisions of EU Directive 2081/92 of 17.07.1992.
- Law on the legal protection of Topographies of semi-conductor products No. 5(I)/2002. This Law adopts the provisions of EU Regulation 87/54 of 16.12.1986.

Cyprus

Chapter 7:
Czech Republic

Czech Republic

By Barbora Rovenska
(Horák & Chvosta)

Introduction
Major issues affecting intellectual property legislation

Recent developments in Czech intellectual property legislation have primarily dealt with the implementation of the EU directives, reflecting the forthcoming accession of the Czech Republic to the EU, and the need to incorporate into Czech legislation the principles of the international treaties and conventions to which the Czech Republic is a party (e.g., Patent Cooperation Treaty).

Treaties and conventions

The Czech Republic is a the party to the following international treaties and conventions, among others:

- Convention Establishing the Word Intellectual Property Organization (WIPO Convention)
- Paris Convention for the Protection of the Industrial Property
- Madrid Agreement Concerning the International Registration of Marks
- Protocol Relating to the Madrid Agreement Concerning the International Registration of Marks
- Madrid Agreement for the Repression of False or Deceptive Indications of Source on Goods
- Patent Cooperation Treaty
- Nice Agreement Concerning the International Classification of Goods and Services for the Purposes of the Registration of Marks
- Locarno Agreement Establishing an International Classification for Industrial Designs
- Strasbourg Agreement Concerning the International Patent Classification
- Budapest Treaty on the International Recognition of the Deposit of Microorganisms for the Purposes of Patent Procedure
- Berne Convention for the Protection of Literary and Artistic Works

---

Barbora Rovenska is a partner with the law firm of Horák & Chvosta in Prague. The firm's practice includes advice on the registration and protection of intellectual property rights as well as representation in intellectual property related litigations. Horák & Chvosta is a member of The Interlex Group, a worldwide association of leading law firms.

Czech Republic

- Trade Mark Law Treaty
- TRIPS

Patents

Definition of the patent

The Act No. 527/1990 Coll., on patents and improvements, as amended (the "Patent Act") defines a patent as the exclusive right to the invention. Patents are recognized and registered by the Industrial Property Office of the Czech Republic ("IPO").

Criteria for registration

Patents are granted only in relation to inventions which are new, have been developed as a result of the inventor's activities, and are industrially applicable. The invention is considered to be new provided it does not create a part of the existing status of technique (prior art). Provided the invention is non-obvious for an expert (a person skilled in the art) from the current status of technique (prior art), it complies with the condition that it be developed as a result of the inventor's activities. If the subject of the invention can be produced or otherwise exploited in industry, agriculture or other sectors of the economy, it is considered to be capable of industrial application.

It is crucial that the invention not be disclosed to the public before filing the patent application, so that the invention is not considered as prior art and, therefore, not in compliance with the definition of a patentable invention. In cases where the invention is disclosed to the public during a six-month grace period prior to the filing of the patent application, such disclosure does not prevent future granting of the patent provided that:

- the disclosure resulted from obvious misappropriation in relation to the applicant or applicant's legal predecessor;
- the applicant or applicant's legal predecessor disclosed the invention to the public when presenting the invention in the course of the official or officially recognized exhibition.

The patent may not be granted to:

- discoveries, scientific theories and mathematic methods;
- esthetic works;
- plans, principles and methods of intellectual activities, playing games or performance of business activities, software programs;
- provision of information.

Czech Republic

Inventions created during the inventor's employment

In cases where the inventor creates an invention while performing the duties determined in his employment contract, the right to seek issuance of the patent is automatically transferred to the employer. The employer has to exercise such right and apply for a granting of the patent within three months from the day when it becomes aware that the invention has been created. If the employer does not exercise such right within that time, the right to apply for issuance of the patent is returned to the inventor.

Owner of the patent

The patent may be granted only to the inventor or to the inventor's legal successor. Special rules apply in cases of inventions created by employees as specified in the section above.

Effects of the patent

The owner of the patent has the exclusive right to use the invention, to authorize third parties to use the invention (license) or to assign the patent to third parties. The effects of the patent registration originate as of the date on which granting of the patent is published in the Bulletin of the IPO.

Patent application procedure

The process of applying for the patent is to be initiated by filing the patent application with the IPO. The patent application must specify the inventor and the applicant and must contain a detailed description of the invention as well as the patent claims, which will determine the extent of the future patent protection.

The right of priority regarding the invention is established in favor of the applicant as of the moment of filing of the patent application.

After filing the patent application, the IPO carries out a preliminary examination to make sure that the application complies with all formal requirements of the Patent Act. The patent application is published after the lapse of 18 months from the priority date in the Bulletin of the IPO. It is possible to request that the patent application be published no later than 12 months after the priority date, upon payment of special fees.

Any person may object to patentability of the invention after the patent application is published in the Bulletin. The IPO takes such objections into account when carrying out the full examination of the patent application. The application requesting the IPO to carry out the full examination must be filed no later than 36 months after filing the patent application. The patent certificate may be granted

Czech Republic

only after the IPO has carried out a full examination. The granting of the patent is published in the Bulletin of the IPO.

Term of patent protection

The patents are granted for a period of 20 years from the date of filing of the patent application, provided that annual renewal fees are paid.

The patent may be cancelled during the term of the patent protection for various reasons, such as when the granting of the patent was in contradiction to the Patent Act (e.g., the invention was not new or industrially applicable). Another reason for canceling the patent would be that the patent was granted to a person not meeting qualification requirements to be the patent owner.

Patent infringement

Protection against patent infringement can be sought through the courts.

Registered Designs

Definition of a registered design

The Act No. 207/2000 Coll. on protection of registered designs (the "Act on Registered Designs") defines a design as the appearance of the product or its part resulting particularly from the lines, contours, colors, shapes, texture or materials of the product itself or its ornamentation. Designs complying with the definition of the design contained in the Act on Registered Designs can be registered with the IPO.

Criteria for registration

The design may be registered with the IPO provided it is new and has an individual character.

The registered design is considered to be new if the identical registered design has not been disclosed to the public before the day of filing the application with the IPO.

The Act on Registered Designs holds that public disclosure of the design in a twelve month grace period prior to filing the application with the IPO does not prevent the registration of the design, provided that the exact conditions specified by the Act are met.

If the overall impression produced by the design on the informed user differs from the overall impression produced by another registered design disclosed to the public before the filing of the application requesting the registration of the design with the IPO, the design qualifies for registration.

Czech Republic

Designs created during the creator's employment

If the design was created during the inventor's employment, the rights attached to the design belong to the person who commissioned the design. The person who commissioned the design may seek registration within a three month period from the date he becomes aware that the design has been created. If the right to seek registration is not sought within the said deadline, it passes back to the creator.

Owner of the registered design

The creator of the design or his legal successor may seek the registration of the design with the IPO. Special rules apply regarding registration of the commissioned design as specified above.

Effects of the registered design

The owner of the registered design has the exclusive right to use the registered design, to prevent third parties from using the registered design without the owner's approval, to authorize third parties to use the registered design (license) or to assign the right to use the registered design to third parties.

The rights resulting from the registered design do not prevent third parties from using the registered design if such using:

- is made for non-commercial, experimental or educational purposes;
- is compatible with fair business practice;
- is not unreasonable; and
- the source is mentioned.

Registration process

An application seeking registration of the design must be filed with the IPO in order for the registration proceedings to commence. The application must specify the creator as well as the applicant, the name of the design, and it must specify the products on which the design is to be applied, including the classification of the products according to the applicable international classification. The depiction of the design, which clearly illustrates the nature of the design, must be attached to the application.

If the application complies with the formal requirements of the Act on Registered Designs, the applicant benefits from the priority rights attached to the design as of the date of filing of the application with the IPO.

IPO examines the application after the application is filed. If the design to which the application relates qualifies for registration in accordance with the Act

Czech Republic

on Registered Designs, the IPO registers the design and publishes the registration in its Bulletin.

The applicant may request that the registered design be published in the Bulletin of the IPO after the lapse of a period not to exeed thirty months from the date of filing of the application, upon payment of special fees.

Term of protection

The registered design remains in force for five years from the date of filing the application. The protection period may be renewed for additional five year terms. The total protection period may not exceed 25 years.

Infringement

The owner of the registered design who believes that his rights attached to the registered design are subject to infringement may seek protection by initiating court proceedings.

Trade Marks

Definition of the trade mark

The Act No. 137/1995 Coll. on trade marks (the "Trade Mark Act") defines the trade mark as a sign which enables consumers to differentiate the goods or services of one entrepreneur from goods or services of another. The IPO registers trade marks in its register of trade marks.

Criteria for registration

A trade mark can consist of words, letters, digits, drawings or shapes of the product or its packaging, or by a combination of these elements.

The following signs are specifically excluded from registration:
- signs not capable of graphic presentation;
- signs consisting exclusively of marks or indications usually used in common language;
- signs consisting exclusively of marks or indications used to specify the type, quality, amount, purpose, value or other qualities of goods or services or geographical origin of goods or services;
- signs formed solely by the shape of the product given by its nature or which is necessary for reaching certain technical results;
- signs confusing for the consumers in respect of the nature, quality or geographical origin of products or services.

A sign not able to differentiate products or services may be registered as a trade mark only if the applicant proves that such sign acquired distinctiveness for

Czech Republic

his goods or services by having been used prior to the application date.

Classes of goods and services

Trade marks may be registered for goods and services, as divided into 45 international classes.

Effects of the registration

The owner of a registered trade mark has the exclusive right to use the trade mark for marking goods and services for which the trade mark is registered. The owner of a well-known registered trade mark has the exclusive right to use the trade mark for any goods or services, not just the goods or services for which it is registered.

Furthermore, the owner of a registered trade mark has the exclusive right to prevent third parties from using the trade mark or a sign confusingly similar to the trade mark without the owner's approval, to authorize third parties to use the trade mark (license), or to assign the right to use the trade mark to third parties.

Registration process

The registration process is to be initiated by filing the trade mark application with the IPO. The application must specify the applicant, the sign to be registered as the trade mark, the goods or services to be marked with the trademark including the classification of the goods or service in the relevant international classes.

The priority rights regarding the respective sign originate in favor of the applicant as of the date of filing the trade mark application. The IPO examines the application in order to make sure that the sign qualifies for the registration as the trade mark and meets the requirements of the Trade Mark Act. After completing the examination, the IPO publishes the application in its Bulletin.

Persons explicitly specified in the Trade Mark Act (particularly owners of prior trade marks or prior trade mark applications related to the same or confusingly similar signs) may oppose the registration within three months from publication. The IPO has to either reject the opposition or declare it founded before it decides whether to register the trade mark, referring to the claims mentioned in the opposition.

In cases where the application is not opposed, the IPO registers the trade mark and publishes the registration in its Bulletin.

Term of protection

The initial period of trade mark protection is 10 years from the application date. The protection period may be renewed for additional 10 year periods.

Czech Republic

The trade mark may be cancelled during the protection period for various reasons, including the non-compliance of the registration with the Trade Mark Act or not using the trade mark for a continuous period of five years without an acceptable reason.

Infringement

Trade mark infringement cases shall be dealt with by competent courts.

New Act on Trade Marks

The new Act on Trade Marks (Act No. 441/2003 Coll.) will become effective on April 1, 2004 with the exception of a few provisions that will become effective on May 1, 2004 (the date of accession of the Czech Republic to the EU).

Copyright

Definition of copyright

The Act No. 121/2000 Coll. the Copyright Act, defines the subject of copyright protection as a literary or other artistic or scientific work which is the result of the unique creativity of its author and is expressed in any objectively perceivable form including electronic form despite the extent, purpose and meaning of the work. The protection provided by the Copyright Act covers literary works, music, dramatic works, choreographical and pantomimic works, photographs, audiovisual works, graphic, architectural and cartographic works. The authors of software programs and databases also enjoy the protection granted by the Copyright Act.

Registration of copyright

The registration of copyright is not possible in the Czech Republic. Therefore, it is recommended to attach the copyright notice © including the name of the author and the date of publication to the work.

Extent of the copyright

The copyright consists of the author's moral and proprietary rights. The author may neither waive nor license nor assign the moral rights attached to the work.

The author has the exclusive right to use the work, to authorize a third party to use the work (license) or to assign the right to use the work to any third party and to prevent third parties from using the work without the owner's approval.

Czech Republic

Works created by authors during their employment

The employer exercises the proprietary rights to the work provided that his employee created the work when performing his obligations ensuing from the employment contract.

Term of copyright protection

The copyright protection lasts for the whole term of the author's life and 70 years following his death.

Infringement

Only the courts are competent to award judgments in copyright infringement cases.

Chapter 8:
Denmark

Denmark

By Martin Sick Nielsen
(Zacco Hofman Bang)

Introduction

Intellectual property is not only becoming increasingly important to Danish industry, but is also recognized as such. This is reflected in the fact that more and more Danish corporations are developing and implementing strategies for the protection and exploitation of their intellectual property rights, and are considering intellectual property as an integral part of their decision making process.

Denmark generally has up-to-date intellectual property legislation, and is signatory to the key international treaties and agreements. Exceptions are the Madrid Arrangement and the Haag Agreement.

Further, Denmark is complying with its obligations as a member state of the European Community by implementing the necessary national law, and aligning is examination practice to that of OHIM (and EPO).

The Danish PTO is efficient and modern, allowing for e-filing and on-line access to the Danish patent and trademark register via the Internet.

The enforcement system is also efficient, and the Danish courts have contributed substantially to European jurisprudence on issues relating to the parallel import of pharmaceutical products.

In particular, the Danish customs authorityis seizing a substantial amount of counterfeit goods at the Danish borders, and is among the most efficient customs authorities in the European Community.

No major changes in the Danish intellectual property legislation are expected in the near future. In the more distant future, an accession to the Geneva Agreement may be expected, and a committee is presently considering the domain name system under the .dk top-level domain, including whether the allocation of domain names shall come under public administration.

Martin Sick Nielsen is a partner with Zacco Hofman Bang, one of Europe's leading firms of patent and trademark attorneys with six offices throughout Denmark, Norway and Sweden. The firm provides a full range of IP services, including representation of overseas clients towards the EPO and OHIM, and litigation through its correspondent law firm, Zacco Legal.

Denmark

Patents

Legislation

Patents in Denmark are regulated under the Patents Act of August 30, 2001.

A patent covers the Kingdom of Denmark, which includes Greenland and the Faroe Islands.

The Utility Models Act of June 9, 1998 provides for the protection of utility models, which shall not be dealt with here.

The application procedure

A patent can be obtained either as a Danish patent or as a European Patent validated in Denmark, in both situations either by filing directly with the Danish PTO or the EPO as appropriate, or by entering into the national phase of a PCT application.

A Danish patent is obtained by application to the Danish PTO in accordance with the Patents Act and its implementing regulations. The Danish PTO carries out a full formal and material examination. If granted, the patent will be published, giving third parties a nine month period to oppose. The decision of the Danish PTO in the opposition proceedings can be appealed to the Danish Patent and Trademark Appeal Board and further to the Maritime and Commercial Court.

If a European Patent is granted, the patent becomes valid in Denmark only if a full Danish translation of the patent is filed with the Danish PTO together with the publication fee no later than three months from the date of grant.

On June 10, 2003 the Parliament amended the Patent Act so that in the future it will be possible to file the European Patent in English (or in an English translation) with a Danish translation only of the patent claims. This amendment will enter into force by decision of the competent Minister when the London Agreement on cost reduction enters into force.

How long does a patent last?

Patents are granted for a period of 20 years from the filing date of the application, subject to the payment of annuities starting at the third year after filing. It is possible to obtain SPC's as discussed in the European Community chapter.

To whom can a patent be granted?

The right to apply for a patent belongs to the inventor(s) or his or her assignees. If a patent application is filed by a person or entity other than the inventor, the name of the inventor must be stated in the application.

If an employee has made an invention during the course of his or her normal duties, and the invention relates to the activities of the employer or to a specific assignment given by the employer to the employee, the employer is entitled to have the invention assigned to itself—under certain circumstances against payment of compensation to employee.

It is possible to make different arrangements under individual employment contracts, but the employee's right to compensation is mandatory.

The right to inventions made by employees at universities, public research institutions, hospitals, etc. is governed under a separate act, which shall not be dealt with here.

Once granted, is the patent safe?

A patent may be declared invalid, in whole or in part, either by an administrative cancellation action or by a decision of the courts. The validity of a patent can be challenged throughout the life of the patent, and even after the patent has expired or ceased.

What rights does a patent give?

Once a patent has been granted, the patentee is entitled to prevent others from exploiting any invention which falls within the scope of the patent.

Infringement Proceedings

In Denmark, a patent is enforced either by applying for an injunction to the competent High Court or by applying for a preliminary injunction to the competent bailiffs' court if the conditions to obtain a preliminary injunction are fulfilled.

If a preliminary injunction is obtained, the claimant must start a legal action before the ordinary courts no later than two weeks from the decision of the bailiffs' court to confirm the preliminary injunction.

Designs

Legislation

Designs are regulated under the Designs Act of December 20, 2000, which implements the Directive 98/71/EC on the legal protection of designs.

A Danish design registration covers Denmark, excluding Greenland and the Faroe Islands, where it is not possible to obtain a design registration.

What is a design?

The definition of a design is as discussed in the European Community Chapter. In Denmark the distinction between trade marks and designs is also blurred, as discussed in the UK chapter.

It is possible to obtain a design registration for spare parts, but only for 15 years, as opposed to other designs where the design registration lasts for 25 years provided renewal fees are paid every 5 years.

Denmark

Design registrations have an overlap with copyrights, but it is expressly provided for in the Copyright Act that a copyright does not exclude the owner from also obtaining a design registration.

The application procedure

A design registration is obtained by application to the Danish PTO in accordance with the Designs Act and its implementing regulations, and the application procedure is substantially as discussed regarding registered community designs in the European Community chapter.

The Danish PTO carries out a formal examination, but no material examination specifically as to whether the design is new and has individual character.

On the request of the applicant and the payment of an additional official fee, the Danish PTO conducts a limited search of other facts of which the Danish PTO has knowledge. The search report is provided for the guidance of the applicant only. A straightforward design application should be registered within two months of filing.

The design registration is published, but it is possible to defer publication for a period of six months from the date of application or the date of priority, if priority is claimed.

There is no opposition procedure, but it is possible to claim cancellation of the design registration. The decision of the Danish PTO in the cancellation action can be appealed to the Danish Patent and Trademark Appeal Board and further to the Maritime and Commercial Court.

Prior disclosure - 12 month grace period

In Denmark registered designs also benefit from the 12 month grace period in respect of the applicants prior disclosure as discussed regarding registered community designs in the European Community chapter.

The employment relationship

There is no provision in the Danish Designs Act similar to that in the Community Design Regulation that designs created in an employment relationship belong to the employer, but it is generally acknowledged that designs created in an employment relationship are assigned to the employer also without an express provision to this effect in the employment contract. This does not include a possible copyright in the work created by the employee, which is governed by the Copyrights Act, and it is therefore recommend to include an express provision to this effect in the employment contract.

Denmark

Infringement

The owner of a design right has the exclusive right as discussed regarding registered community designs in the European Community chapter.

There is no precedence under the Designs Act, but in the doctrine it is expected that design registrations will have a rather narrow scope of protection.

Trade Marks

Legislation

Trade marks in Denmark are regulated under the Trade Marks Act of August 30, 2001, which implements the Directive 89/104/EEC to approximate the laws of the member states relating to trade marks.

Trade mark rights can be established by registration or by use.

A Danish trade mark right covers the Kingdom of Denmark, which includes Greenland and the Faroe Islands. Neither a CTM registration nor a designation of Denmark under the Madrid Protocol covers Greenland and the Faroe Islands.

Registered trade marks

A registered trade mark right is established by application to the Danish PTO for the goods and services covered by the registration.

Registrability and the application procedure

The types of marks that can be registered and the application procedure are substantially as discussed in the European Community chapter.

The Danish PTO conducts a search of trade mark registrations and applications covering Denmark (including Danish collective marks, CTM's and International trade marks designating Denmark), company names, family names and works protected by copyright. However, as it is not necessary or possible to register copyrights in Denmark, the last part of the search is impossible to conduct in practice.

If the mark is accepted, it will be registered and advertised, giving third parties a two-month period to oppose the registration. The decision of the Danish PTO in the opposition proceedings can be appealed to the Danish Patent and Trademark Appeal Board and further to the Maritime and Commercial Court.

A straightforward trade mark application, without office actions other than the search report, should be registered within two months of filing.

How long does a trade mark registration last?

A trade mark registration is valid for 10 years from the date of registration, but is renewable in perpetuity for further 10 year periods upon payment of renewal fees.

Denmark

The registration can be cancelled, in full or in part, by a decision of the courts or in an administrative cancellation action brought by a third party for substantially the same reasons as discussed in the European Community chapter.

Unregistered trade marks

An unregistered trade mark is established by use of the trade mark in Denmark, and covers the goods and services for which the trade mark is used and continues to be used. The trade mark right thus expires if and to the extent the trade mark is not used. It is not possible to establish an unregistered trade mark right in a mark that cannot be registered.

In principle, an unregistered trade mark enjoys the same protection as a registered trade mark.

Advantages of registration

A trade mark registration constitutes prima facie evidence of a trade mark right, which makes it substantially easier to enforce, assign and license registered trade marks. Further, a registered trade mark can be enforced for 5 years after the trade mark was last used, and if the use is resumed (without the trade mark registration having been cancelled), the registered trade mark preserves its priority date.

While trade marks do not need to be registered, it is recommended not to rely on an unregistered trade mark right at least for important marks.

What rights does a trade mark give?

A trade mark gives the owner exclusive rights to prevent others from:

1. using a sign identical to the mark in relation to identical goods or services, or
2. using a sign identical or similar to the mark in relation to identical or similar goods or services, if there is a likelihood of confusion, including a risk of association, on part of the public, and
3. irrespective of the limitation in 2. to identical or similar goods or services, also in relation to dissimilar goods or services, if the mark has a reputation in Denmark and the use takes unfair advantage of or is detrimental to the reputation of the mark.

Domain names and brand protection on the Internet

The right to use a .dk domain name is derived from a contract between the registrant and DK Hostmaster A/S who is administrating the .dk top level domain, and the registration of a domain name does not give the registrant any exclusive rights by law.

However, on the basis of the Marketing Practices Act it may be possible for the registrant of a domain name to prevent others from using a sign identical to the domain name or another sign in a way which may cause confusion.

The internet activities discussed in the UK chapter may also amount to trade mark infringement in Denmark.

Copyright and Related Rights

Legislation

In Denmark, copyright is regulated under the Copyrights Act of March 12, 2003.

Do I need to register copyright?

It is not necessary or possible to register copyright in Denmark.

Copyright notice

It is not necessary, but common to attach a copyright notice to the work, e.g. setting out the © symbol followed by the copyright owner's name and date of publication. There is no precedence as to its value in infringement proceedings.

Term

The term of copyright in Denmark is as discussed in the European Community chapter.

Related rights

Rights similar to but distinct from copyright also apply in Denmark to protect:

- the work of performing artists (such as musicians, actors and dancers) in respect of recording and distributing copies of their performances;
- sound and movie recordings in respect of copying or making such recordings available to the public;
- radio and TV broadcasts in respect of their broadcast or otherwise being made available to the public;
- photographs in respect of their copying or being made available to the public;
- titles by prohibiting the publication of literary and artistic works under a title, which may cause confusion with the title of a prior work or its author; and
- catalogues or databases, where there has been a substantial investment of financial, human or technical resources in obtaining, verifying or presenting the material constituting the database.

Further, the author has moral rights in his or her copyright works. They prevent, among other things, 'derogatory treatment' of works and can require the author's name to appear with the work.

Status of latest European Community directive on copyright
The Info-soc directive has been implemented in Danish law by the amendment of the Copyright Act enacted by Parliament on December 17, 2002.

Confidential Information

Confidential information is protected most efficiently by identifying the information as confidential and carefully managing the disclosure process.

Disclosure should be made on a "need to know" basis only, and only subject to the recipient (whether an employee, a consultant or other business partner) undertaking an express obligation to secrecy.

If the recipient has not undertaken an express obligation to secrecy, he or she will in most situations (in particular in an employment relationship) be under an implied obligation to secrecy which follows from a general obligation of confidence in the contractual relationship between the parties. Obviously, such implied obligation to secrecy is generally more limited that an express contractual obligation.

Also, without an express or implied obligation to secrecy, the Marketing Practice Act prohibits a person in a contractual relationship to a business to gain unjustified access to the trade secrets of that business, and if having obtained justified access, not to disclose or use the trade secrets during the relationship and for a period of three years from the termination thereof. If a trade secret is disclosed to a third party in violation of the above, the law further prohibits the recipient to use the information. Violation of the relevant provision in the Marketing Practice Act is a criminal offense and subject to a fine and imprisonment in up to two years.

"Trade secrets" are defined narrowly and the Marketing Practice Act has limited practical importance in protecting confidential information. It is recommended not to rely on the protection under the Marketing Practice Act as an alternative to an express contractual obligation to secrecy.

Competition

In Denmark, the European Community competition law applies directly together with the national competition law as regulated under the Competition Act of June 28, 2002.

Denmark

Since 1997, the Danish competition law has largely been harmonized with the European competition law.

Generally, the Danish Competition Authorities deal with matters that only or primarily affect Denmark, irrespective that they may affect trade between member states, whereas the Commission deals with matters that affect more member states and thus has Community dimension.

Useful Industry Contacts

Danish Patent and Trade Mark Office ("Patent og Varemærkestyrelsen") grants patents and designs and registers utility models and trade marks in Denmark:
www.dkpto.dk

Danish Competition Authority ("Konkurrencestyrelsen") is administrating the Danish competition act: www.ks.dk

DK Hostmaster A/S is administrating the .dk top level domain: www.dk-hostmaster.dk

Copy-Dan, Koda and Gramex are joint collecting societies in Denmark: www.copy-dan.dk, www.koda.dk, www.gramex.dk

DI ("Dansk Industri") is the confederation of Danish industries: www.di.dk

Håndværksrådet is the Danish federation of small and medium-sized enterprises: www.hvr.dk

HTS ("Handel, Transport og Serviceerhvervene") is the Danish Chamber of Commerce: www.hts.dk

LIF ("Lægemiddelindustriforeningen") is the Danish federation of pharmaceutical industries: www.lifdk.dk

Danish Design Center ("Dansk Design Center") is a promotion organisation established to increase the awareness of design: www.ddc.dk

Danish IT Society ("Dansk IT") is an organisation for IT professionals: www.dansk-it.dk

Chapter 9: Estonia

Estonia

By Pirkko-Liis Harkmaa and Viive Näslund
(Lepik Ja Luhaäär AS)

Introduction

Legislative basis for protection of intellectual property

In general, the protection of intellectual property is based on Articles 32 and 39 of the Constitution of the Republic of Estonia. Article 32 of the Constitution foresees that the property of every person is inviolable and equally protected, whereas everyone has the right to freely possess, use, and dispose of his or her property and any restrictions thereto shall be provided by law. Property shall not be used contrary to the public interest. Article 39 of the Constitution foresees that an author has the inalienable right to his or her work, whereas the state shall protect the rights of the author.

There have also been laws passed providing legal protection to different categories of intellectual property. Namely:

Trademark Act

Patent Act

Utility Model Act

Industrial Design Protection Act

Act on the Protection of Layout Designs of Integrated Circuits

Geographical Indication Protection Act

Copyright Act

The said laws are based on the principles foreseen in the TRIPS Agreement of WTO, of which Estonia has been a member since 1999, and the agreements administered by WIPO, of which Estonia has been a member since 1994, as well as the respective legislation of the European Union. The European Commission has acknowledged that the Estonian legal protection system of industrial property meets the requirements of the European Union, and during the accession negotiations the chapter on company law was closed in 2000.

Pirkko-Liis Harkmaa and Viive Näslund are attorneys with Lepik Ja Luhaäär AS in Tallinn. Lepik Ja Luhaäär AS provides a wide range of legal services covering corporate and commercial law, corporate finance, banking, investments, intellectual property, employment, taxation, construction, and insolvency law. The firm works in close cooperation with law offices in Sweden, UK, Finland, US, France, Denmark and Switzerland.

Estonia

Treaties and Conventions

Estonia is a party to several multilateral international treaties. They are:

Industrial Property

Paris Convention for the Protection of Industrial Property (1883)

Berne Convention for the Protection of Literary and Artistic Works (1886)

Paris Convention for the Protection of Industrial Property (Stockholm Act, 1967)

Convention Establishing the World Intellectual Property Organization (Stockholm, 1967)

Patent Cooperation Treaty (Washington, 1970)

Nice Agreement Concerning the International Classification of Goods and Services for the Purposes of Registration of Marks (1957)

Budapest Treaty on the International Recognition of the Microorganisms for the Purposes of Patent Procedure (1977)

Locarno Agreement Establishing an International Classification for Industrial Designs (1968)

Strasbourg Agreement Concerning the International Patent Classification (1971)

Protocol Related to the Madrid Agreement Concerning the International Registration of Marks (1989)

Final Act of the Diplomatic Conference of Trademark Law Treaty

New Act of the Hague Agreement Concerning the International Deposit of Industrial Designs (1999)

National Regulatory Authorities

Protection of industrial property comes under the purview of the Ministry of Economic Affairs and Communications which administers the Estonian Patent Office. The Estonian Patent Office provides legal protection to the objects of industrial property in the name of the state and informs the public about the providing of said legal protection. In addition, the Office participates in the development and implementation of legislation within its area of activity and submits proposals for the amendment and supplementation of such legislation; participates in the development of policies, strategies and development plans within its area of activity; and prepares and implements projects connected with its area of activity, including participation in the preparation and implementation of international projects.

The other institution that operates under the Ministry of Economic Affairs and Communications is the Industrial Property Board of Appeal, which carries out pre-court examination of appeals and makes decisions on the appeals. The decisions of the Board of Appeal may be appealed against to an administrative court.

Regulatory issues related to copyright protection, however, are under the authority of the Ministry of Culture, which administers the Committee of Copyright Experts.

Inventions—Patents and Utility Models

Inventions can be protected either by applying for patent or utility model protection.

Patents
Scope of protection

Patent protection is granted to inventions belonging to all fields of science and technology, including medicinal products. Patent protection is not granted to plant or animal varieties or to methods for treatment of the human or animal body and diagnostic methods practiced on the human or animal body.

Who can apply?

The right to apply for a patent, and to become a patentee, belongs to the author of the invention, i.e. a natural person who through his or her inventive activities has made the invention.; co-authorship is also possible. A legal person cannot be an author of the invention. Authorship is inalienable and unspecified in term.

In cases where the invention is made in the course of fulfilling a contractual or work assignment, the right to become a patentee shall belong to the author or to another person pursuant to the contract or employment contract. If such contract exists, the patent application should indicate it. The employer and the employee who made the invention may also file the patent application jointly. In this case, it is recommended that they agree upon the conditions of patent ownership, use and command of the invention before filing a patent application. If the patent belongs to the employer, the author shall be entitled to a fair income from the income received from the use of the invention.

Application procedure

The application for registering an invention and granting patent protection is submitted to the Estonian Patent Office by the author or by the person who has the right to apply for the patent.

As a rule, the patent application should be in the Estonian language; foreign language patent applications are not accepted. In the case of foreign applicants,

Estonia

the additional documents could be in a foreign language, but they should be accompanied by Estonian language translations. The patent application should be filed in a specific format available at the Patent Office and on their web-page, www.epa.ee. The text of the patent application and main documents should be typed, as hand-written documents are not accepted. The patent application should be sent by post or handed over personally. Electronic filing either by telefax, diskette or e-mail is not yet possible.

A state fee of 3500 EEK is payable for filing a patent application.

In order to get legal assistance upon compiling and filing a patent application, the applicant may use an Estonian patent attorney. If the application is filed through a patent attorney, the applicant should give a respective power of attorney to the patent attorney authorizing the patent attorney to file the application and communicate with the Patent Office.

In addition, free consultation in the general matters of patenting of inventions can be obtained from the Patent Office itself.

The Estonian Patent Office acknowledges the first to file principle in filing a patent application. The filing date shall be the actual date of receipt or arrival of documents, provided that the application is in compliance with the formal requirements.

First, the Patent Office will examine whether the patent application complies with minimum requirements. If so, then the Patent Office accepts the application for processing and the applicant will be notified of the filing date and number of the patent application. Thereafter, the Patent Office will examine the compliance of the application with the formal and substantive requirements. If any deficiencies are discovered, additional explanations may be requested from the applicant. Incorrect documentation or failure to follow formal requirements prevents the publication of the patent application, and the applicant is asked to remove the shortcomings within three months. If the applicant fails to do so, the application will be rejected. The patent application is published after 18 months from the filing date or priority date. After publication of the patent application, the Patent Office will carry out substantive examination of the invention, examining the novelty of the invention worldwide, the inventive step and industrial applicability of the invention. If the Patent Office considers that the invention meets the criteria of novelty, the state of art and industrial applicability, and the application documents are in compliance with the formal requirements, the Patent Office shall make a decision on the granting of a patent. Decisions of the Patent Office can be appealed at the Industrial Property Board of Appeal or in the administrative court. The average duration of the examination of patent application is 4.5 years.

Estonia

Registration

Inventions that meet the patentability requirements shall be registered in the State Register of Patents. Upon registration of the invention, the patent is considered to be granted and the person who applied for the patent shall automatically become the patentee and shall receive the traditional *litterae patentes* as proof of the invention's registration in the patent register. A state fee of 1500 EEK is payable for registering the invention in the State Register of Patents. The state fee has to be paid within three months from the date of making the decision.

If the applicant fails to pay the state fee during the said time, the decision of the Patent Office will not come into force and the patent application is deemed to be withdrawn. The three-months deadline cannot be prolonged or restituted.

A notice of the grant of patent shall also be published in the Patent Gazette. As of the date of publishing the said notice, the patent applicant shall have the exclusive right to possess, use and dispose the invention.

Term of protection

The term of the patent is 20 years from the filing date. In order to renew and keep the patent valid, a state fee must be paid each year. Medical and plant protection products are given an additional protection that is valid for five years after the termination of the term of the patent.

Utility Models
Protected inventions

Utility model protection is granted only to inventions that are novel worldwide and industrially applicable. Utility model registration applications can be submitted for a device, method or substance. Basically the same kind of inventions can be protected as utility models as those protected by patents, except inventions belonging to the field of biotechnology. Compared to patentable inventions, the inventions protected as utility models do not have to involve such a high inventive step. The inventive step of a utility model is a new engineering solution providing a useful technical result.

Who has the right to apply?

The right to apply for the registration of a utility model belongs to the author of a utility model or the inventor.

In cases where the invention is made in the course of fulfilling a contractual or work assignment, the right to apply for the registration of a utility model shall belong to the person indicated in the contract or employment contract.

Estonia

Application procedure

The application for registering a utility model is submitted to the Estonian Patent Office. Compiling and filing of the application is done according to the same principles as in the case of patent applications. The difference is that the registration application may comprise only one invention, and thus combinations of inventions related to the inventive idea cannot be registered as a utility model.

The Patent Office will examine the compliance of the application with the formal requirements. The novelty and the industrial applicability of the invention is the sole responsibility of the applicant and the Patent Office will not check it.

If it appears that the invention is not new or industrially applicable, any interested person may file an appeal with the Industrial Property Board of Appeal and an action in court for invalidation of the legal protection. The claim of a utility model cannot be amended in cases where litigation proceeding has been started against the utility model in the court. Therefore, although registration of a utility model is cheaper, faster and easier than registration of a patent, the risk of annulment of the protection in case of appellation of the registration is higher.

A state fee of 1600 EEK is payable for filing a patent application.

Assistance with compiling and filing of the registration application can be obtained from patent attorneys.

The average duration of the examination of a utility model application is three months, provided that there is no need to amend the application.

Registration

If the application fulfills the formal requirements, the Patent Office shall decide to register the utility model and make a respective entry into the state registry of utility models. The applicant shall be notified thereof in writing. After publishing the notice of the entry of registration data, the Patent Office will issue a utility model certificate.

Term of protection

The first term of protection of a utility model is four years from the filing date. The term of protection may be renewed initially for an additional four years and thereafter for another two years. The renewal requires the payment of a state fee within six months before the date when the validity of the registration expires.

Industrial Designs

Scope of protection

The proprietor of an industrial design shall have full legal power (exclusive right) over a registered industrial design that fulfills conditions of granting legal

Estonia

protection. The proprietor of an industrial design shall have exclusive right to manufacture products according to an identical or confusingly similar industrial design and to distribute, sell, export and store them on the territory of the Republic of Estonia. The scope of legal protection of the industrial design shall be determined on the basis of the reproduction of the industrial design.

Application procedures

The registration is carried out by the filing system. The registration application may include one industrial design or a set of industrial designs. Registration applications of industrial design can be filed within one year after making it public.

The Patent Office does not examine the novelty, individual character and applicability of the industrial design, nor does it examine the right of the applicant to file a registration application. The Patent Office examines the compliance of the application documents with the formal requirements of registration of an industrial design and the compliance of the industrial design with the definition of industrial design. Legal protection is not granted to an industrial design which derives solely from the technical function of the product (except designs which make it possible to join module system products in different ways and take the product into pieces and put it together several times and combine the parts), is contrary to good practice, is unstable, is a layout design of integrated circuits or is a spare part or component which is not visible upon normal use when assembled in the product.

Registration

After entering the industrial design in the state register of industrial designs, the industrial design is published in the Estonian Industrial Design Gazette, the official gazette of the Estonian Patent Office.

Term of validity

The term of the rights of the owner in the industrial design is five years from the filing date of the registration application; after that, upon paying the state fee, the term of the rights in the industrial design may be renewed four times for five years each. The maximum term is 25 years.

Trade Marks

Registered trademarks

Any sign or combination of signs that is capable of being represented graphically and consists of letters, words, numerals or designs or is three-dimensional may be registered as a trade mark provided that such signs distinguish the goods

Estonia

and services of one natural or legal person from those of others. A trademark may be registered in black-and-white or color, whereas a trade mark registered in black-and-white shall be protected in all color combinations.

The scope of legal protection of a trademark is determined by the reproduction of the trademark and the specification of goods and services to which the trade mark applies, set out in the application for registration of the trademark. The specification is a list of goods and services classified according to the Nice Agreement Concerning the International Classification of Goods and Services for the Purposes of the Registration of Marks.

Application procedures

To acquire legal protection of a trade mark, an application should be filed with the Patent Office as soon as possible, because although legal protection will start after registration of the trademark, the trademark will be retrospectively protected as of the date of filing the application.

Before filing a registration application with the Patent Office, it is possible to make inquiries on registered and pending trademarks and to use the internet database of trademarks, which also includes international trademarks (where Estonia has been marked).

Trademarks well known in Estonia do not have to be registered.

The registration application can be submitted either by hand delivery, by post or by fax, whereas in case of a faxed application the original documents should be filed in one month of the date of receiving the fax. The text of the registration application should be typed. Each registration application should contain only one trademark.

Foreign applicants should file the registration applications only through Estonian patent attorneys. Estonian applicants may file the registration applications themselves.

The documents of the registration application should be in the Estonian language in the established format available from the Patent Office or from its homepage.

A state fee is payable for the registration of a trademark.

Upon processing trademark applications, a substantive examination system is used. Trademarks are examined as to the absolute grounds for refusal (he distinctive character) and as to the relative grounds for refusal (the earlier rights). The duration of the examination of trademark applications is approximately 10 months.

Estonia

Registration

If a trademark is registered, then the holder of the trademark shall be issued a traditional trademark certificate. The owner of the trademark shall thereafter have the exclusive right to use the respective trademark. The rights granted by registration are limited by the territory.

Term of protection

The registered trademark is valid from the date of filing the registration application for 10 years from the date of its entering into the Register of Trademarks.

The trademark holder is obliged to use the trademark; if it has not been used for five years, the registration could be invalidated.

Geographical Indications

Geographical indication means the name of or a reference to a geographical area which indicates the specific geographical origin of a good or service if the given quality, reputation or other characteristic of the good or service so identified is essentially attributable to the geographical area.

Geographical indication does not have an owner and legal protection of the geographical indication is perpetual. A registered geographical indication may be used for identifying goods or services by a person who acts as the producer, processor or preparer of the good specified in the registration or as the renderer of the service in the geographical area specified in the registration, and whose good or service has all the qualities, reputation or other characteristics specified in the registration.

A geographical indication may be figurative or in word form. The applicant may apply for the registration of only one geographical indication. The applicant may be a person who acts as the producer, processor or preparer of the goods or renderer of the service, an association of such people or consumers or a competent office of the country of origin.

The Patent Office does not examine the protectability of the geographical indication for which registration is applied. The Patent Office examines the compliance of the application documents with the formal requirements of the registration of a geographical indication.

The legal protection of the geographical indication is granted by registration in the State Register of Geographical Indications and by publishing a relevant announcement in the official gazette of the Patent Office. The registration of the geographical indication may be contested in court pursuant to administrative or civil court procedure.

Estonia

Domain Names

Domain names are registered in Estonia by EENet (Estonian Educational and Research Network), a governmental non-profit organization that manages the Estonian top level domain (.ee).

Top level domain .ee is a symbol representing the Estonian State. This sets limits to the registration of the second level domain under the .ee. The subdomain registration process is open only to companies registered in the Estonian Commercial Register, as well as to other organisations registered in Estonia and individuals, insofar as they have permanent Internet connection in Estonia. The subdomain ends with .ee.

The registration is currently free of charge (one cannot, however, exclude the possibility for possible registration fees, annual fees etc. in the future).

The applied second level domain should refer to the organization's name or to it's principal activities. It should not be misleading and should not be with prejudice to another person's interests. The name of the subdomain should not refer to anything obscene in languages represented in Estonia.

If the second level domain coincides with a well-known trademark or international company name, the applied second level domain will not be registered (except when the trademark belongs to the applying organization itself). Also, the registration of computer terminology, place names and several general words (for example shop.ee) as second level domains is restricted. When applying for 2-3 letter second level domains it is recommended to follow that it refers uniquely to the abbreviation used by the applying organization. Second level domain cannot be registered if someone else has already registered it.

The domain name has no trademark status. As domains under .ee are meant to be an institution's identification on the Internet (like the register code in the commercial register), registration of an additional domain in the defense of a trademark or a name form is not possible.

In order to register second level domains under .ee domain, an application in 'plain text' format should be sent to hostmaster@ns.kbfi.ee using the electronic application forms available at www.eenet.ee/info/domreg_ver4.html. Questions or requests for help can be referred to hostmaster@eenet.ee.

As a general rule, one organization can register only one domain. In case an organization needs more than one second level domain, a well-grounded application should be sent and the upper nameserver administrator (hostmaster@ns.kbfi.ee) has the right to make the decision. If his/her decision is contested, the final decision will be made by a person who is registered as an administrator of the .ee domain in INTERNIC. A well-grounded application is also needed in case an organisation is applying for a subdomain that does not cohere with its' name.

An organization applying for a second level domain is liable for the presented information and that it corresponds to the law and good practices. This responsibility stays with the applicant after the subdomain is registered. In cases where the applicant has presented false data, the hostmaster may annul the registered domain.

The subdomain registration applications and requests for the changes in the nameserver configurations will usually be processed in seven workdays.

Copyright and Related Rights

The Estonian Copyright Act provides for:
1) the protection of a specific right (copyright) of authors of literary, artistic and scientific works for the results of their creative activity;
2) the persons who may acquire rights to literary, artistic or scientific works created by an author and the rights of such persons;
3) the rights of performers, producers of phonograms and broadcasting organisations (related rights);
4) the rights of makers of databases and conditions for the exercise and protection thereof;
5) the related rights of producers of first fixations of films and of other persons specified in this Act;
6) limitations on the exercise of copyright and related rights upon the use of works in the interest of the public;
7) guarantees for the exercise of copyright and related rights and the protection of such rights.

In general the Estonian Copyright Act applies to works:
1) the author of which is a citizen or a permanent resident of the Republic of Estonia;
2) first published in the territory of the Republic of Estonia or not published but located in the territory of the Republic of Estonia, regardless of the citizenship or the permanent residence of the creator of the works;
3) which must be protected in accordance with an international agreement of the Republic of Estonia.

Copyright subsists in literary, artistic and scientific works, i.e. any original results in the literary, artistic or scientific domain which are expressed in an objective form and can be perceived and reproduced in this form either directly or by means of technical devices. A work is original if it is the author's own intellectual creation.

Estonia

The author of a work is the natural person or persons who created the work. Copyright shall belong to a legal person only in the cases prescribed in the copyright law.

The author of the work shall acquire the copyright to the respective work upon the creation thereof. Creation of a work means the moment of expression of the work in any objective form that allows the perception and reproduction or fixation of the work.

The registration or deposit of a work or completion of other formalities is not required for the creation or exercise of copyright.

The copyright constitutes of moral rights and proprietary rights.

The author's moral rights include right to authorship, right to author's name, right to integrity of the work, right to additions to the work, right to protection of author's honor and reputation, right to disclosure of the work, right to supplementation of the work, right to withdraw the work, right to request the removal of the author's name.

The moral rights of an author are inseparable from the author's person and non-transferable. The moral rights may be limited only in the cases prescribed by the copyright law.

The author's proprietary rights constitute of the author's exclusive right to use the author's work in any manner, to authorize or prohibit the use of the work in a similar manner by other persons, and to receive income from such use of the author's work. In addition, the author has the right to grant or restrict the right to reproduce the work, distribution right, right to translate the work, right to alter the work, right to collections of works, right of public performance, right to exhibition of the work, and right to transmit the work.

The proprietary rights of an author are transferable as single rights or a set of rights for a charge or free of charge. The proprietary rights of an author may be limited only in the cases prescribed by the copyright law.

Authors exercise their proprietary rights either independently or through collective management organizations.

The copyright law also foresees certain limitations to the proprietary rights of authors. In certain cases, provided that this does not conflict with a normal exploitation of the work or does not unreasonably prejudice the legitimate interests of the author, it is permitted to use a work without the authorization of its author and without payment of remuneration. In general, a lawfully published work of another person may be reproduced for private use without the authorization of its author and without payment of remuneration.

Estonia

The term of protection of copyright shall be the life of the author and seventy years after his or her death, irrespective of the date when the work is lawfully made available to the public.

The authorship of a certain work, the name of the author and the honor and reputation of the author shall be protected without a term.

Useful Industry Contacts

The Estonian Patent Office
Toompuiestee 7
15041 Tallinn
Estonia
phone: 372 627 7900
fax: 372 645 1342
e-mail: info@epa.ee

Ministry of Culture
Committee of Copyright Experts
Suur-Karja 23
15076 Tallinn
Estonia
phone: 372 6 282 250
fax: 372 6 282 200
e-mail: min@kul.ee

Estonian Authors' Society
Lille 13
10614 Tallinn
Estonia
phone: 372 6 684 360
fax: 372 6 684 361
e-mail: eau@eau.org

Chapter 10: Finland

Finland

Leif Nordin
(Berggren Oy Ab)

Patents

Finland entered the European Patent Convention on March 1, 1996. Therefore, the Finnish Patent Act, as well as the procedures of the National Board of Patents and Registration (also cited as the Finnish Patent Office, are substantially harmonized with the practice of the European Patent Office and thus there does not exist any significant differences between the systems and procedures in the field of patents. One of latest harmonization practices has been the patentability of computer-related inventions, which have been completely harmonized with the practices of the EPO.

National practice

As already mentioned, there are no significant differences between the contents of the Finnish patent law and the EPC. However, regulations and practices seem to be documented in more detail within the EPC regulations, whereas such regulations are only adapted in practice by the Finnish Patent Office.

In addition to the international co-operation with the EPO and the WIPO, the Finnish Patent Office takes an active role in searching, examining and granting patents. The Office has over 80 examiners and is actively seeking to broaden its examination staff. Typically, the applicant who first filed his application in Finland obtains the result of the search within six to ten months from the filing date. Thus, the result is helpful to the applicant when deciding whether to pursue the application abroad within the priority year. In order to ensure continuity, the Finnish Patent Office has established a quality assessment program for controlling the smooth handling of the application while maintaining high quality.

Official languages of the Finnish Patent Office are Finnish and Swedish. An interesting feature of the Finnish patent practice is that the first filed application can even be filed in English. Of course a translation into the official language shall

---

Leif Nordin is Managing Director of Berggren Oy Ab in Helsinki. Berggren Oy Ab has more than 65 years of experience in industrial property rights. The firm offers a wide range of services covering all industrial property (IP) rights including patents, trademarks, utility models and designs.

Finland

be provided later. Also, the fees of the Finnish Patent Offices are substantially lower than those of international offices.

One of the special characteristics in Finnish IPR laws is the utility model, which Finland has adopted. Utility model applications are examined only as to formal requirements. Novelty and validity can be evaluated by administrative procedure through the Patent Office, whereas infringement requires court procedure. It is also possible to convert a patent application into a utility model application.

The Finnish Patent Office provides electronic services such as electronic filing and follow-up of the application.

International cooperation

The Finnish Patent Office acts as a national patent authority in many respects to the European Patent Convention and also to the Patent Co-operation Treaty, thus enabling, for example, the filing of both the European and International applications as well as providing the translations of the European Patents.

The Finnish Patent Office also started preparations for undertaking the tasks of a PCT authority. Finland's application was addressed for the first time in the General Assembly of the PCT Union. The Assembly stated that Finland is fully entitled to apply for this authority status and that the National Board of Patents and Registration of Finland has the resources required and capability to act as a PCT authority. WIPO's Secretariat also supported Finland's application. The handling of the matter was postponed for later decision in the General Assembly of the PCT Union.

Trade Marks

The Finnish Trademark Act as well as the procedures concerning formal requirements for the registration of trademarks are harmonized with the European Community Regulations and thus, there does not exist any remarkable differences between the systems and procedures in the field of trademarks.

There are no differences between the contents of laws, but the usage of the Finnish Patent Office is somewhat stricter than the usage of the Office for the Harmonisation of the Internal Market (OHIM). In contrast to the usage of OHIM, the Finnish Patent Office will examine relative grounds of the marks. The registration of three-dimensional marks is also rather difficult at the moment, for the Patent Office considers most of them as lacking distinctiveness.

As concerns the registration of indications of origin, the Finnish Patent Office used to reject all marks indicating geographical names, but the Examiners have now somewhat loosened the practice in this respect. Nowadays it is possible to register a geographical name, if it is not yet a well-known place, for certain goods. Eg. 'Havanna' is famous for cigars and thus not available, but 'Key West' is available for clothing, for example.

Chapter 11: France

# France

By Jacques Beaumont, Isabelle Brenn and Frédéric Dumont
(Deprez Dian Guignot)

Patents

A patent is an industrial property right issued by governmental institutions, which grants the patentee an exclusive right to exploit the invention for a limited period of time, currently twenty years.

The modern idea of protecting inventions first appeared during the French Revolution, with two statutes passed in 1790 and 1791; it was then governed for a century by an 1844 Act. Then, a January 2, 1968 Act was followed by a July 13, 1978 Act. After being modified several times, the 1978 Act became the July 1, 1992 Act which was codified in the French Intellectual Property Code (hereinafter referred to as the "CPI"). The codification was completed by an April 4, 1995 decree.

French companies tend to file fewer applications for patents than companies in other countries. National patent legislation is progressively replaced by European and international legislation.

Obtaining a Patent
What is a patentable invention?

- An industrial product, defined as every material item, every unique good distinguished from other goods by its mechanic composition or chemical structure.
- A process, defined as a system composed of a method or of any substance or composition and means that allows obtaining a product or a result.
- A new implementation of known means, defined as the use of one or many means already known which fulfills a new function.
- A combination of known ways, defined as an original combination of known means, which results in a new industrial product or a general industrial result different from the one resulting from each mean separately.

Jacques Beaumont, Isabelle Brenn and Frédéric Dumont are attorneys with Deprez Dian Guignot (Ddg) in Paris. Mr. Beaumont acts on behalf of a wide range of French and foreign clients on tradmark matters and has extensive experience in litigation involving luxury brands. Ms. Brenn handles a wide variety of Internet, computer, advertising and mass media matters. Mr Dumont has extensive expertise in the fields of copyright litigation, especially entertainment (broadcast TV), advertising, IT and publishing matters.

France

Patentability requirements

The industrial creation must necessarily be an "invention", defined as a technical solution to a technical problem. It must have a concrete application. French law only provides for exclusions, such as discoveries, scientific theories and mathematical methods, aesthetic creations, computer programs, and information presentations (Article L611-10 2 CPI).

An invention must comply with three conditions (Article L611-10 CPI):

- It must show an element of novelty, so it should not form part of the current state of art. The state of art comprises everything made available to the public before the date of filing of the patent (Article L611-11 CPI).
- It must involve an inventive step (Article L611-14 CPI). It should not be obvious to a person skilled in the art, having regard to the state of the art.
- It must be susceptible to industrial application (Article L611-15 CPI). The object of the invention should be possible to make or use in every kind of industry, including agriculture.

Exclusions of patentability

Some inventions complying with the conditions of patentability are nevertheless excluded from this protection (Article L611-17 CPI):

- Inventions of which publication or exploitation would be contrary to public order and morality.
- Plant varieties of a kind or species protected by a certificate of plant variety.
- Animal varieties and especially biological processes for the production of plants and animals.

How is a patent granted?

The patent application can be filed by any French person or legal entity. A foreign person or legal entity can file an application in some cases:

- If it benefits from the Convention of Union of Paris or from the ADPIC Act, or
- If it has its residence or an industrial plant in France, or
- If French citizens and legal entities have mutual rights in the country of the foreign person or legal entity (Article L611-1 CPI).

The right to a patent belongs to the inventor (or his assignee/successors) who has first filed the application (Article L611-6 CPI). Inventions made by employees are governed by specific rules (Article L611-7 CPI):

- Inventions made in the course of a mission belong to the employer ("Inventions made by the employee in accomplishment of an employment contract containing an inventive task fitting with his effective duties, or of studies and research expressly allocated to him.")

- Inventions which are not made in the course of a mission but in the area of the company's activities, or thanks to the knowledge or the use of techniques or ways specific to the company or of data brought by it, can be granted to the employer at his demand, and with the payment of a fair price.
- Other inventions made out of the mission belong to the employee.

The patent application must relate to one invention only, or to a group of inventions so linked as to form a single general inventive concept (Article L612-4 CPI).

The patent application must contain the following formal elements: a request for the grant of a patent, the identification of the applicant, a description of the invention, one or more claims, an abstract of the technical contents of the invention, the drawings referred to in the description, a copy of the anterior filings from which some elements come (Article L612-2 CPI). The description must be clear and precise enough so that a man of the art would be able to use it; on the contrary the patent could be invalidated for lack of description (Article L612-5 CPI).

The claims, which define the matter for which protection is sought, must be clear and concise and be supported by the description. If not, the application may be dismissed and the patent invalidated (Article L612-6 CPI).

Procedure

The application can be filed at the National Institute for Industrial Property (INPI), at a date that should be considered as the official starting point of the protection. It is subject to the payment of a filing fee (35 euros) and a search fee (320 euros). The patent application is published in the Official Bulletin for Industrial Property (BOPI) 18 months at the latest after its filing. The Minister of Defense reviews all patent applications, and deems them "secret" if it is in the interest of national security.

The INPI proceeds with an administrative and technical review of the compliance of the application with the form and substance conditions (Article L612-11 and L612-12 CPI).

The INPI then drafts a research report, via the European Patent Office (EPO), evaluating the patentability of the invention. A preliminary research report presents the state of the art at the filing date. The applicant can make observations on it and modify his demand, particularly the claims. During the three months following the drafting of the preliminary report, observations can be made by anyone on the invention's patentability. A final report is drafted, which will be at-

France

tached to the granted patent.

The INPI director grants the patent. The text of the patent must be published. The granting decision is notified to the applicant who receives a copy of the patent. The granting gives a definitive content to the patentee's right. The granted patent is considered valid. The applicant must then pay a granting fee (85 euros).

Specificities of the French procedure

The French patent system is dual, as no cross-examination of the invention's patentability is done but a detailed priority search is made during the granting procedure.

The French procedure of granting patents is simple and fast, as 95% of the patents are granted within a two-year period. Its cost is low (about 440 euros), compared to other industrialized countries. After its 20-year period of validity, the cost of the patent for its filing and renewal comes to approximately 5300 euros.

The priority search performed by the EPO is of high value. However, guarantees given by the patent are low compared to other countries.

In the past, patents were granted "with no government's guarantee". Today, the INPI mainly grants patents on the basis of a formal examination, with no real checking of the patent's compliance with the legal conditions. Thus, the majority of applications lead to the granting of a patent.

Patent Protection
Rights and obligations of the patentee

The patent gives the patentee an exclusive right to work the invention, the patentee being the only one allowed to manufacture and commercialize it.

The patent can be assigned to a third party or brought into a business. It can also be licensed or pledged. The patentee can be forced to waive or to license his patent, for example through: expropriation by the State of the patented inventions for the purpose of national security (Article L613-20 CPI); mandatory licenses granted by judges to demanding third parties, in case of lack of exploitation of the patent by its patentee (Article L613-11 CPI), although it rarely happens in practice; granting of automatic licenses by the administrative authority in three cases—economic development (Article L613-18 CPI), public health (Article L613-16 CPI) and national security (Article L613-19 CPI).

The patent gives its patentee protection in the national territory for 20 years from the date of the application filing (Article L611-2 1° CPI). In practice, the duration can be extended for about a year by applying for a European patent designating France, made during the priority period. The protection may also be extended in the case of patents concerning a medicine, a process of obtaining a medicine, a product necessary to obtain a medicine or the manufacturing process of such a product, when the patent is used for the making of a medicine subjected to marketing authorization (Article L611-3 CPI). A Supplementary Protection Certificate protects the inventor starting on the legal term of the patent, for a maximum period of 7 years from this term and of 17 years from the granting of the marketing authorization (Article L611-2 3° CPI).

Patentee's rights

The following acts of exploitation of the patent by third parties are forbidden without the patentee's consent, because of the protection given by the patent (art L613-3 CPI):

- Manufacturing, supply, marketing, use, importing or possession for the aforementioned purposes of the patented product.
- Use of a patented process or offer to use on the French territory,
- Supply, trade, use, importation or possession for the aforementioned purposes of the product obtained by the patented process.
- Acts of assistance to these operations are also forbidden, such as providing or offering to provide, on French territory, to a person not allowed to exploit the invention, the ways of implementing, on this territory, the invention or an essential element of it (Article L613-4 CPI).

The following acts are authorized for third parties:

- Acts renowned as being non commercial (Article L613-5 CPI),
- Acts authorized in consideration of the termination of the patent right (Article L613-6 CPI),
- Acts allowed due to an anterior personal possession right (Article L613-7 CPI).

Patentee's obligations

The patentee shall pay annual renewal fees so as to maintain his patent (Article L612-19 CPI). The fee amount increases incrementally, from 25 euros in the first year (2002) to 530 euros in the final year.

The patentee must also exploit the invention, unless an automatic license is granted to all demanding third parties (Article L613-11 CPI).

Sanctions of violations of patent rights
Non-infringement action

A manufacturer who considers manufacturing a product or implementing a process can get around an action for patent infringement through an "action in declaration of non infringement" (Article L615-9 CPI). The manufacturer asks the patentee to declare the manufacturer a potential infringer of his patent. If the patentee doesn't answer within three months or if the manufacturer challenges his answer, the latter can bring a legal action against the patentee before a first level court ("Tribunal de Grande Instance") to establish the absence of infringement. An infringement action cannot be initiated later on the basis of the same facts.

Conditions of the action for infringement of a patent

An infringement action compensates the patentee for acts of patent exploitation where the patentee's consent has not been obtained. This action can be brought by the patentee, as well as exclusive licensees and licensed parties after unsuccessful prior formal notice to the patentee (Article L615-2 CPI). The action is taken before first level courts—tribunaux de grande instance—(Article L615-17 CPI). The action is prescribed by a three-year period from the date of infringement (Article L615-8 CPI).

Only ten courts in France entertain jurisdiction over the action for infringement or nullity of patents (Article L615-7 and R631 CPI).

Procedure

The infringing act is defined as any offense to the patentee's rights. Bad faith of the counterfeiter is necessary in the following cases: every act made by a non-manufacturer (use, supply, trade, marketing, possession in order to use or trade, provision of ways to exploit the patent) and a party (provision of ways to exploit the patent). Conversely, bad faith is not necessary for any act done by the manufacturer of the infringing item, or for importation onto French territory by a non-manufacturer (Article L615-1 al3 CPI).

The applicant must establish the existence of similarities of essential elements between the patented invention and the item exploited by the defendant. The patentee can prove the offense by all means. He also benefits from the specific procedure of seizure of counterfeited goods (Article L615-5 CPI); the President of the court then decides to make a detailed description of the litigious products or processes, with or without seizure of these products or processes.

Sanction of the infringement action

The applicant can request from the President of the court, competent for urgent matters, to temporarily prohibit the continuation of the acts or to subordinate this continuation to the constitution of guarantees for the applicant (Article L615-3 CPI).

Finally the court can opt for the following sanctions: cessation of the unlawful acts; confiscation of the unlawful items and instruments or means which contributed to the realisation of the infringement (Article L615-7 CPI); compensation for the infringement aimed at repairing the injury caused to the patentee (punitive damages are not allocated); publication of the judgment in the press.

Penal action for infringement, taken before criminal courts ("tribunal correctionnel"), can lead to criminal sanctions (restored by a 26 November 1990 Act): two years of imprisonment and 150,000 euro fine for parties who knowingly violated the patentee's rights (Article L615-14 CPI).

Action for infringement of a patent in France

Disputes relating to patents are often settled by transaction, with only an average of 300 litigations pending in courts every year.

The trial in infringement cases is long. For instance, it takes one and a half to three years in first instance jurisdictions, and an average of three years in appeal. Competent judges are not technicians although ten courts only are competent in patent litigation matters. Judges are often assisted by experts to evaluate the damages and trial attorneys are helped by patent attorneys for all technical matters, even often for the draft of written pleadings (but not oral advocacy).

The evaluation of damages varies with the way the invention is exploited. When the patentee works his patent himself, he can be compensated for loss of profits. On the contrary, when the patent is licensed, the licensee only gets compensatory royalties; those royalties are priced higher than the market's rate. Companies usually complain about the low level of royalties granted by the courts, which affects the deterrent effect of the damages.

Proceedings costs allocated by judges that can be reimbursed by the opponent, under Article 700 of the French Code of Civil Procedure, were low but are significantly increasing (about 4,000 euros).

Designs and Models in France

The "unity of art" rule

Designs/models protection was developed in two directions in France:

On the one hand, a non-specific set of rules concerning literary and artistic property appeared during the French Revolution in 1793. This legislation didn't expressly concern industrial designs/models. It was later completed by a 1902 law extending its application to specific areas such as architects or sculptors. An Act passed on March 11, 1957 replaced the 1793 act.

On the other hand a specific legislation, implemented in 1806, organized an application procedure before the "Conseils de Prud'homme", this system being still used until recently. This legislation was later abrogated by a 1909 law, creat-

France

ing the "unity of art" rule according to which protection conferred by the 1909 law combines with the protection given by the 1793 law. The 1909 act was repealed by a law passed on November 26, 1990.

These two legislations were finally codified in 1992 in the French Intellectual Property Code (hereinafter referred to as the "CPI"). A European directive was adopted in 1998 to harmonize the protection of designs and models in the EU, which was transposed by the French decree of July 25, 2001.

The designs and models protection system is specific in France in regard to the "unity of art" rule, according to which designs and models can be both protected by their specific legislation and by the author's rights legislation; the designs and models must then comply with these regimes' conditions.

Cumulative protection

A design/model can also be protected by a trademark if the specific conditions are complied with. This design/model could then enjoy three protections: specific protection of designs and models, trademarks protection and author's rights protection. The trademarks' protection shall be refused to signs exclusively constituted by the shape imposed by the nature or function of the product or which gives the product its substantial value (Article 711-2 c) CPI).

In contrast, cumulative protection by designs and models and by patents is forbidden (Article L511-3 al2 CPI). When the design/model fulfills a technical function, the specific legislation of designs and models is excluded and the patent rules should be applied.

How to Obtain the Specific Protection of Designs and Models
The designs and models that can be protected

A registered design/model protects the aesthetic, visible aspect.
A design or model can be every "product", meaning every object (three dimensions) or every decorative motif (two dimensions), which presents an apparent character (Article L511-1 CPI[1]), excluding computer programs. The protection can be given to the product or every part of the product.

To be apparent, the design/model should be able to be perceptible to the eye. Excluded from protection are:

- Computer programs,
- Ideas,
- Forms solely dictated by the technical function of the product (Article L511-8 1 CPI),
- Pieces of interconnection, excluding pieces that are part of modular systems (Article L511-8 2 CPI),

- Designs and models contrary to public policy or accepted principles of morality (Article L511-7 CPI).

Conditions of the protection

The design or model can be protected only if it is new and has a peculiar character (Article L511-2 CPI).

The design/model shall be deemed new if, on the date of the filing of the registration's application or on the date of priority claimed, no identical design or model has been disclosed (Article L511-3 CPI), with no limit of time or space. This condition won't be satisfied in certain cases:

- If the design/model is absolutely identical to, or only has immaterial details that differ from an anterior design/model.
- If the holder of the design/model has disclosed it before his registration, except if he applies for registration of the design/model in the year following this disclosure. The disclosure is appreciated in regard to a public composed of professionals operating in the EU in the designs/models' area.

The design/model shall present a particular character if the overall visual impression it produces on the informed observer differs from that produced by any design/model disclosed before the date of the filing of the application for registration or before the date of priority claimed. The degree of freedom of the creator in developing the design or the model is taken into consideration when assessing this condition.

Obtaining the protection

<u>Owner of the protection:</u> The protection of the design/model is granted to the creator or to his successor-in-title (Article. L511-9 CPI). There is a presumption according to which the design is the creation of its applicant, failing proof to the contrary. This presumption has stronger effects than the authors' rights presumption, according to which the author is the person who commercializes the work.

If a design/model was registered so as to defraud another person's rights or in violation of a statutory or contractual obligation, any person who believes he has a right on the design/model may claim its ownership (Article L 511-10 CPI). In case of successful legal proceedings brought before a court, the claimant will get the property of the design/model. The claimant should be aware of the term of limitation (3 years from the design/model's registration's publication, or from the expiration of the protection in case of bad faith of the registration's owner).

<u>Registration application:</u> The applicant has to register his design/model with the National Institute for Industrial Property (INPI) to get the specific protection of the designs/models (Article L511-9 CPI).

France

The application must contain the following elements: a registration application, graphical and photographical representations of the design/model, and proof of the fee payment.

The registration application will mainly contain the identification of the applicant, the number of designs/models and reproductions registered, a description of the design/model, and the claim for priority right.

Procedure

Usual application. The owner of a design/model must file an application for its registration with the INPI. The date of this application will be considered as the official starting point of the protection. It is subject to the payment of an application fee.

The INPI first examines the application's compliance with the form conditions (documents needed and payment of the fees). In the case of an incomplete application, the applicant has two months in which to regularize his application, otherwise it will be refused.

The INPI will only examine the conformity of the application with public policy and morality; it won't check the novelty or the particular character of the design/model. The applicant should be asked to present comments on INPI's objections, prior to filing's refusal. An application may be refused under various circumstances, such as when it is not in compliance with the conditions of protection mentioned above, or if it infringes the copyright of a third party (Article L512-4 CPI).

Designs/models registrations shall be published in the Official Bulletin of Industrial Property, unless the applicant has requested, at the time of the filing, the postponement of such publication for three years.

Postponement of publication may only concern the filing as a whole.

The registration allows the holder to extend abroad the protection of his design/model, claiming in the same moment the benefit of International conventions and the priority right of 6 months from the French registration ("Convention d'Union de Paris" of 1886).

Simplified application: In the case of designs pertaining to industries that frequently change the form and presentation of their goods, filing may be made in a simplified form. The form of the presentation of the graphical and photographical representations is simplified and the filing shall be subject to proof of payment of a fee independent of the number of reproductions.

Postponement of the publication is automatic in this case, and it doesn't necessarily only concern the filing as a whole. This simplified procedure is often used in the fashion business. The postponement of the publication allows for the selection of some designs/models in a collection that will be effectively protected.

France

Specifics of the French procedure

<u>*Application of the "unity of art" rule:*</u> The creator shall automatically benefit from the authors' rights protection if his design/model complies with the condition of originality. Even if this protection doesn't need any registration, it can be useful to prove the date of the creation. In this case, the creator can get a "Soleau" envelope issued by the INPI, allowing him to constitute proof of the date of his creation; this envelope's size is limited to 5-7 papers. This kind of filing doesn't confer to the applicant the benefit of the specific protection of designs/models.

Moreover, the applicant should be aware of the fact that designs/models' protection through author's rights is not admitted in every country.

<u>*General:*</u> Whereas the 1998 directive created the condition of "individual" character for the specific designs/models protection, the French decree of 2001 that transposed this directive referred to the condition of "particular" character. One might wonder about the way that French courts will interpret this new condition. The number of applications for designs/models registration has increased in the last ten years, particularly because of the authorization of simplified application.

Protection of Designs and Models

Rights and obligations of the owner of the design/model

The registration of a design/model gives its creator an exclusive right to exploit it. He can exploit it directly, or assign or license it to a third party (Article L513-2 CPI). These acts transferring the exploitation rights of a registered design/model can only be opposed by third parties if they have been registered in the National Register for Designs and Models (Article L513-3 CPI).

The specific protection of the designs/models starts from the date of the application's filing and for a period of five years, which may be extended by periods of five years with a maximum limit of twenty-five years (Article L 513-1 CPI). This protection duration was much longer before the 1998 European directive, as the initial period of protection of twenty-five years could then be renewed for another twenty-five years.

If the creator benefits from the author's rights protection, his economic right will last as long as the author lives and will belong to eligible parties for 70 years after his death. The creator also benefits from his moral right.

Creator's rights

Acts of exploitation of the design/model are forbidden to third parties, without the creator's consent, including the making, offering, putting on the market, importing, exporting, using, or possession for these purposes, of a product comprising the design/model (Article L513-4 CPI).

The protection conferred by the registration of a design/model shall be extended to any design or model which does not produce on the informed observer a different overall visual impression.

Third-parties are allowed the following acts without the creator's consent (Article L513-6, L513-7 and L513-8 CPI):

- Acts done privately and for non-commercial purposes.
- Acts done for experimental purposes.
- Acts of reproduction for the purposes of making citations or teaching, if these acts mention the registration and the name of the right's holder, provided they are compatible with fair business practices and do not prejudice the normal exploitation of that design/model.
- Acts concerning the equipment on ships and aircraft registered in another country when these temporarily enter French territory. Acts of importation into France of spare parts and accessories for the repair of these ships or aircraft and the acts of repair.
- Acts covering a product comprising this design/model, when this product has been put on the market in the European Community or in the European Economic Area by the owner of the design/model or with his consent.

Creator's obligations

The creator shall pay renewal fees to maintain his exclusive right on his design/model.

Sanctions of violation of the design/model rights

In the case of a violation of his rights, the creator of the design/model benefits from two actions: infringement action and unfair trading action.

Infringement action

Conditions: Acts of infringement of a design/model can be condemned on the basis of author's rights or of specific designs/models rights.

The infringement action can only sanction the violation of the rights on a design/model that was previously registered. This action can be initiated by the creator or his assignee. In contrast, this right is not given to the licensee, even benefiting from an exclusive license.

The claimant can bring the action either before a civil court ("Tribunal de Grande Instance" or "Tribunal de Commerce") or a penal court ("Tribunal

Correctionnel"). These two actions are prescribed in different time limits starting from the realization of each infringement act: three years for the penal action, ten years for the civil one.

Procedure: The infringement action sanctions any knowingly committed infringement of the creator's rights on his design/model (Article L521-4 CPI). It will then be punished only if the following elements exist: a material element and a moral one:

- The material element is an act of infringement defined as any offense to the creator's rights.
- The moral element is the intention of the third party to infringe the creator's rights, the fact that he knows he has violated the design/model.

Case law has created a presumption of bad faith in penal subjects. In civil procedure, the proof of the good faith of the infringer doesn't exempt him from his responsibility.

The claimant can prove the offense by all means. Even before the filing's publication, the claimant benefits from a specific procedure of seizure of counterfeited goods (Article L521-1 CPI). The President of the first level civil courts ("Tribunal de Grande Instance") then decides to make a detailed description, with or without seizure, of the incriminated articles or instruments.

The customs' administration may also, at the written request of the owner of a deposited design, withhold in the course of its inspections, goods alleged by him to be infringing the said designs (Article L521-7 CPI). This withholding measure shall be lifted as of right where the plaintiff fails to prove to customs services, within ten days following notification of the goods' withholding, either that precautionary measures have been ordered by the President of the "Tribunal de Grande Instance", or that he has instituted proceedings before the civil court or the court of misdemeanours and has provided the required guarantees to cover his liability in the event of the infringement claim being eventually considered unfounded.

Sanction of the infringement action: Both natural persons and legal entities may be declared criminally liable (Article L521-5 CPI). Legal entities might get stronger sanctions, as mentioned in Articles 131-38 and 131-39 of the Penal Code.

The infringement act is punished by the following criminal sanctions: two years imprisonment and a 150,000 euro fine (Article L521-4 CPI). It might also lead to the closure of the establishment that served for the commission of the offense, for a maximum period of five years; in this case specific rules are applied for employment contracts[2].

In both penal and civil actions, the infringer might be condemned to pay damages to the claimant. Both penal and civil courts can decide the confiscation of the

France

articles infringing the creator's rights, even in the event of a discharge (Article L521-3 CPI).

Action in unfair competition

The action in unfair trading, which condemns disloyal behaviour on the trade market, can complete the action in counterfeiting as it is different from it in terms of nature of the action and conditions.

This action belongs to the design/model's creator or his licensee.

The claimant shall prove the existence of an act different from the infringement of his design/model. He must establish the third party's responsibility, according to the conditions of Article 1382 of the Civil Code. He must then prove that the third party's act constituted a fault that created a prejudice to him.

The responsible third party shall be condemned to pay damages to the claimant.

Specificities of the French infringement actions

Two specificities of the French designs/models protection system have to be highlighted.

The creator has a risk to destroy the novelty of his design/model if he has disclosed it before its registration and if he hasn't applied for registration of his design/model in the year following this disclosure.

The consequences of the postponement of a design/model's registration's publication on the novelty of a later registered design/model. In the case of an infringement action, the presumed infringer tries to avoid infringement conviction, by alleging the existence of a previous design/model that destroys the novelty of the infringed design/model. This previous design/model has been disclosed by a third party and the publication of its registration has been postponed after the registration's date of the design/model. The consequences of the postponement of the registration's publication are different if the infringement action is based on authors' rights or on designs/models specific protection. If the action is based on the authors' rights, the design/model previously created will destroy the originality of the design/model, and the infringement conviction will be avoided. In contrast, if the action is based on the specific designs/models protection, the previous design/model whose registration was not published will not destroy the novelty of the design/model, and the infringer might be convicted.

Infringing designs/models are assessed in an analytical way, as they are examined and compared with the original design/model; control is then meticulous and detailed.

Infringement actions are rarely taken before the criminal courts.

© 2004 WorldTrade Executive, Inc. and Deprez Dian Guignot

France

Trade Marks

The first statute on trademarks was the Act of June 23, 1857, which remained in force for almost a century. At that time, trademark rights belonged to the first user. Trademark filing was then facultative and merely declarative.

French trademark law has been heavily influenced by the concept of property rights. Trademark protection has thus been largely defined, although trademark owners' obligations were few, even non-existent at the origin.

The Act of December 31, 1964 rendered trademark filing mandatory. It also introduced a form of examination of the trademark application and, above all, imposed the actual use of trademarks, by allowing a revocation action after five years of nonuse.

The current Trademarks Act of January 4, 1991 has transposed the European Directive of December 21, 1988 on the approximation of trademarks laws.

The salient feature of this Act was the introduction of an opposition procedure, which has transferred an important part of trademark litigation (nullity requests and infringements actions) from the courts to the Trademarks Office.

Previously, all conflicts were dealt with in court. Furthermore, the conditions to a revocation action were widened, the rule of acquiescence introduced, and the grace period for trademark renewals abolished.

While coexisting with the European Community system, the French trademarks system still offers some original and interesting features for companies, particularly low filing costs and a relatively quick registration period, such that a French tradmark can be enforced shortly after its filing. In addition, certain French overseas territories, such as New Caledonia and Pacific, are only covered by national trademarks.

Although French Courts and the Trademark Office today comply with European Community case law and apply a less analytical approach when comparing litigious marks, some uncertainties remain. Due to the rather reasonable costs and simplicity, one can say that some signs are abusively subject to a trademark filing, many signs being systematically filed, although they do not correspond to any genuine product or service.

What is a trademark?

French courts have adopted the definition of "trademark" in the Paris Convention and, more precisely, in European Community Law.

French law recognises that any sign capable of being represented graphically, and of distinguishing the goods and services of one undertaking from those of another can be registered as a trademark.

France

French law has always had a liberal approach to signs likely to be registered, such as packaging, numerals, colours, letters etc., contrary to UK or German trademarks laws. Registrability is thus less tricky than in other E.U. countries, although French examiners are becoming more and more severe.

For instance, to be distinguishable, a nuance of colour is only required to be clear and precise (e.g. : the colours 'Rouge fuchsia' or 'Rouge Congo' and 'green' have been considered as being able to be specifically associated to a washing liquid.)

However, with respect to odours, French Courts have never as yet recognised that a reliable graphical representation was possible for this kind of 'sign'.

Outside of trademark law, the impact of specific statutes should be mentioned. Indeed, the French "anti-smoking law", for example, commonly known as "Loi Evin" of January 12, 1991 forbids the use of a registered trademark designating tobacco for the advertising of other goods and services.

A statute aimed at the protection of the French language, la "Loi Toubon" of February 2, 1994, does not prevent the filing of English words as French trademarks, but requires the advertisements to include their French translation.

Classes of goods and services and the wording of specification

France applies the International classification of goods and services, today divided into 45 classes.

In practice, French trademarks are often filed in at least three classes, because the filing fee is the same for up to three classes.

Until recently, the wording used to specify French trademarks was often the citation of the International classes' general headings, and thus, today, most French trademarks renewed merely covers these headings. With the growth in trademark conflicts, due in particular to the rapid development of the opposition procedure and the influence of filings made by US and overseas companies, the wording of the specification of goods and services tends to be much more precise and specific.

Examination process

The French system of trademark registration is one of the fastest in the world. The average period to obtain a registration is between 4 to 6 months from the filing date, provided that no opposition has been lodged by a third-party or that no objection has been raised by the appointed Examiner.

The application is officially published 6 weeks from the filing date in the Official Bulletin for Industrial Property (Bulletin Officiel de la Propriété Industrielle or BOPI) which starts the two-month opposition period.

During the same period, any party can also file observations regarding the trademark application (most often, its registrability).

France

The National Institute for Intellectual Property (Institut National de la Propriété Intellectuelle or INPI) does not examine the availability of the mark applied for, but only considers legal grounds for refusal.

Therefore, one could say that the legal 'value' of the French trademark registration is somewhat affected by the lack of examination of prior marks. This lack of examination also places emphasis on the necessity to watch trademark applications in order to oppose on time.

The Preservation of a Registered Trademark
Obligation of use

A trademark registration must be used within five years from registration. If no use has been made, it can be expunged by the court at the request of any party having an interest. The use must be public, actual and not fictitious or token. It is not required, however, that the use be commercially important. It must encompass all the products and services of the specification or partial revocation can be sought with respect to unused products or services. Unlike the former Trademark Act of 1964, the use of a trademark for certain goods or services does not protect similar goods and services for which it is not used.

If the work is used by an authorised third party where there is no license recorded, or even no written license, the trademark is still "used" within the meaning of the law.

A second ground for revocation was set out by the Trademarks Act of 1991. It is the ground of *genericism*, which was previously recognised by the courts. However, in this matter, little case-law exists since the defense available to the registrant, based on the distinctive character of the trademark, is generally considered as being sufficient to maintain the trademark's existence.

Renewal of the trademark

The French registration is valid for a 10-year period from the initial filing date. The registration can be indefinitely renewed. The renewal application must be filed at INPI six months before the expiry date.

INPI does not send any reminder letter to the registrant or its agent, contrary to WIPO for International Registrations.

Thus, if the renewal application is not filed on time, the only way is to submit a petition for reinstatement together with an application for renewal to the Director of INPI provided, however, that a legitimate excuse can be alleged and established. This legitimate excuse often lies in the failure of the agent in charge of the renewal.

France

The Trademarks Law of 1991 suppressed the six-month grace period which previously existed, although this seems to contradict the wording of the Paris Union Convention.

Enforcement and Litigation
Substantive rules

<u>General principles:</u> The identical reproduction or apposition, imitation or use of a trademark without the owner's consent constitutes an act of infringement.

Before 1991, trademark law distinguished between two separate actions : (i) infringement *by identical reproduction* of the trademark and (ii) infringement *by imitation*, i.e. when the prior mark was not reproduced but imitated, for which a risk of confusion was to be shown.

Since 1991, a statute has merged both legal actions, although both grounds are still distinguished within the infringement action. Thus, today, infringement by reproduction and infringement by imitation coexist, the latter requiring the demonstration of a likelihood of confusion between the marks in the consumer's mind (see Article L. 716-1 of the Intellectual Property Code).

Under the Trademarks Act of 1964, influenced by the concept of property rights, French Courts widely protected trademarks and held in favour of plaintiffs even when a prior registration was only partially reproduced.

This lenient and very questionable approach was then abusively extended by the Opposition Division of INPI when comparing conflicting trademarks. The reproduction of a first syllable or of the first term of a denomination made up of two terms became automatically considered as an infringement, even for weak and barely distinctive terms.

This tendency became more criticised with the implementation of the European Directive of December 21, 1988, since there partial reproduction was not mentioned, so that the construction of the term "reproduction" became a sensitive issue in trademark litigation.

As a consequence, plaintiffs and defendants could avoid the demonstration of any likelihood of confusion, instead of alleging the reproduction of part of their prior trademark.

French Courts and the Opposition Division of INPI today assess the existence of a risk of confusion each time the litigating marks are not identical or almost identical. They then apply the Community "overall" approach when comparing litigious marks, even if they may instinctively refer to the analytical method used for assessing the existence of a partial reproduction.

France

France is very concerned about infringement and tries to set an example in Europe for the respect of applicable legislation.

Lobbying groups are very active and influence French legislation. The CNAC (National Anti-infringement Committee) has just made the French strategy public and, more precisely, has argued for the creation of a new law on infringement by the end of the year. This law would aim to apply many of the European provisions included in the propositions of last January.

The protection of trademarks having a reputation: French trademark law operates a binary classification for trademarks which, from the point of view of clients, are recognisable by the public beyond the specific goods or services they cover. Trademarks which have gradually become recognisable over years of use are the focus here.

The first category is that of trademarks "having reputation", the existence of which was recognised in Article 6 of the Paris Convention of 1883.

French trademark law distinguishes between trademarks "having reputation" and "well-known" trademarks, protected by Article 6bis of the Paris Union Convention.

The main difference between them is that trademarks "having reputation" are registered, whereas "well-known" trademarks are normally not registered.

Trademarks having a reputation are protected beyond the rule of speciality against non similar products and services.

The fact that a trademark is well-known does not exclude the application of the speciality principle.

Article L713-5 protects marks having a reputation only against identical signs and not imitations which can be attacked under the general provisions of Article 1382 of Civil Code only.

Opposition and Litigation

The opposition procedure: The opposition procedure was gradually introduced, by groups of classes, over a 5-year period (1991-1996), by the Trademarks Act of January 4, 1991. Only prior trademark registrations or applications, or well-known trademarks, can be used as the basis for an opposition.

The opposition procedure is open to the registrants, as well as to their exclusive licensees, unless otherwise stipulated in the license contract. Similarly, the owner of a well-known trademark can form an action in opposition.

The opposition procedure is strictly framed by rather short time limits. If no suspension of the time limit is asked for by both parties, an opposition is adjudicated within 6 to 9 months, depending on whether or not the opposition is defended.

France

When the prior trademark has been registered for more than five years, the defendant may request that the INPI request the opponent to submit evidence of use over the course of the past five years.

If no evidence is produced by the opponent, the INPI will automatically close the opposition proceeding. However, the INPI is not entitled to pronounce the cancellation, for lack of use, of the prior registration, this matter being reserved for the courts.

Likewise, INPI will merely acknowledge the material filing of evidence showing the use of the prior trademark, but is not entitled to appreciate the strength and validity of such use.

The Opposition Division first issues a preliminary decision. If it is not contested, it then becomes final. However, both parties can challenge the preliminary decision and then exchange briefs, and more rarely, ask for an oral hearing. Then, a final decision is issued by the INPI which can be challenged before the competent Court of Appeals. Generally, the Court of Appeals upholds the INPI decision, particularly in Paris where most appeals take place.

<u>Trademark litigation:</u> In the case of an infringement, an abusive use of the trademark, or an alteration or suppression of a registered trademark, the registrant can initiate an action before a civil or criminal court.

The assistance of an attorney at law (*Avocat à la Cour*) is required for all infringement and unfair competition actions before court.

The criminal procedure is rarely opted for, in particular since damages awarded are much lower, unless the plaintiff is eager to severely punish the defendant in order to set a precedent.

The trial takes place before the Court of First Instance, (*Tribunaux de Grande Instance*) and a judgement is usually rendered in 12 to 18 months. An appeal usually takes an additional year.

Trademark cases are heard by specialised Chambers. The main trademark jurisdictions are the Third Chamber of the Court of First Instance of Paris, and the Fourth Chamber of the Court of Appeals of Paris.

<u>Summary proceedings and injunction:</u> An injunction can be sued for before trial if the infringement action has been undertaken by the plaintiff expediently, within a short period of time ("bref délai") from learning of the infringement. The short period of time is generally held to be six months.

Before suing for an injunction, the plaintiff first needs to initiate an infringement action on the merits.

Damages allowed by French Civil Courts are compensatory damages, as is set forth by Article 1382 of the Civil Code. They are usually not high in practice and do not always compensate the prejudice suffered, nor deter the infringement. There is no such thing as punitive damages under French law.

Reimbursement of part of the legal fees can be obtained by the winning party from the losing party, under Article 700 of the French Code of Civil Procedure. The recovered amount does not usually exceed 5,000 euros although recent decisions have awarded up to 10,000 euros for very complex cases. However, contrary to the situation in common law countries, there is no indemnity rule, since the adverse party's attorney fees are not to be fully paid by the losing party.

Restriction to the actions

<u>Use of the trademark:</u> In relation to infringements resulting from the use of a similar trademark, the First Court has recently made clear what degree of use constitutes damage to the right. (First Court of Paris, March 11, 2003 "Sa BD Multimedia / M. Joachim H".) In this case, the BD Multimedia company, exploiting its trademark "Domina" via a website "domina.fr", instituted proceedings against the German owner of the domain name "domina.net" used to provide the same services as the BD Multimedia company. The Court of First instance decided that to prohibit a domain name similar to a French registered trademark, the plaintiff has to prove firstly that the website can be accessed from France and then secondly that the goods and services offered can be delivered in France.

<u>Parody:</u> For a long time, the parody of a trademark was considered, in France, to be an infringement of the trademark owner's rights. At that time, the owner's property rights took precedence over freedom of expression.

However, since the Supreme Court's decision of July 12, 2000 (*Les guignols de l'info v. Jacques Calvet*), French case law tends to admit the defense of parody. In this case a comic television programme, "Les guignols de l'info" was parodying the Director of a famous car company - Peugeot - and the Peugeot 605's car whose name was a registered trademark. The Supreme Court holds that the words were caricature and did not infringe the litigious trademark.

This judicial tendency has been recently confirmed by two decisions of the President of the Court of First Instance rendered in summary proceedings. Greenpeace was sued by a French company specialising in nuclear energy, Areva and Esso (the mark Esso being turned into an E).

These first instance decisions given in summary proceedings have been confirmed by the Court of Appeals of Paris on February 26, 2003 on the grounds of the constitutional principle of freedom of expression.

On April 30, 2003, a Court of Appeal invalidated a summary decision which held the *Réseau Voltaire* (French association for the defence of freedom of speech)

France

liable for trademark infringement. The *Réseau Voltaire* had reproduced the trademark "Danone" (a famous yogurt brand) with satiric, although not disparaging, comments. The trademark figured in the sentence: "jeboycottedanone" (meaning "I boycott Danone").

The defense developed by the Court based on parody is similar to the defense developed on the basis of America's First Amendment. This defense to trademark infringement leaves more latitude for the exercise of freedom of expression.

Rule of acquiescence: Article L. 714-3 CPI specifies that the owner of a prior registration cannot ask for the invalidity of the latter registration, which is similar to his, if this similar registration has been registered in good faith and if the plaintiff has acquiesced to its use during a period of five years.

This disposition has been imposed in the French law by the European Directive of December 21, 1988. The underlying to this rule is that, when acquiescing to the use of his sign, the prior owner has eroded the distinctive character of his sign whereas he should have protected it via opposition or litigation proceedings.

The debarment of the action is submitted to the reunion of three conditions. First, the prior owner must have acquiesced to the use, meaning that, although he was aware that his trademark was used he did not react against it. Secondly, he must have acquiesced to this use without initiating an infringement action during five years. The sending of a cease and desist letter does not suffice to stop acquiescence and a judicial action is requested. Lastly, the similar registration must have been registered in good faith.

Nevertheless, the inadmissibility of the infringement action is limited to the goods and services for which the use has been acquiesced.

In this action, the prior owner will have to prove that the similar registration has been registered in bad faith whereas the owner of the similar sign will prove that the prior owner knew about the registration and did not react.

The question of the infringement to the selective distributorship: Article L. 713-4 paragraph 1 CPI specifies that *"the right conferred by a mark shall not entitle an owner to prohibit its use in relation to goods which have been put on the market in the European Economic Community or the European Economic Area under that mark by the proprietor or with his consent."*

This rule is called "the rule of the right's exhaustion". Consequently, the owner of a trademark cannot claim the infringement of his right as soon as the goods have been put on the market by him or an authorised licensee. However, the action will still be allowed as long as the owner can prove that during the further act of marketing, the goods have been subsequently changed or impaired.

France

Since 1993, French case law has admitted that the existence of a selective distributorship, conforming to the admissibility conditions of the European law, constituted a legitimate reason to dismiss the rule of right's exhaustion (*See Supreme Court, Section Com., Feb. 23, 1993, Chanel*). Moreover, in 1997, the Appeal Court expressly ruled that because of the existence of his selective distributorship, the owner was fully justified by acting on the infringement action via the notion of illicit use or by acting on the grounds of unfair trading. (See *Appeal Court of Paris, October1, 1997, Ste Piaggo and CSPA and others /SARL Finetti.*)

Sanctions

Civil sanctions have to be distinguished from penal ones.

Regarding civil remedies, the owner can obtain the cessation of the infringements, damages and the publication of the judgement.

The cessation of infringement will usually consist in the prohibition of using the trade mark However, the judge will not prohibit the confection of the goods themselves. The infringer will just have to produce them under another sign.

Damages are not punitive, but merely cover lost profits and proven loss.

Furthermore, the legislator regularly intensifies penal sanctions (currently a new project tightening the fight against counterfeiting is being discussed in the Ministry of the Economy, Finance and Industry). Nowadays, in cases of infringement, the police can seize all counterfeit goods and the material used to fabricate these goods.

According to Article L. 716-9 CPI, "shall *be punished with a two-year prison term and a fine of Euros 150.000 any person who has:*

- *Reproduced, imitated, used, affixed, removed or altered a mark, a collective mark or a collective certification mark in violation of the rights conferred by the registration thereof and the prohibitions deriving there from;*
- *Imported, under any customs regime, or exported goods presented under an infringing mark."*

A bill on the evolution of criminality partially adopted by Parliament would increase the penalties for infringement. Offenders would incur a three-year prison term and a fine of 300,000 euros. This bill also establishes that the commitment of such offense by an organized group will be an aggravating circumstance, increasing the penalties incurred to a five-year prison term and a fine of 500,000 euros.

Moreover, the Court may order total or partial, permanent or temporary closure, for a period not exceeding five years, of the establishment that has served for the commission of the offense.

France

The legal person's responsibility can also be involved because of infringements done by its directors or representatives. The responsibility of the legal person does not exclude the one of persons naturally responsible of the acts.

Sanctions are stronger; the maximum amount of the fine applicable to legal persons is five times the sum laid down for natural persons by the statute that sanctions the offense.

Legal entities may be condemned to other sanctions such as dissolution, prohibition to exercise directly or indirectly one or more social or professional activity, either permanently or for a maximum period of five years, placement under judicial supervision for a maximum period of five years, permanent closure or closure for up to five years of the establishment, or one or more of the establishments of the enterprise that was used to commit the offenses in question, disqualification from public tenders, either permanently or for a maximum period of five years, prohibition, either permanently or for a maximum period of five years, to make a public appeal for funds, confiscation of the materials which were used or intended for the commission of the offense, or of the thing which is the product of it, the public display of the sentence or its dissemination either by the written press or by any type of broadcasting.

France is concerned with infringement and tries to set an example in Europe for the respect of applicable legislation.

Lobbying groups are very active and influence French legislation. The CNAC (National Anti-infringement Committee) has just made the French policy public and, more precisely, has called for the creation of a new statute on infringement, by the end of the year. This statute would include many of the European dispositions contained in last January's proposals.

Civil actions

The basis of unfair competition action and parasitism: As long as the behaviour of the infringer does not directly infringe the sign itself, the owner will have to sue the infringer for unfair competition or parasitism. The most important action is unfair competition.

Unfair competition constitutes a civil wrong, which renders its author liable if any damage occurs.

The basis for the unfair competition action: This action consists in showing that, by his behaviour, the offender has infringed the freedom of commerce claimed in 2d and 17th of March, 1791 Acts (Acts named "Loi le Chapelier" and "Decret d'Allarde"), these Acts being still in force today and this freedom being now a general principle of law. Today, such an action is based on Article 1382 of the French

Civil Code and these texts.

Competition between the actors of the market has to be done in respect with the principle of loyalty and of fair use. Therefore, a disloyal behaviour scorns and infringes business freedom.

Conditions of action in unfair competition: Article 1382 of the French Civil Code provides that the plaintiff first has to prove the existence of a fault committed by the defendant and a damage arising therefrom and, secondly, has to demonstrate a link of causality between this fault and the damage sustained.

When the owner of a trademark alleges "unfair competition" action, he has to prove an act distinct from the mere infringement of his sign. The French Courts appreciate very strictly the notion of "an act distinct from the trademark infringement." The infringer may, for instance, have imitated not only the trademark, but also the packaging of the good, its colours, have lowered its price, etc.

The prerequisite is the existence of a fault, which consists of the bad faith behaviour of the competitor on the trade market. This action is different by its legal nature and condition from the infringement action.

Unfair competition and infringement action: Action in unfair competition and action in infringement can be cumulative.

In order to sanction the infringement of his sign, the owner can initiate his action on two grounds:

- the infringement action, in case of infringement, abusive use of the trademark, alteration or suppression of a registered trade mark;
- the action based on civil liability or on the violation of the freedom of commerce, as long as the infringement is not related to the sign itself.

The action based on civil liability or on a violation of the freedom of commerce has some advantages. It can be initiated even if the sign has not been registered as a trademark.

Comparative advertising: Comparative advertising may lead in France to an action in unfair competition for disparagement. In France indeed, comparative advertising is allowed under three conditions:

- the advertisement must not be false or likely to mislead;
- it must relate to goods or services fulfilling the same requirements or pursuing the same objective;
- it must objectively compare one or more essential, pertinent, verifiable and representative characteristics of these goods or services, one of which may be price.

When those three requirements are not met, the unfair competition action cannot succeed.

France

Administrative actions

<u>The customs withholding</u>: Two systems of customs withholding cohabit in France. France is indeed at the origin of a strong customs control in order to create a greater protection for trademarks. This can be explained by the existence of an important number of trademarks concerning luxury goods.

First, the "Loi Longuet" of February 5, 1994 has assimilated the infringement of trademarks to the importation of prohibited merchandise. Nowadays and since 1994, importation and exportation of infringing goods are completely prohibited. Regarding circulation of the infringing goods, they are submitted to the European Union restrictions.

According to the French Customs Code, the Customs Agency can keep, on the request of the owner of the infringed trademark, the contentious goods for 10 days.

The Customs Agency can also intervene on its own initiative. (In practice, before intervening, it must contact the owner of the trademark to be assured that goods are not imported via a system of parallel importation.)

According to the French Customs Code, the author of the customs infraction can be punished by:

- a three-year prison sentence;
- the confiscation of the goods;
- the confiscation of all the ways used to infringe;
- a fine between one and two times the estimation of the goods infringing the trademark;
- a temporary interdiction to practice any industrial, commercial or liberal activity.

Furthermore, according to the European regulation of December 22, 1994, CPI also provides, under Article L. 716-8, for a procedure of customs withholding.

Therefore, the Customs Agency may, upon written request from the owner of a registered mark or from the beneficiary of an exclusive right of exploitation, withhold, during customs inspection, any goods claimed by the owner or beneficiary to be designated by a mark that infringes the mark for which he has obtained registration or with regard to which he enjoys an exclusive right of use.

Withholding shall be lifted automatically if the plaintiff fails, within 10 working days from the notification of the withholding of the goods, to furnish evidence to the customs authorities:

- either of the withholding measures decided by the President of the First Instance Court;
- or of having instituted legal proceedings by civil action or criminal action

and having furnished the required securities to cover possible liability in the event of infringement not being subsequently recognized.

For the purpose of the institution of the legal proceedings referred to in the foregoing paragraph, the plaintiff may require the customs administration to communicate the names and addresses of the sender, the importer and the consignee of the goods withheld or of the holder thereof, and also the quantity thereof, notwithstanding the provisions of Article 59bis of the Customs Code on professional secrecy to which all officials of the customs administration are bound.

The Customs withholding can be done anywhere in France and concerns goods coming from all countries, even from European countries. (European regulation limits the right of retention of goods coming from third countries, but France has completed this disposition by including the European countries too. Nevertheless, judges are the only ones authorised to qualify the offense.)

According to Article L. 716-9 CPI, the person who has imported, under any customs regime, or exported, goods under an infringing mark, shall be punished with a two-year prison term and a high fine.

Sanction of fraud: Several agencies fight against trademark infringement. Since the adoption of the "Loi Doubin" of December 31, 1989, the General Direction of competition, consumption and fraud repression (DGCCRF) can intervene on all the French territory among importers, manufacturers, wholesalers and in every commercial place selling goods with infringed trade marks.

Agents of the DGCCRF are authorised to search and record by statement evidence of offenses to trademarks regulations.

DGCCRF may investigate on its own initiative, or upon request of a professional or of a consumer.

Trademarks and Domain Names

Using another's previously registered trademark to name a website can be deemed an infringement.

Trademarks against domain names (cybersquatting)

An infringement action is possible where products or services of the domain name in question are identical or similar to those of the registered trademark. Cyber squatting relies upon the notion of fraud. Undue deposition or undue use must have been done with the evident intention of blackmailing. General civil liability may also be incurred if there is a risk of confusion, an abusive use of rights or free-riding behaviour.

Lastly, an arbitration procedure has been established by the ICANN. Accord-

France

ing to this procedure, a complaint is filed at the WIPO, and a sentence is delivered within 45 days.

In France, contrary to the U.S. position, courts consider that French law is applicable when the litigious trademark appears on a screen located within their territorial jurisdiction.

For example, the Court of Nanterre enjoined, under threat of daily penalty payments of 50,000 francs, a Canadian resident and an Egyptian resident to stop using and relinquish possession of the domain name "lorealparis.com", "cacharel.com", "lancome-paris.com" and "guylaroche.com", all being well-known trademarks.

However, if the website is established and exploited actively prior to the registration of a trademark, such registration is excluded.

The registration of a trademark in class "38" no longer impedes the registration of a domain name: a comparison between the contents of the site and the nature of the product or service for which protection is sought is necessary for a trademark to be an obstacle to the deposit of a domain name.

The registration of a trademark for communication services does not grant the owner an absolute protection against all forms of use of the sign on the internet. The specialty principle must allow trademarks to coexist with others, similar or identical signs used on the internet to identify different activities.

In fact, in the "ZE BANK" case, French Courts (*Tribunal de Grande Instance de Nanterre*) held that, in order to assess the risk of confusion between two litigious web sites, it was necessary to examine the contents of the sites. There was no risk of confusion in light of the differing activities of the two sites.

Various sanctions, such as the payment of financial damages, radiation or restitution of the litigious domain name can be pronounced by French courts. Restitution of the name is a frequently pronounced sanction. It consists of an injunction from the judge condemning the squatter to transfer the name to the person who summoned him. It is also possible to obtain a complementary sentence for unfair competition or parasitism and therefore obtain extra damages. Finally, criminal sanctions can also be considered on the basis of extortion (Article L. 312-1 of the French criminal code).

<u>*Domain name against trademarks:*</u> A domain name registered prior to an identical trademark, renders that trademark unavailable. (TGI Nanterre November 4, 2002, Temesis v/ Association Afaq, *a contrario*.)

According to French Courts, online establishment of a website does not make the corresponding trademark unavailable.

According to Article L.711-4 CPI, a trademark cannot be registered if it infringes previously registered or generally-recognised rights. This article contains a non-exhaustive list of situations in which there is such a previously established right.

A French Court (TGI Le Mans, June 29, 1999 Microcaz v/ Océanet) declared void the registration of a trademark, in light of the prior exploitation of a web site bearing the same name prior to the registration, on the basis of Article L.711-4 CPI). This was also held in two other cases: TGI Paris September 23, 1999, and Agraphone and TGI Paris June 27, 2000, No Problemo. It is important to underline that, in order to annul the trademark, products and services designated by the trademark in the registration act must be identical or similar to those designated by the domain name.

Finally, if the registration of the trademark was fraudulently made, it is possible to obtain its annulment on the basis of Article L 712-6 CPI. According to this article *"where registration has been applied for, either fraudulently with respect to the rights of another person or in violation of a statutory or contractual obligation, any person who believes he has a right in the mark may claim ownership by legal proceedings."*

Copyright

In France, copyright (called "droit d'auteur") results from old tradition. French copyright law has influenced legislation in several European countries, the drafting of international conventions (such as the Berne Convention), as well as European Directives.

Under French law, the copyright is a personal right. This main principle entirely founds the status of the author. The author benefits from the protection of his work without formality (registration of his work) and without having to exploit it.

The two main French statutes are: the Act of March 11, 1957, listing the different categories of rights, the scope of the protection they provide, and their limits; and the Act of July 3, 1985, which seeks to balance the author's rights and the managers' interests. These Acts have been codified in the French intellectual property Code (hereinafter mentioned as the "CPI"), chapters 1 and 3.

What can be protected?
Features of the work to be protected

<u>The work must be original:</u> According to case-law, originality is the stamp of the author's personality (this criterion differs from that retained in American copyright, which considers that a work will be protected as long as it is not a copy).

France

For example, in a case concerning Margaret Mitchell's book <u>Gone with the Wind</u>, and Regine Desforges' novel <u>La bicyclette bleue,</u> the French Supreme Court held that, regarding literary works, "the form and the style" were as important as the story itself. Thus, the Court considered, on the basis of form and style differences, that there had been no infringement of Margaret Mitchell's work.

When evaluating originality, the Pachot case (French Supreme Court, March 7, 1986) is frequently referred to. In that specific case, the French Supreme Court defined originality as "a personalised effort, beyond the mere implementation of an automatic logic (...) the materialization of such an effort reflecting the personal effort of its author."

We can also recall the Duchamp case in which a urinal was smashed by an admirer. It was considered that the value of the work, mere industrial item, relied on Duchamp's signature; therefore the originality of the work also depended on his signature.

Thus, signature, consequently assimilated to trademark, therefore authenticates the work which, in the absence of such a signature, would only be a common urinal.

The work must be formalised: However, French law does not protect ideas, concepts, or processes, which are subject to the subsidiary protection of unfair competition and passing off actions. According to Article L. 111-1 of the CPI, *"the author of a work of the mind shall enjoy in that work, by the mere fact of its creation, an exclusive incorporeal property right."* This is contrary to American copyright, where registration is necessary.

For the time being, notions such as audiovisual works have not been defined by statute.

Audiovisual works include the title, the concept and the configuration of the television program. It can also define the structure and the chain of programs that will compose the television series.

The scope of protection will depend on the degree of development of the work. If not elaborated enough, it could only be considered as the medium of an idea.

However, if the degree of development is important enough to be considered as original, the audiovisual work is likely to be protected by copyright, similar to film scripts.

It should be noted that even though mere creation falls into the copyright scope of protection, it can be useful to establish, via registration, the material existence of the work.

Various works, varied status

The "unity of Art" theory: The artistic or aesthetic value of a work is not taken into consideration. Protection is available regardless of the genre, the form of expression, the quality or the destination of the work (Article L 111-3 of the CPI). The checklist provided by Article L. 112-2 of the French Intellectual Property Code is, therefore, not exhaustive. For instance, French case-law offers copyright protection to book titles, as long as they are original (the Court held that the French translation – Les Hauts de Hurlevent - of the title of Emilie Brontë's Wuthering Heights was original and copyrightable).

In spite of the apparent unity of copyright protection, some specific regimes that take account of the influence of European law, have recently appeared. It is now difficult to conflate, under French law, fine arts and industrial arts.

Beyond the protection of titles, specifically provided by article L 112-4 of the CPI (as long as the title is original as regards the work it designates) we can also evoke:

- advertising work, for which the order for a work is subject to a specific regulation favourable to the advertiser (Article L. 132-31 of the CPI);
- audiovisual work, whose legal regime attempts to reserve the ownership of rights for the producer (article L 132-24 and following of the CPI);
- Software (see below).

Who is protected?

Sole author: Article L. 113-1 of the CPI provides that "authorship shall belong, unless proved otherwise, to the person or persons under whose name the work has been disclosed."

There is a presumption according to which the work is the creation of its author, even if the author chooses to disclose his work under a pseudonym, or to remain anonymous, or if the author is employed by an undertaking.

In case of a salaried author, Article L. 111 paragraph 3 of the CPI provides that "the existence or conclusion of an employment agreement shall in no way derogate from the enjoyment of the right."

French law prohibits global assignments of future works. Nevertheless, an employer can get around this rule when the author is hired to make a specific work by obtaining an assignment of rights, provided that the author retains all moral rights. Indeed, French courts have validated clauses providing for automatic assignment of an author's rights to his employer when circumstances make it possible, at the time of the signature of the agreement, for the work to be identified and isolated.

France

Regarding advertising, an agreement between a producer and an author is an assignment of exploitation rights to the producer if the contract provides for a distinctive remuneration for each means of exploitation of the work (Article L. 131-31 CPI).

In the case of journalists, the employment agreement implies an automatic assignment of the economic rights, which is strictly limited to the publication in the journalist's newspaper. The journalist retains rights of exploitation and reproduction by any other means, in particular on the internet. This issue has recently been the subject of many proceedings.

French law, as regards salaried authors, is very constraining for employers. The French government recently appointed a Commission in order to study possible reforms. However, without a consensus, such reform seems indefinitely postponed. In the meantime, the transmission of rights via contract should be adapted.

Plurality of authors: Two hypotheses should be distinguished. The first has to do with "works of collaboration" in the creation of which several persons have participated equally. As long as each person's participation is personal and creative, and can be individualised, each participant is considered to be an author, and the work is the property of all. Authors will then exercise their rights together, while being authorised to exploit their own part provided that this exploitation does not infringe the overall work. Usually, comics and movies are considered to be works of collaboration.

The second hypothesis concerns "collective works". A work is collective if initiated by one person, or one company who produces it under his own name and direction. Here, the participation of each person cannot be distinguished from that of the others. The owner of the copyright is considered to be the author of the work. Nevertheless, contrary to the situation of an American work "made for hire", each participant retains the moral right attached to his individual contribution. Participants receive a lump sum. For instance, periodicals and dictionaries, designs, jewelry and fashion designs are usually deemed collective works.

What rights does the author have?

There are two categories of right: the patrimonial right and the economic right.

Attributes of the patrimonial right: French law distinguishes the right of reproduction from the right of representation. The economic right lasts as long as the author lives and belongs to eligible parties for 70 years after the author's death.

French law has a peculiarity: the "droit de suite" (literally speaking, right of pursuit). This right belongs only to authors of graphical or plastic works or to authors of literary works. Authors of graphical or plastic works receive financial compensation for the sale of their work in the case of auction or of any sale by a dealer. Since the transposition of the European Directive on the "Information Society" to French law, authors of literary works should be able to claim compensation in the case of library loans.

Exceptions to the economic right: Article L. 122-5 of the CPI lists several uses of the author's work, which do not require any authorisation. Whenever the work has already been disclosed once, the author cannot forbid:

- Private and gratuitous performances carried out exclusively within the family circle. The notion of "family circle" only concerns persons, parents or very close friends, who belong to the author's family or have an intimate relationship with him. The fact that the display is free of charge does not in itself permit any display. Associations and elector's assemblies do not satisfy the notion of "family environment".
- Copies or reproductions reserved strictly for the private use of the copier, and not intended for collective use. Software purchasers are only authorized to make one back-up copy of it (See below for the specificities of software protection).
- Citations and analysis, as long as the author and the origin of the work are mentioned. Regarding parodies and caricatures of his work, there is no need to mention the latter elements.
- Acts useful for gaining access to electronic databases, which are necessary and foreseen by the contract.

These exceptions are exhaustive. For any other use, the authorisation of the author will be necessary. The exceptions are thus more narrowly defined than the American "fair-use doctrine".

The moral right

This right is a French peculiarity.

Features of the moral right: The author can require the recognition of the paternity of the work and of the respect of the work (for instance, adding music to a silent film is reprehensible).

Even after the transfer of the work, the author can prohibit any foreseeable alteration, modification or addition.

The author has the choice whether or not to disclose his work. Even if he sells it, he can always withdraw his work from the market, by expressing his repentance (in which case, he would have to compensate the purchaser). This faculty of repentance is not transmissible to eligible parties. It is a personal right.

(Note: French law recognises more moral rights for authors than does the Berne Convention.)

France

Characteristics of the moral right: It is a perpetual, inalienable and indefeasible right which can be transmitted at the death of the author.

This right can not be given away. It may be exercised by eligible parties after the death of the author or by a third party selected by the author. Nevertheless if the eligible parties use this right abusively, the Minister of the Culture can submit the case to a judge at first instance.

Software

From the perspective of the rights-holder, software is subject to a specific regime. Unless there are provisions or clauses to the contrary, patrimonial rights to software and related documentation created by one or several employees during their working hours or according to their employer's instructions are automatically transferred to the employer who is the only one entitled to exploit them.

The author of software cannot, unless there are provisions or clauses to the contrary, prohibit the alteration of software by the transferee, so long as his honour or reputation is not affected.

Further, he is not allowed to withdraw his creation or to express repentance for it. Theoretically, the author should be paid a lump-sum.

The transferee has the benefice of the patrimonial right (right of reproduction and right of representation).

Nevertheless, the purchaser of the software can examine it, study it, and explore the principles which govern each part of the software, without the authorisation of the creator.

Furthermore, the purchaser can copy the software only for security reasons. The use of the software has to be personal, or familial, professional use normally being excluded. However, the law of January 3, 1995, has provided for the automatic transfer of reproduction rights by reprography to collective management societies as soon as the work is published, in order to mitigate the severity of this rule and to adapt it to the practical necessity of reproduction for professional use, subject to the condition that the name of the author and the origin are indicated.

The length of the protection is the same as that for others works, meaning for the life of the author and for 70 years after his death.

The "droits voisins"

The Rome Convention for the Protection of Performers, Producers of Phonograms and Broadcasting Organisations (1961) was the model the French legislator employed for drafting French legislation regarding "droits voisins". The "droits voisins" concern the rights of the artist-performers, producers of phonograms or videos and audiovisual communications holdings.

These rights are separate from and independent of the author's rights. The length of their protection is up to 50 years from the year of the first communication to the public. The rights of the owner of the "droits voisins" vary according to each category of protected party.

Artist-performers: With regards to patrimonial prerogatives held by this category, they can claim the right of first fixation of their performance, the right of reproduction and the right of the communication to the public of their performance.

Concerning their moral rights, artist-performers do not have the benefit of the right to divulge the work, nor do they have the right of repentance. The right to the respect of their performance is similar to the general personal right and is not as well-protected as the right to respect which belongs to the author. The right to paternity of the performance is completely recognised in the same way as for the authors.

The producer of phonograms and videos: They have the right of reproduction and of communication to the public but no moral rights.

The audiovisual communications holdings: They can claim a right of reproduction, communication to the public and broadcast of their programmes, but they do not have any fixation right distinct from the reproduction right.

All these patrimonial rights are subject to the same exceptions as the patrimonial rights of the author.

Moreover, Article L. 214-1 paragraph 1 CPI, specifies that where a phonogram has been published for commercial purposes, neither the performer nor the producer may oppose its direct communication in a public place where it is not used in an entertainment or by broadcasting or by the simultaneous and whole cable distribution of such a broadcast.

However, the artist-performer, as the producer, will be remunerated on the basis of the receipts of the exploitation or by a lump sum.

The producer of databases

According to the European Directive of March 11, 1996, the database maker has a *sui generis* right over the database, whose duration is 15 years. From this right, he can control the extraction or reutilisation of a part or of the entirety of the database, so long as the database itself demonstrates that a substantial investment, either qualitative or quantitative, was made in obtaining, verifying or presenting the material constituting the database. The investment can be financial, material or human and can be present at any moment in the creation of the databases.

France

The owner cannot forbid the extraction or reutilisation of an unsubstantial part of his work, nor can he forbid the extraction of data in a private purpose.

The exploitation of rights

The support of the work must be distinguished from the work itself.
If the moral right is indeed inalienable, the patrimonial rights can be transferred for a price or gratuitously.

The exploitation of patrimonial rights usually requires an exploitation contract between the author and the transferee. However collective management societies act as representatives of the authors who have transferred rights to them.

Exploitation contracts

<u>The formalism of the contract:</u> Except for the performance, publication, or audiovisual production contracts, it is not necessary to make any written statement regarding the assignment of the patrimonial right.

However, according to Article L. 131-3 CPI, the "transfer of authors' rights shall be subject to each of the assigned rights being separately mentioned in the instrument of assignment and the field of exploitation of the assigned rights being defined as to its scope and purpose, as to place and as to duration." Thus, a written statement is almost obligatory, at least for evidentiary issues.

Article L. 122-7 CPI lays out that where a contract contains the complete transfer of either of the rights referred to in the article, its effect shall be limited to the exploitation modes specified in the contract: the author is thus presumed to keep for himself all the rights and all the modes of exploitation which are not expressly mentioned in the transfer.

<u>The remuneration of the author:</u> Usually this is proportional to the price of sale. Nevertheless, Article L. 131-4 CPI lists six special situations in which a lump sum payment is authorised. Generally, a lump sum payment will be permitted where a basis for the calculation of a proportional participation either cannot be determined, or cannot be controlled (for example, for collective works or where the work is a mere accessory of the principally exploited object.)

The collective management of author's rights

Author's rights are managed collectively when several authors confide their rights, for specific works, to a management society.

This is the case, for example, in relation to music, where the authors confide the management of their rights to the Society of Authors, Compositors and Musical Editors (SACEM).

These societies collect, on behalf of the authors and their assistants, the proceeds of the exploitation of the authors' rights or neighbouring rights before distributing them appropriately.

Authors' societies can sue in order to defend the interests they have been entrusted with and can, notably, sue for infringement or seek to obtain compensation for the damage incurred by their members. However, they cannot defend the members' moral rights.

They also have to keep a complete list of the French and foreign authors they represent for potential users.

Compensation due by users is fixed by the contract signed between the authors and the management company, or, alternately, through collective bargaining via agreements with socio-professional groups.

Protection of Author's Rights

The constitutive elements of an infringement of rights

An infringement of rights is established each time previous author's rights are disregarded. The export or import of an infringed work is punished identically.

An intention to infringe is presumed as soon as the factual elements of an infringement are materially established. Sincerity is evaluated by the judge, who can be very strict, especially with "infringement professionals".

Infringement is determined according to degree of resemblance, rather than according to the differences, between the works submitted to the court's appreciation.

Infringement action

Just as for the infringement of trademarks, the action can be introduced before the civil or criminal courts.

There are no limits on the types or forms of evidence which may be introduced. The author can also prove the existence of an infringement on the basis of mere declarations that can be relative, not only to the infringed specimens, but also to the objects used for the illicit activities.

The plaintiff must introduce an action before the court that has jurisdiction for the matter, at most, 30 days after the seizure; otherwise the restitution of the property could be ordered.

The seizure of counterfeit goods will be exercised by the superintendent's agent, or, if there is no police precinct with jurisdiction, by the magistrate's agent.

France

Footnotes

[1] Article L. 511-1 CPI, "the appearance of the whole or a part of the product, resulting from the features of, and in particular its lines, contours, colours, shape, texture or materials, is eligible for protection as a design or model. These features can be those of the product itself or its ornamentation.
Is deemed to be a product any industrial or handicraft item, including inter alia parts intended to be assembled into a complex product, packaging, get-up, graphic symbols and typographic typefaces, but excluding computer programs."

[2] Temporary closure may not be a cause of either termination or suspension of employment contracts, or of any monetary consequence prejudicial to the employees concerned. Where permanent closure causes the dismissal of staff, it shall give rise, over and above the indemnity in lieu of notice and the termination indemnity, to damages as provided in Articles L122-14-4 and L122-14-5 of the Labour Code for the breach of employment contracts. Failure to pay those indemnities shall be punishable with a six-month prison term and a fine of FRF 25,000.

France

Chapter 12: Germany

Germany

By Alexandra Barth, Christian Meister,
Mathias Ricker, Richard Schloetter
and Monica Warchhold (Jones Day)

Patents

Preliminary remarks

Patent law in Germany is regulated by the German Patent Act (1981).

The right to a patent shall belong to the inventor or his legal successor for providing an invention that is new, involves an inventive step and is susceptible to industrial application.

What is the patent application procedure?

The patent application has to be filed with the German Patent and Trademark Office or with special *"Patentinformationszentren"*. Basically, there is no need for the applicant to appoint any representative before the Patent Office.

The patent application has to comprise a request for grant, the names of the inventors, at least one patent claim, a description of the invention, drawings referred to in the description (if desired) and an abstract of the invention. Furthermore, the applicant is entitled to claim priority of a previous application. A declaration of priority has to be filed by the end of a 16-month period after the priority date. It is to be noted that the application may be filed in any language if a certified translation into German will be provided within three months after the filing date.

Once the application has been filed and examination has been requested (and the respective fees have been paid), the Patent Office conducts a prior art search and examines the application under formal and material aspects. A request for material examination may be filed up until 7 years after filing. In case any (formal or material) deficiencies are detected, the applicant is requested to remedy the same. In most cases, discussions take place related to novelty and/or inventive-step issues, subsequently leading to a patent grant or refusal.

Christian Meister and Richard Schloetter are Partners, and Alexandra Barth, Mathias Ricker and Monica Warchhold are Associates, in the Munich office of Jones Day. Mr. Meister specialises in trademark law, including litigation, portfolio management and seizure at the border, copyright and competition law. Mr. Schloetter specialises in IP and patent litigation, licensing, and competition law. Jones Day is a global firm with offices in a number of major cities in Europe, the United States and Asia, with some 2,000 lawyers worldwide.

Germany

It is important to disclose the invention as completely as possible in the application as originally filed, since this disclosure will be the reservoir of information to be used during examination. In particular, it is not possible to add further information without losing the first filing date.

Eighteen months after first filing, the patent application will be published. In case a patent has been granted already, the patent will be published instead.

A divisional application can be filed relating to any pending patent application–even after grant–and based on any patent pending in opposition proceedings.

How long does a patent last?

A patent is granted for a period of 20 years from the filing date of the application. Renewal fees are due the third year and each subsequent year, calculated from the day of filing.

Once granted, is the patent safe?

Within three months from the publication of the patent grant any person is entitled to file an opposition. Up to 2007 the German Federal Patent Court ("Bundespatentgericht", BPatG) decides on opposition cases. As a result, no second judicial authority (appeal stage) is available for opposition cases. In the past, opposition cases were handled by the Patent Office (Opposition Divisions) and the subsequent judicial authority dealing with an appeal, if filed, was the Federal Patent Court. In 2007 it will be decided how to pursue oppositions in the future.

Another possibility to challenge a patent is to file a Nullity Suit with the Federal Patent Court. This is only admissible after the period for filing an opposition has expired. The second judicial authority for Nullity Suits is the Federal Supreme Court, which here investigates material facts (normally, the Federal Supreme Court deals with legal questions only).

Infringement

Actions of patent infringement are brought to specialised chambers of selected District Courts which are entitled to deal with intellectual property rights, the most prominent for patent cases being the District Courts of Munich, Mannheim and Düsseldorf. Plaintiff as well as defendant need to be represented by an attorney at law. The subsequent judicial authority is the respective Higher Regional Court. An appeal on legal matters may be filed with the Federal Supreme Court.

Utility model

Another useful tool is the German Utility Model that can be branched off from any pending patent application as well as any patent pending in opposition proceedings. A utility model will be registered (usually within a period of 2 to 3 months after filing) only without material examination. Consequently, a protective right may be obtained within a short time via this route. The utility model is particularly useful if a patent examination proceeding turns out to be protracted or infringing product(s) comes to the owner's attention, either at a stage where the patent application is still under examination or while opposition proceedings are pending.

A utility model may be also branched-off from a PCT-application or an EP-application/patent in cases where Germany is one of the designated states.

Designs

Legislation

Registered designs in Germany are regulated under the German Design Act 1976. According to the German Design Act, protection is only provided for registered designs, not for unregistered designs. Protection for unregistered designs in Germany may only be sought under Copyright Law.

Furthermore, Germany has not yet implemented EC Directive 98/71/EC, although it was obliged to do so at the latest by October 28, 2001 (see European Chapter). According to the jurisdiction of the ECJ, the German Design Act currently in place has to be construed in the light of the directive.

What is a design?

The German Design Act does not define the term "design". However, according to established German jurisdiction, the definition of a design is as discussed in the European chapter.

Registration process

Registration of a design has to be applied for at the German Patent and Trademark Office.

A design is an unexamined right, i.e. the German Patent and Trademark Office does not examine either absolute or relative grounds of refusal of an application. Rather an application will be registered, as long as it is not contrary to public policy and fulfills the following formal requirements:
- The applicant has to complete an official application form and submit it to the German Patent and Trademark Office;
- The application must be accompanied by either photographs or other graphic illustrations of the design or model, which clearly illustrate the features the applicant wishes to register.

Germany

The German Patent and Trademark office only conducts a simple examination of the application and if it meets the formal requirements for registration it will generally qualify for registration. Therefore, a design enjoys full protection as soon as registration has been applied for at the German Patent and Trademark Office. Registration and publication of the design are merely declaratory.

Duration

A registered design can remain in force for a maximum of 20 years, provided renewal fees are paid every five years.

Criteria for protection under the German Design Act

In order to enjoy full protection under the German Design Act, a design has to:

- be **new** (i.e. at the time of application the design has not yet been made available to the relevant public circles and with regard to the existing prior art its esthetical effect was not known to the public before);
  The German Design Act, however, foresees a grace period of 6 months, whereby disclosure to the public in a 6-month period prior to the date of application will not preclude the design from registration, if registration is applied for without alteration.
- have **individual character** (i.e. with regard to the features relevant for the esthetical effect, especially color and form, the design appears to be the result of an individual and inventive activity, which exceeds the average capability of a designer having the relevant expertise in this area.)
  Whereas the Council Regulation and the EC Directive focus on the *"overall impression of the informed user"* when determining, whether a design has individual character, the German Design Act, as it is in force at this point of time, still focuses on the *"average capability of a designer having the relevant expertise in this area"*. Therefore, this differing perspective may lead to differing judgments on whether a design actually has individual character. However, as soon as the German legislator implements the EC Directive, this problem will not occur any longer.

Since a design is an unexamined right, novelty and originality are not registration requirements. However, if a registered design lacks novelty or originality it can be attacked by third parties by way of a nullity action before the civil courts.

Infringement

The owner of a registered design has the exclusive right to use the registered design including duplication, distribution, offer, sale and importation thereof. The design owner also has the correlating right to restrain third parties from any such use.

Germany

Trade Marks

Registered trade marks

Trademarks in Germany are regulated under the Trademarks Act of 1994.

Registrability and the application procedure

The types of marks that can be registered in Germany are as discussed in the European Community chapter. Additionally the Trademark Act explicitly mentions acoustic signs.

The German Patent and Trademark Office will only reject an application based on absolute grounds, not on relative grounds. Therefore the German Patent and Trademark Office will reject registration if the trademark:

(i) is not sufficiently distinctive;

(ii) is merely descriptive;

(iii) has become a generic term;

(iv) is likely to deceive or confuse the public; or

(v) is contrary to public policy.

The Patent and Trademark Office does not issue a search report to the other side and will not search the Register for any conflicting prior applications or registrations. Proprietors of earlier trademarks, domains or company names are able to oppose registration within three months after the date of publication of the registration. A straightforward trademark application should be registered within 4 to 6 months of filing.

How long does a trade mark registration last?

The duration of a trademark registration is as discussed in the UK and European chapter (i.e., ten years with the possibility to extend for subsequent ten year periods). A trademark must be used within five years in order to avoid cancellation upon application of third parties.

What rights does it give?

The exclusive rights are also as discussed in the UK chapter. A trademark protects its owner against the use of later signs (including trademarks) and—for example— domains, if the signs are in danger of confusion and cover similar goods and services. Well known trademarks can enjoy protection even if the goods and services are not similar.

Company names and— for example—the titles of printed publications, movies and similar works are also protected.

Germany

Unregistered trademarks

If a sign has not been registered as a trademark, it may also receive trademark protection under the German Trademark Act, if:

(i) the sign has been used in such a way as to establish a reputation with regard to the relevant public circles;

(ii) the sign is well-known in the sense in which the words well-known are used in art. 6 bis of the Paris Convention; and

(iii the sign has been used as a company name.

It is a lot easier to bring an action for trademark infringement before German courts with regard to a registered trademark, since the burden of proof generally lies on the applicant. Therefore, in the case of an unregistered trademark, the applicant/claimant not only has to evidence the use of such trademark/sign, but in case of (i) and (ii) also has to evidence its good reputation by way of independent surveys. According to German jurisprudence the trademark has to be known by more than 70 % of the relevant public circles.

Copyright and Related Rights

What is copyright?

Eligible literary, scientific and artistic works can be embodied in many forms, including any sort of writing, speeches, computer programmes, music, drama, dance, sculpture, architecture, the applied arts, photography, films, drawings, maps, or charts. Substantial adaptations of another work–which require the original author's approval–collections and databases are also included. All forms qualify for protection under German copyright, provided they result from a natural person's creative effort.

Unlike some European countries, Germany has a rather strict standard for attaining copyright protection. Instead of individuality and originality, German copyright law has demanded for many years a rather high level of artistic creativity to be expressed in the author's work in order to attain protection. In the wake of the European harmonisation process, this strict standard has been eased to some degree. Still, merely functional or technical works are excluded from copyright protection for lack of creativity.

Copyright law in Germany is governed by the "Urhebergesetz" (commonly abbreviated to "UrhG").

Do I need to register copyright?

There is no registration for copyrighted works in Germany. With no formalities required, a work will be protected under copyright law upon its creation, provided it meets the prerequisites outlined above.

Germany

Copyright notice

It is not necessary to attach a copyright notice ©. Nevertheless, attaching a notice © as a warning sign and escrowing records with a notary public may be helpful.

What rights does copyright give?

A copyright owner may enjoin unauthorised use or copying of her work. In particular, authors' rights include the right of reproduction, distribution and exhibition. If an infringer is found to have acted negligently or intentionally, the author may also claim damages for material and immaterial harm done. However, copyright protection is not available for independent development of the same ideas. Furthermore, an author may not assert her rights against certain kinds of uses that serve educational purposes or informational purposes for the public.

An integral part of copyright are moral rights. While an author may enter a contract to assign the exploitation of a work to someone else, the moral right as a consequence of the author's personal creative effort shall always vest in the author, or his heir. The principle that copyright vests in the author also applies to employees hired to create a work.

The author may request to be identified as author. The author is also entitled to enjoin even rightful owners of his work from effacing it.

Term

Copyright protection ends 70 years after the author's death.

What else does copyright protect?

The German copyright act also governs certain related rights. The term of protection for related rights differs, but is generally much shorter than that for copyrights. While restrictions apply, related rights include protection for:

- scientific volumes;
- the posthumous publication of works after the copyright term has expired;
- the work of performers (such as musicians, actors and dancers) in respect of recording and distributing copies of their performances;
- the exclusive right of the record producer for reproductions; and
- databases.

The functionality of industrial design works usually forecloses copyright protection due to a lack of creativity expressed in the work. Instead, German law grants protection that is distinct from copyright protection for registered designs through the "Geschmacksmustergesetz".

Germany

Status of latest European Community directive on copyright

Effective September 13, 2003, Germany has implemented the recent European Directive on copyright on new economic rights discussed in the European Community chapter[1]. Already in 2002, Germany had also bolstered authors' positions in contractual assignments of their rights by amending the copyright act.

Further reforms are planned. For instance, photocopiers and recordable cassettes/CDs are currently subject to a levy that benefits authors as a group to compensate them for reproductions. In turn, it is legitimate to reproduce works for private use under some circumstances. An amended version of the German copyright act might well abolish the levy and curtail the right of private reproduction.

Confidential Information

A source for protecting confidential information in the context of most commercial relationships can be found within the Unfair Competition Act ("Gesetz gegen den unlauteren Wettbewerb" – "UWG"). In particular, sec. 1 UWG, a general clause, can be applied to most cases in commercial life related to misappropriation and abuse of confidential information. Moreover, there are particular provisions explicitly focusing on employer/employee relationships (sec. 17 UWG) and generally the unauthorized use of specifically entrusted secret information (sec. 18 UWG).

Trade secrets and confidential information

German Law does not distinguish between technical and purely commercial information. Both are, in most cases, equally covered. However, the protection ends where any third party can generate the same knowledge or have access to it, if a modest amount of money and time is invested.

Protection of trade secrets

Generally speaking, any unauthorized use of entrusted information will be regarded as "unfair" in the sense of sec. 1 and thus be regarded as illicit. Consequently, the trade secret owner can enjoin another party from distributing a product the manufacture of which was at least facilitated by using his trade secret. Also, enticing away of employees with particular skills with the intention to have access to the former employer's trade secrets is unfair.

During an employment, any employee is bound to secrecy. Any violation of this obligation will not only constitute a breach of the employment contract (where confidentiality is at least subject to implied duties) but, moreover violates sec.17 UWG. Sec. 17 has a twofold character and protects trade secrets in employment relationships by civil law and criminal law means. Simultaneously, the provision is not restricted to any kind of unauthorized disclosure of the employer's trade secret. Rather, any kind of misappropriation can be prosecuted. However, the statutory protection of trade secrets is, in this context, associated with the existence of the employment contract. Once the employment relationship has been terminated, the employee will no longer be bound to secrecy. Theoretically, the general clause (sec. 1 UWG) would enable the court to apply post-employment secrecy obligations. However, the courts are rather hesitant to do so. Therefore, it is strongly recommend to provide post-contractual secrecy covenants in employment contracts.

Thirdly, sec. 18 UWG covers any misappropriation of entrusted models, samples, documents, prototypes, patterns and the like.

Remedies

Theoretically, remedies for breach of confidence and misappropriation of trade secrets include injunctions, account of profits and damages payment.

Competition

What is competition?

In Germany, the term competition law encompasses two different concepts: First, the "Gesetz gegen Wettbewerbsbeschränkungen" (commonly abbreviated to "GWB") denotes an act against restraints on competition. It prohibits anti-competitive behaviour and abuse of market power that could prevent, restrict or distort competition in Germany. In addition, European Community law may apply.

Second, the "Gesetz gegen den unlauteren Wettbewerb" (commonly abbreviated to "UWG") denotes an act against unfair competition. It prohibits unfair trade and advertising practices. Protection of confidential information and trade secrets are also part of the UWG. Therefore, it is an important legal tool in Germany.

What does the UWG protect?

Though the act takes a very generalising approach to defining what unfair trade means, case law has established a number of categories. These include nuisance of consumers, interference with competitors, exploitation of competitors, breach of law and market disturbances. In addition, the UWG contains rules on comparative advertising and prohibits consumer deception.

While many of the UWG's categories aim to protect the consumer, only competitors or certain associations may take action based on this act. Associations in particular have contributed to a great extent to the development of the German case law. However, their litigious efforts are often regarded as vexatious by the industry.

Germany

It is important to note that this act's provisions can be used as a fall-back position if other, more specialised IP laws fail to provide protection. For example, when the owner of a design takes action against an alleged infringer, she may also invoke protection from the UWG by claiming that the alleged infringer imitated her product and therefore exploited efforts that are rightfully hers. Thus, the UWG often serves as a fall-back position to more specialised IP rights.

Status of the UWG

The UWG is about to undergo major legislative reform that aims to further strengthen consumer rights. The categories established by case law will remain, however, and be integrated into the act's wording. It is expected that the new UWG shall be enacted later in 2003.

Footnotes

[1] 2001/29/EC of the European Parliament and of the Council of May 22, 2001 on the harmonisation of certain aspects of copyright and related rights in the information society.

Useful Industry Contacts

The German Patent and Trade Mark Office ("Deutsches Patentamt") is responsible for German patents, designs and trade marks.
http://www.dpma.de/index.htm (German only)

The European Patent Office is located in Germany.
http://oami.eu.int

The Max-Planck Institute for Intellectual Property, Competition and Tax Law is a research institute with an emphasis on international comparative legal analysis.
http://www.ip.mpg.de/Enhanced/English/Homepage.HTM

The IPR-Helpdesk Service is a European Commission pilot project aiming to assist potential and current contractors taking part in Community funded research and development projects with IPR issues.
http://www.cordis.lu/ipr-helpdesk/en/home.html (in 5 languages)

The GEMA ("Gesellschaft für Musikalische Aufführungs- und Mechanische Vervielfältigungsrechte") is Germany's musical copyright society.
http://www.gema.de/engl/home.shtml

The VG Wort ("Verwertungsgesellschaft Wort") is Germany's copyright society for literary works.
http://www.vgwort.de/ (German only)

The VG Bild-Kunst ("Verwertungsgesellschaft Bild-Kunst") is Germany's copyright society for artists, photographers and movie makers.
http://www.bildkunst.de/ (German only)

Germany

Chapter 13: Greece

Greece

Nicolas K. Dontas
(Dontas Law Offices)

Patents

Patent grants and protection are regulated by Act No. 1733/1987 (the Patents Act). Greece has also ratified the Patent Cooperation Treaty (via Acts No. 1883/1990 and No. 2385/96) and the European Patent Convention (via Act No. 1607/1986).

Requirements for a patent to be granted
Substantive

A patent will be granted for an invention, which (a) is new, (b) involves an inventive step and (c) is capable of industrial application. Further it should not fall within the categories of subject-matter excluded under article 5 (2) of the Patent Act (e.g. mathematical methods, aesthetic creations).

Procedural

Applicants for a patent grant must file with the Industrial Property Organisation (OBI) an application including a detailed description of the patent claims and relevant data. Provided that the application meets the formalities of the Patents Act, it will be made available to the public eighteen months (18) following the filing date. OBI will then proceed to basic substantive examination of the patent application and, provided that it is satisfied, a patent will be granted to the applicant.

Duration

Patents are granted for a period of 20 years from the filing date of the application, subject to the payment of renewal fees.

Nicolas K. Dontas regularly advises clients on matters involving trademark, design and copyright protection, licensing and Internet related disputes, as well as unfair competition law claims. His litigation experience covers all the above areas with particular emphasis on trademark dilution and trade dress infringement cases. Mr. Dontas has been included in the Euromoney guide on the "World's Leading Trademark Law Practitioners" and has written and lectured widely on IP matters.

Greece

Protection

A patent grant confers upon the patentee a legal monopoly over the invention entitling him to prevent any third party from exploiting any invention within the patent specification. However, a patent may be invalidated, for lack of novelty, inventive step or industrial applicability, following a nullification action by any third party establishing legitimate interest.

Utility model certificate

Under article 19 of the Patents Act, a utility model certificate shall be granted for three-dimensional objects which do not present the inventive step required for patents, but are novel, industrially applicable and capable of giving a solution to a technical problem. The duration of the the validity of such a certificate is seven (7) years.

Industrial Designs

Presidential Decree No. 259/1997 (the Decree), which was issued in implementation of Act No. 2417/1996 ratifying the Hague Agreement, sets out the requirements for registration of industrial designs in Greece.

Registration

Provided that the application to register an industrial design meets the formal requirements set out under the Decree, a registration certificate is issued by the OBI four months after the filing of the application.

Rights conferred

The registrant of an industrial design enjoys an exclusive right to exploit the design and prevent any third party from exploiting it. Still, as is the case with patents, an industrial design registration may be invalidated if it is not new or does not present individuality, under article 12 of the Decree.

Term of protection

An industrial design registration is valid for five (5) years, as of the date of filing of the application with the OBI. The term may be renewed for periods of further five years, up to a total term of twenty-five (25) years, subject to payment of renewal fees.

Trade Marks

In implementation of the EC Directive 89/104, Act No. 2239/1994 on Trademarks (the Trademarks Act) was enacted to govern registration and protection of trademarks in Greece. The Trademarks Act embodies the principles set out by the Directive, essentially reiterating the majority of its provisions.

Greece

Application procedure

The application for registration of an indication as a trademark is filed with the Trademarks Administrative Committee. When examining the application, the Committee, unlike the OHIM, may raise objections based on either relative (i.e., earlier identical or similar trademarks) or absolute grounds of refusal.

If the mark is accepted it will be advertised in the "Industrial Property Bulletin", allowing third parties to file a notice of opposition to the application (on relative or absolute grounds).

Famous trademarks

Under article 4 of the Trademarks Act, famous trademarks are afforded a greater degree of protection even against signs, which are not identical or strongly similar. As a general rule, which is applied consistently by the Greek courts, the greater the reputation and market recognition of a mark, the easier to establish consumer confusion in case of a conflict with a similar sign.

Duration

A trademark registration will remain in force for an initial period of 10 years, which may be renewed in perpetuity for further 10 year periods upon payment of renewal fees.

Revocation

Following a cancellation action by any third party establishing legitimate interest, a trademark may be revoked, in full or in part, if it has not been used for a continuous period of 5 years or if it has been registered in violation of articles 3 and 4 of the Trademarks Act, which set out the absolute and relative grounds for refusal of registration of a trademark. In this case, the cancellation action may only be filed within a period of five years as of the date of registration of the trademark.

Protection

The owner of a trademark is entitled to prevent any third party from using, in the course of trade, any indication identical with or similar to his trademark. As a general rule, any interference with the absolute and exclusive right in and to the trademark will be considered trademark infringement. The civil remedies available comprise (i) an injunction prohibiting the defendant from carrying out or continuing to carry out the infringing activity and (ii) the seizure of the infringing materials. Moreover, damages may also be sought by means of an action for damages, under article 914 or 920 of the Greek Civil Code, provided that the conditions of tort liability are met. However, the claim for damages is very often of little importance, as it is extremely difficult to find out the actual number of infringing products sold and, thus, quantify, on the basis of an objective and concrete method of calculation, the profit lost. Moreover, in most cases a decision awarding damages cannot be enforced, due to the absence of sufficient assets in the name of the infringer.

For obvious reasons, a preliminary injunction action is the most effective civil action in most cases of trademark infringement. In such an action, the plaintiff should satisfy the requirement of urgency. Generally, tolerance of the infringement for a considerable period of time may render the preliminary injunction action inadmissible for lack of urgency. The hearing of the preliminary injunction action is usually scheduled within 5 to 7 weeks as from the date of filing of the said action.

Unregistered Marks

Unregistered marks are protected under Act No. 146/1914 on unfair competition. Distinctive signs (including a product's trade dress) are protected under article 13 of the Unfair Competition Act, provided that they have become known in the relevant circle of consumers and territorial boundaries (inside Greece) as a distinctive sign of the goods and/or the company that markets them.

Copyright and Related Rights

Copyright and related rights are governed by Act No. 2121/93 (the Copyright Act), as amended to implement EC legislation.

Fundamental principles

Unlike US law, there is no registration procedure for intellectual works in Greece. Further, only a natural person may be the author of such work and legal persons may obtain copyright only via assignment or licensing (although in cases of works created by virtue of an employment relationship, article 8 of the Copyright Act provides that the copyright is automatically transferred to the employer). Moreover, the Copyright Act draws a distinction between copyright and moral rights, which may not be assigned, although practically, can be significantly restricted.

Protection

In case of copyright infringement, the author is, pursuant to article 65 of the Copyright Act, entitled to seek an injunction and damages, while the courts are under an obligation to grant preliminary injunctions and even ex parte orders to stop copyright infringement. Moreover, in Article 66 of the same Act, criminal sanctions of significant deterrent value are threatened against anyone exploiting without the author's permission, a copyrighted work by, among other things, dealing in or with products of any kind, bearing or incorporating any of the copyrighted works. More specifically, the infringer may receive a jail sentence of at least one year and a fine ranging from three to fifteen thousand Euros. In cases where the illegal activity is carried out habitually, or the damage inflicted on the copyright owner and the illegal profit of the infringer are very substantial, the criminal courts may impose a jail sentence of at least two years and a fine ranging from fifteen to sixty thousand Euros.

Duration

In Greece, the duration of copyright is in accordance with the European Community directive discussed in the European Community chapter. As a general rule, a work is protected for 70 years after the author's death.

Database right

In implementation of the EC Directive 96/9, a recent amendment to the Copyright Act provides for the protection of databases. The database owner has the right to prevent any third party from extracting or re-utilising all or a substantial part of the contents of the database. The duration of a database right is 15 years from creation.

Chapter 14: Hungary

Hungary

By Dr. Tamás Éless and Dr. Zita Tamás
(Réti Szegheo & Partners)

Patents

Which are the relevant measures?

Act XXXIII of 1995 on the Protection of Inventions by Patents (Patent Act) sets out the rules on patentable inventions, including the criteria of granting patents, the rights and obligations arising from the invention and the protection by patent, and the rules regarding national and international procedures.

Hungary has been a party to the Patent Cooperation Treaty (PCT) since 1980[1], and joined the European Patent Convention (EPC) in 2002[2].

Hungarian law has been harmonized with Directive 98/44/EC on the legal protection of biotechnological inventions. General rules regarding supplementary protection certificates come into effect on the date on which Hungary becomes a Member State of the European Union (May 1, 2004). Up to now, the regulation gives only the background for the eventual regulation of supplementary protection certificates regarding medicinal and plant protection products.

What is the application procedure?

Before submitting the patent application it is advisable to conduct a preliminary research on the patentability of the invention, whether a similar patent has been granted or a similar patent application has been submitted before. The registry of patents and patent applications is public.

The patent application containing the application for registration, the patent description with the claims, the abstract and—if necessary—drawings and other schedules shall be submitted to the Hungarian Patent Office (HPO). An application and research fee shall be paid within two months. If the schedules of the patent application are in a foreign language, a translation shall be submitted within four months following the date of application.

Dr. Tamás Éless is a partner at Réti Szegheo where he heads the IP, competition and litigation practice. Dr. Éless is also an honorary professor of law at ELTE University and a lecturer on international commercial arbitration at Asser College Europe. Réti Szegheo provides clients with services in the legal fields of corporate and commercial; banking and finance; competition; labour and employment; intellectual property protection and IP enforcement; IT, e-commerce and data protection; real estate; and dispute resolution.

Hungary

Following the submission of the patent application, the HPO conducts a formal examination. Throughout the procedure the applicant is given the opportunity to make any necessary corrections. If the patent application is not correct, it shall be deemed to be withdrawn.

Thereafter HPO conducts a research on novelty, prepares a search report and publishes the termination of the research in the official journal of the HPO. The patent application shall be published after eighteen months from the application date. Following the publication, anybody may submit observations to the HPO on the patentability of the invention.

The HPO performs the substantive examination of the patent application only upon request of the applicant, who shall submit the request within six months following the date on which the completion of the research on novelty is published. The applicant shall pay the examination fee within two months after the submission of the application.

Before granting the patent, that version of the patent description, the claim and the drawings, which would serve as basis for the granting, shall be sent to the applicant who may state within three months whether he agrees with this version. If the applicant agrees, a granting fee and a printing charge shall be paid within the above-mentioned time-limit. The HPO issues a patent document following the granting of the patent. The HPO registers the granting of the patent in the patent register.

The decision of the HPO on granting may be modified or set aside by the Metropolitan Court of Budapest upon request of a party to the case that is filed within a 30-day time limit.

How long does the patent last and to whom can it be granted?

The protection lasts for twenty years from the application date. A maintenance fee shall be paid annually. During the term of protection, anybody may submit an application to the HPO for the annulment of the patent if in her/his opinion the patent application should have been refused because it had not met the requirements of granting.

The property rights arising from the patent may be transferred. A patent can be granted only to the inventor and his/her legal successor (the employer is qualified as the legal successor of the employee in case of an employee's invention).

Infringement

On the basis of patent protection, the patentee has exclusive right for the utilization of the invention. Therefore the patentee may act against anybody who utilizes the invention without her/his authorization. The patentee may initiate a lawsuit against the infringer, which procedure falls within the exclusive competence of the Metropolitan Court of Budapest.

A procedure known as 'negative finding' may be initiated at the HPO to the effect that the product or process utilized—or intended to be utilized—does not infringe a specific patent. Such procedure might be initiated by anyone who expects that a lawsuit for patent infringement may be brought against him. The negative finding may be initiated only before the commencement of the procedure for patent infringement. The decision pronouncing a negative finding precludes the commencement of a procedure for patent infringement.

Designs

Registered and unregistered designs

In Hungary, unlike in the UK, there is no protection for unregistered designs. Therefore it is necessary to have the design registered. However, it can be protected by copyright rules if it qualifies as an author's work. Protection can also be obtained by applying unfair competition rules. The registry of designs and design applications is public, therefore a preliminary research may be conducted before the application.

It is possible to request the registration of more than one design if the designs have external characteristics in common.

Which are the relevant measures?

Act XLVIII of 2001 on designs contains the regulation regarding designs. The Hungarian rules are harmonized with directive 98/71/EC on the legal protection of design, and Hungary is a party to the relevant international treaties. As mentioned in Chapter 3, the existing Community applications and registrations will automatically extend to the new Member States (i.e. to Hungary as well) at the Enlargement Date.

Registration procedure

An application shall be submitted to the HPO which contains the request for registration, the illustration of the design, the name of the product and—if necessary— other schedules. The application fee shall be paid within three months. The registration procedure is similar to the application procedure of patents (formal examination, research on novelty, substantive examination). The main differences are the following:
- there is no research fee, granting fee or printing charge;
- the termination of the research on novelty is not published in the official journal;

Hungary

- the design application shall be published after nine months from the application date, which may be postponed upon request of the applicant in cases where the postponement fee has been paid, but the application shall be published within thirty months from the application date at the latest;
- the applicant does not need to submit an application to have the substantive examination commenced, because the HPO has the right to conduct substantive examination before the publication of the application;
- the design can be registered only a month after the publication to assure the right of submitting observations.

Design protection

The protection lasts for 5 years from the application date and may be renewed for five years four times (a total of 25 years) upon payment of the renewal fee. The owner of the design may be the author and its legal successor.

In case of infringement, a lawsuit may be brought against the infringer. The possible infringer may initiate a procedure on negative finding.

Trade Marks

Registered trademarks

Which are the relevant measures?

Registered trademarks in Hungary are regulated by the Act XI of 1997 on the Protection of Trademarks and Geographical Product Markings.

Hungary has joined the main international treaties regulating trademarks. Hungary became a party to the Madrid Agreement in 1909[3] and the Madrid Protocol in 1997[4]. Since Hungary is a party to the Nice Agreement[5], the Nice Classification is used in the trademark registration procedure.

Hungarian law is harmonized with 89/104/EEC Directive on trademarks. In Hungary, Regulation no. 40/94/EC on Community Trademarks comes into force the date on which Hungary becomes a Member State of the European Union (on May 1, 2004) and on the same day the community trademark applications and registrations will automatically extend to Hungary.

What are the conditions of registration?

The main conditions of registration are in accordance with the regulation of the other EU countries, however there are some differences.

Hungarian law does not specify the use or the intention to use the trademark as a condition of registration. However, the trademark protection terminates if the owner of the trademark has failed to begin the use of the trademark within a period of five years from the date of registration, or has failed to use the trademark for a period of five successive years. It is possible to register trademarks in joint ownership (joint trademark protection).

Registration procedure

An application shall be filed to the HPO containing the application request, the device, the specification of goods and services and—if necessary—other schedules, and the application fee shall be paid. The documents may be filed in a foreign language, although the HPO may request a Hungarian translation. English, German and French are accepted in practice. In the procedures before the HPO, foreign persons shall be represented by lawyers or patent attorneys.

The rules concerning trademark registration procedure have been recently modified; the new provisions come into effect on May 1, 2004. As a result, the registration procedure will be significantly different from the present procedure.

The main difference is that currently, the HPO may reject an application on relative grounds as well as on absolute grounds, and it has to examine all possible causes of refusal. As of May 1, 2004, the HPO will only examine the absolute causes of refusal and it will be up to the owner of the earlier trademark to file an opposition based on relative grounds.

During the procedure, the HPO will conduct a search on the prior trademarks in the registry, but the results are only for the applicant's information. However, the owner, the user of a prior trademark or the applicant will be able to request that the HPO inform her/him if the results of a search report carried out in respect of a later application refers to her/his earlier trademark. A fee shall be paid for this service.

According to the new procedure, the owner of the trademark may file an opposition within three months from the publication of the trademark application. The HPO will only examine the reason of refusal contained therein. While an opposition refering to relative causes of refusal has to be filed within the time limit mentioned above, observations concerning absolute causes of refusal may be submitted during the whole procedure. The decision of the HPO regarding registration may be changed or set aside by the Metropolitan Court of Budapest upon request.

It is advisable to conduct a preliminary research in the trademark registry regarding earlier trademarks before filing an application. In practice, the first impression of the consumer shall be taken into consideration to decide whether the devices are similar or not. In the case of the consent of the earlier trademark owner, the similar trademark can be registered.

Hungary

How long does a trademark last?

The trademark protection lasts for 10 years from the application date, and may be renewed every ten years upon payment of the renewal fee.

Trademark infringement

In the case of trademark infringement, the owner of the trademark may submit an action to the Metropolitan Court of Budapest against the infringer. The applicant may commence such procedure as well; in that case, the lawsuit for infringement shall be suspended until the the HPO makes its decision on the registration of the trademark.

Under Hungarian custom law, it is possible to submit a general or a singular request to customs to prevent the importing of products infringing other trademarks as well as the export of such products. After May 1, 2004, the provisions of the 3295/94/EC regulation has to be applied.

Unregistered trademarks

According to the Trademark Act, a mark may not be granted trademark protection if it has been in actual use on identical or similar goods from an earlier date by a third party on the domestic market without registration, where the use of the mark sought to be registered would breach the law due to lack of consent from the user of the earlier mark. For example, Act LVII of 1996 on the Prohibition of Unfair and Restrictive Market Practices, forbids the competitor to manufacture, place on the market, advertise and use a device by which the competitor or its goods or services are normally recognized.

Geographical Product Markings

Geographical indications and designations of origin used to indicate the geographical origin of products on the market may be granted protection as geographical product markings.

An application shall be submitted to the HPO and the application fee shall be paid to have the geographical product marking registered. The application procedure is the same as the trademark application procedure. The protection of a geographical product marking is not limited in duration. The owner of the geographical product marking may initiate a procedure at court in casse of infringement of protection.

Domain Names

The Council of Hungarian Internet Providers (CHIP) is the national registry adopting rules of domain name registration under the .*hu* ccTLD[6]. CHIP has a

Policy which regulates the procedure of domain registration. Under this Policy, a legal advisory board and a Court of Arbitration ad hoc helps CHIP to prevent illegal and abusive registration attempts. Owners of trade marks registered by the Hungarian Patent Office can register under *.hu* even if they are not seated in Hungary or do not have Hungarian citizenship. The registration procedure of such trade marks by the owner is simpler than the general procedure.

Copyright and Related Rights

Relevant measures

In Hungary, copyright is regulated by Act LXXVI of 1999 on Copyright (Copyright Act). Hungarian law is harmonised with EU law and the country is party to the main treaties, such as the Berne Convention since 1922.

What is copyright?

The Copyright Act protects all literary, scientific and artistic works that have an individual character.

Copyright protection

In Hungary, copyright cannot be registered. Copyright protection comes into existence the moment the work is created. The term of protection is harmonized with the Council Directive 93/98/EEC, discussed in chapter 3 on the European Community.

The moral rights of an author are the following:
- the author may decide whether her/his work can be published
- the author has the right to be indicated as author on her/his work as well as to publish the work anonymously
- protection of the integrity of the work

The author has the exclusive right to utilize her/his work and to grant licenses for the use of the work. The license contract shall be in writing and authors are entitled to a fee which has to be in proportion with the utilization of the work. The license may be limited to a specific area, duration, manner of use, extent of use, the license may be exlusive or not, and may give the right to transfer it to third persons. In the case of a discrepancy, the interpretation that is most favourable for the author shall be taken into consideration when interpreting the license agreement.

The following, in particular, are considered uses of a work:
- reproduction of a work
- distribution of a work
- public performance (stage performances, concerts etc.)
- presentation to the public by broadcast or some other manner

- adaptation
- exhibition

The moral and property rights of an author cannot be transferred (the property rights may be transferred in certain cases, for example the property rights of the works for advertising, software, databases).

The Copyright Act regulates the protection of software and databases which are harmonized with the Directives discussed in the European Community chapter.

In the event the author's rights are infringed, the author may turn to court.

Related rights

Related rights give protection:
- to the work of performers (mainly in respect of the recording, distribution, broadcasting, reproduction of her/his work), of the producers of music, of the radio and television organizations and of the producers of films; and
- to the authors of databases.

General Protection of Intellectual Property

The Hungarian Civil Code protects all intellectual property works that are not protected and regulated by other measures and may be utilized widely in the society and are not yet in the public domain.

Competition

Act LVII of 1996 on the Prohibition of Unfair and Restrictive Market Practices provides protection for unregistered product names and markings, appearance, get-up or shape of the products in cases where the competing products or the manufacturer thereof can be identified (distinguished) upon such name, marking or outlook.

Confidential Information

In addition to intellectual property, technical knowledge having commercial value (know-how) is protected by Hungarian law. The protection of know-how utilized or intended to be utilized lasts until the know-how becomes part of the public domain.

In business relationships, it is advisable to sign confidentiality agreements in which the other party is obliged not to disclose to third parties any information that comes to her/his knowledge during such relationship and relating thereto. As the consequence of the breach of contract, penalty may be stipulated and the damages may be claimed for the disclosure.

Hungary

Footnotes

[1] PCT has been published in Law Decree XIV of 1980.
[2] EPC has been published in Act L of 2002, the rules came into force on 1st January, 2003 in Hungary.
[3] The last version of Madrid Agreement adopted in Stockholm has been published in Law Decree XXIX of 1973.
[4] Madrid Protocol has been published in Act LXXXIII of 1999.
[5] Nice Agreement has been published in Law Decree VII of 1967.
[6] Country Code Top Level Domain
[7] Directive 2001/29/EC of the European Parliament and the Council of May 22, 2001 on the harmonization of certain aspects of copyright and related rights in the information society.

Chapter 15:
Ireland

Ireland

By Cliff Kennedy
(MacLachlan & Donaldson)

Patents

Current Irish patent legislation is governed by the Patents Act, 1992. Ireland is a member state of the European Patent Convention (EPC) and the Patent Cooperation Treaty (PCT). Irish law now provides for the grant of full-term and short-term national patents.

The main provisions of the current legislation are set out below.

European Patent Convention

Ireland became a contracting state of the European Patent Convention in 1992.

Patent Cooperation Treaty

Ireland has ratified the Patent Cooperation Treaty and is also bound by Chapter 11 of the PCT. The Irish Patents Office is a Receiving Office for PCT applications, but it is only possible to designate Ireland by way of a European patent designation.

Full-term patents
National law

Irish national patent law is now in line with the European Patent Convention. The term of all national full-term patents is twenty years.

Evidence of novelty

An applicant for a full-term Irish patent must submit evidence of novelty of the invention. The evidence of novelty can take the form of:
(a) a published corresponding patent application (a United Kingdom, European or PCT application) and related search report, or
(b) the specification of a patent granted by one of the prescribed Patent Offices (the United Kingdom, German or European Patent Offices).

Novelty Search: Alternatively, the applicant may request the Irish Patents Office to undertake a search in relation to the invention. The United Kingdom Patent Office normally conducts the search on behalf of the Irish Patents Office.

Cliff Kennedy is a partner at MacLachlan & Donaldson in Dublin, specialising in trade mark law. He is currently the President of the Irish Association of Patent and Trade Mark Agents.

Ireland

Amendment

The applicant must then either amend the claims of the Irish patent application in the light of the prior art, or state that no amendments are necessary. If the evidence of novelty is a copy of the specification of a granted patent, it is necessary to amend the specification of the Irish application to conform with the specification of the granted patent.

Examination

The Patents Office retains the right to examine any patent application, but in normal circumstances there is no substantive examination of new or existing patent applications.

Maintenance fees

Maintenance fees are payable on new applications for full-term patents, but not on existing applications or applications for short-term patents.

Short-Term Patents

Definition

The Irish Patents Act provides for the grant of short-term patents which have a maximum term of ten years. A valid short-term patent is obtainable in respect of an invention which is "new and susceptible of industrial application provided it is not clearly lacking an inventive step". An application for a short-term patent does not need to be supported by evidence of novelty and the patent is obtainable within months of filing the application.

Infringement

Before an infringement action can be taken in the Courts, however, it is necessary to provide evidence of novelty of the invention or request the Patents Office to undertake a search.

Amendment

The specification of the granted short-term patent may need to be amended in the light of the evidence of novelty or the requested search report.

Third party request

A third party may request the Patents Office to undertake the necessary search.

Relationship with full-term patents

It is possible to apply for a short-term patent and a full-term patent at the same time, and in respect of the same subject matter, but the short-term patent will automatically be revoked on the grant of the full-term patent. It is also possible to convert an application for one form of patent to the other and to file a divisional application from either. A short-term patent may be granted while a European application is pending, but will automatically be revoked on the grant of the European patent.

Circuit court

Normally, patent infringement actions are taken in the High Court, but an infringement action may be taken in the Circuit Court in respect of a short-term patent, and should not be as expensive as a corresponding action in the High Court.

Post-Grant Procedures
Revocation

It is possible to apply for revocation of a patent in the High Court or in the Patents Office. However, it is not possible to take an infringement action in the Patents Office.

Restoration

An application for restoration of a lapsed patent or patent application must be filed within two years of the date on which the renewal fee should have been paid. An applicant for restoration of a patent or patent application must show that reasonable care had been taken to ensure payment of the renewal fee within the prescribed period, that the failure to pay the renewal fee was unintentional, and that no undue delay occurred in making the application for restoration.

Licenses

The law relating to voluntary and compulsory licenses remains substantially the same as in the Patents Act 1964, except that it will no longer be possible to obtain, as of right, a license under a patent in respect of food or medicine.

Transitional Provisions
Term

The term of all patents granted under the Patents Act 1964, and in force at the commencement date of the 1992 legislation, has been extended from sixteen to twenty years. There are no license of right provisions as occurred in the United Kingdom.

Ireland

Where the term of a patent granted under the Patents Act, 1964 has been extended from sixteen to twenty years, infringement proceedings cannot be brought against a party who, during the final two years of the extended term, made preparations to exploit the invention when the patent expired.

Trade Marks

Current Irish trade mark legislation is governed by the Trade Marks Act, 1996. This legislation implemented the EC Harmonisation Directive 89/104/EEC. The main provisions are as follows:

Service marks

In addition to registering a trade mark in relation to goods, it is possible to also register a trade mark in relation to services.

Multi-class applications

It is possible to file an application in one or more classes.

Collective/certification marks

Irish trade mark law permits the registration of Collective or Certification Marks. An applicant for a Collective Mark must file the regulations governing use of the mark within 6 months of the date of application.

Registrability

In accordance with the EC Directive, it is possible to register any sign which can be represented graphically and which is capable of distinguishing goods or services from one undertaking from those of another. The definition of a registrable trade mark includes the shape of goods or their packaging but shapes which are purely functional or which are necessary to achieve a technical result or which add substantial value to the goods to be covered by the registration are unregistrable.

Infringement

It is possible to invoke a registered trade mark to prevent the use of an identical or similar trade mark not only in relation to the particular goods or services covered by the registration but also in relation to similar goods or services. It is not an infringement to use a registered trade mark in comparative advertising provided the trade mark is used honestly for the purpose of identifying the goods or services of the registered proprietor or that the use would not take unfair advantage of or be detrimental to the distinctive character of the registered trade mark.

Ireland

Anti-counterfeiting

Where a trade mark, which is identical to or closely resembles a registered trade mark, is used fraudulently for gain, the offense is punishable by fines and/or imprisonment of up to 10 years.

Well-known marks

Irish law extends protection to trade marks, which are neither registered nor used in Ireland, but which are well-known trade marks as defined by the Paris Convention.

Prior rights

The Irish Patents Office examines an Irish trade mark application both on substantive and relative grounds. Thus if there is a prior similar mark registered in respect of the same or similar goods or services, an objection will be raised by the Irish Patents Office. A letter of consent from the proprietor of the cited trade mark will overcome such an objection. A third party can also oppose an application on the grounds of a prior similar registered trade mark or common law rights/ acquired through use of a similar trade mark. The opposition period runs three months from the date of publication of the application in the Patents Office Journal.

Revocation

A trade mark registration may be cancelled at the request of a third party if the trade has not been used by the registered proprietor or with his consent during the previous five years. The onus to establish proof of use rests with the registered proprietor.

Assignments

Trade marks, including pending applications, may be assigned with or without goodwill. An application to record an assignment may be based upon a Certified copy of the original Deed of Assignment although Government stamp duty of 9% is payable on the market value in Ireland of the trade mark being assigned. There are exemptions from payment of stamp duty for transfers between related companies. The original Deed of Assignment is required for the payment of the stamp duty.

Licensing

Use of a registered trade mark with the proprietor's consent automatically accrues to the benefit of the registered proprietor, even when the user is not recorded as a licensee. However, only recorded licensees are entitled to initiate infringement proceedings based on the registered trade mark or to require the reg-

Ireland

istered proprietor of the trade mark to do so. The legislation also provides for recordal of exclusive licenses and sub-licenses.

Renewals

Trade marks registered under the 1996 Act are registered for ten year renewal terms. Under the previous legislation, the initial renewal period was seven years with subsequent fourteen year renewal periods.

Trade marks Register

The previous two-tier Register (Parts A and B) was abolished by the 1996 Act in favour of a single Register. Unlike most jurisdictions, it is possible to alter a registered trade mark provided that the alteration does not substantially affect the trade mark's identify.

International registrations

Ireland is a member of the Madrid Protocol and the Community trade mark system and thus it is possible to secure trade mark protection in Ireland using either system.

Passing off

Ireland is a common law system and recognises that rights can be acquired through use of a trade mark. If a third party represents that his goods or services are that of the plaintiff, the plaintiff may sue for the tort of passing off. Irish law does not recognise the tort of unfair competition.

Industrial Designs

Legislation in relation to Industrial Designs is governed by The Industrial Designs Act, 2001 and The Industrial Design Regulations 2002. The Act gives effect to Directive 98/71/EC of the European Parliament.

What may be registered

Irish law provides that a design may be registered with the Irish Patents Office in respect of any new design which has individual character. Features of the design which are pertinent to registrability include the lines, contours, colours, shape, texture, materials and/or ornamentation of the product. The design need not have any eye appeal, although the features of the appearance of the design must be visible during normal use of the product to which the design is applied.

Novelty

Novelty of a design at the date of application for registration of the design is essential. By way of exception, however, where a design has already been published by its owner, then novelty is retained provided that an application for registration is filed within twelve months of the publication date.

Multiple application

The Act provides for the filing of a multiple application, which may consist of up to 100 designs, provided they all belong to the same class of the Locarno System of International Classification.

Duration of the design

The registration of a design secures for the owner a monopoly in respect of that design which may last for 25 years. The initial period of protection is five years, renewable for four additional periods of five years each.

Copyright

Copyright legislation in Ireland is governed by the Copyright and Related Rights Act, 2000. The Act makes provision for various EU directives relating to the protection of computer programmes on rental and lending rights and other rights, satellite broadcasting and cable retransmission, harmonisation of the term of protection of copyright and legal protection of databases and related matters.

Works in which copyright subsists

Copyright subsists in original literary, dramatic, musical or artistic work, sound recordings, films, broadcasts or cable programmes, typographical arrangements of published editions and original databases.

Performers' rights

An exclusive right to authorise or prohibit certain acts is now vested in the performers, including recording a performance, broadcasting whole or substantial parts of the performance, recording from a broadcast, copying and distributing recordings.

Computer programmes

"Literary work" has been extended to include "a computer programme" which includes any design materials used for the preparation of the programme. There are, however, exceptions to copyright in computer programmes.

Ireland

Moral rights

Moral rights are provided for under the Act and these rights include "paternity rights" which allow a right to be identified as the author (by name or pseudonym). An author may also object to any distortion or other modification of the work.

Duration

The duration of most copyright is now the lifetime of the author and seventy years. There are exceptions, including cable programmes, sound recordings and typographical arrangements.

Ireland

Chapter 16:
Italy

Italy

By Donatella Prandin
(Bugnion S.p.A.)

Patents

The application procedure

The patent application procedure is ruled by the Italian Patent Law No. 1127/39 and implementing regulations.

In order to obtain a filing date, an Italian Patent application must include full details of the applicant, the title of the invention, a description with any drawing mentioned therein, and the evidence of payment of the filing fees and annuity fees for the first three-year period.

Further formal requirements: a description, including a summary and ending with one or more claims; the filing of a designation of the inventor.

Although novelty and non-obviousness are substantial requirements for the validity of a patent under the Italian Patent Law, only a formal and a "prima facie" substantial examination is carried out by the Examiners of the Italian Patent Office on patent applications.

If in the Examiner's opinion either the application does not comply with the formal requirements, or the claimed subject matter does not show any possible novel and inventive feature, a communication bearing the grounds of refusal of the patent application is sent to the Applicant.

After that communication, the Applicant has the opportunity to submit his/her arguments and, if necessary, to amend the application.

In case of final refusal, appeal against the Examiner's decision is still possible before the Board of Appeal of the PTO.

Patents are granted after an average period of 2-3 years from filing.

How long does a patent last?

The rights conferred by a patent last for 20 years from the filing date.

To whom can a patent be granted?

A patent can be granted, under the same conditions, to any legal or natural person, either national or foreigner.

Donatella Prandin is a partner in the Milan office of Bugnion S.p.A. and is the head of the firm's Foreign Department. Ms. Prandin has extensive experience in the IP field, with a particular focus on trade mark matters, copyright protection, designs and domain name issues. Bugnion S.p.A. is one of the leading IP firms in Italy.

Italy

Once granted, is the patent safe?

Opposition procedure is not available after granting of an Italian Patent.

A patent can be invalidated, restricted, or the true owner may be restored in his rights only through a legal action before a Civil Court.

Annuity fees must be paid to avoid lapse of the patent rights.

Rights conferred by a patent

According to Italian patent law, a patent gives the applicant the exclusive right to carry out the invention on the Italian territory.

In particular:

- if the object of the invention is a product, the applicant's exclusive right is to prevent third parties from making, using, selling, offering to sell, or importing the claimed product;
- if the object of the invention is a method, the applicant's exclusive right is to prevent third parties from carrying out such method and from using, selling, offering to sell or importing the product directly obtained by the claimed method.

Exploitation

Patents must be exploited by the owner within three years from the granting or four years from the filing date, whichever is later.

In case of non-exploitation of the patent, a compulsory non-exclusive license may be granted to third parties.

Priority

Applications filed in Italy, as a member of the Convention of the Union of Paris (CUP), benefit from the conventional 12-month priority claim of foreign first filing applications.

Italian patent law does not provide "internal" priority, which means that Italian applications can not claim the priority date of earlier Italian applications.

Infringement

Patent infringement actions have to be brought before the civil courts. It was recently decided that specialised IP departments of the major Italian Courts will be in charge of patent matters.

Precautionary measures

In Italy, it is possible to request to a civil court precautionary measures against the activity of an alleged infringer.

The three possible measures are:
- judicial description;
- seizure; and
- preliminary injunction.

Utility models

Utility models can be filed in Italy under generally the same formal requirements as patent applications, and they benefit from the same priority terms.

Utility model protection lasts 10 years after filing and covers products consisting of a new shape or combination of shapes, having "particular usefulness". Methods and chemical compositions cannot be protect by a utility model.

The utility model protection extends to "equivalent" models, i.e. to models obtaining the same results using the same innovative concept.

Utility models give applicants substantially the same rights as patents against infrigement.

Designs

Legislation

Designs are regulated in Italy by Royal Decree n. 1411 of August 25, 1940 as modified by Legislative Decree No 95 of February 2, 2001 entered into force on April 19, 2001 to implement the Directive 98/71/EC.

What is a design?

The definition of a design is the same for both Italy and European Community forms of protection.

Registration process

To apply for a registered design it is necessary to file with the Italian Patent and Trademark Office an official application form and two copies of the description, as well as the relevant drawings/photographs. There is no limit to the number of views that can be submitted.

It is possible to file both single and multiple applications covering up to 100 designs. There is not any substantial examination; in fact the exam is related to formal aspects of the application.

The Italian Patent and Trademark Office takes three to four years to issue the relevant certificate of registration.

Duration of a registered design is five years from the filing date and the term of protection can be extended for one of more periods of five years each, up to a maximum of twenty-five years from the filing date of the application.

Italy

Prior disclosure – 12 month grace period

Under Italian law, it is possible to file an application for a registered design within twelve months following the first disclosure.

Infringement

The exclusive rights conferred by registration of a design extend to any design or model that does not produce on the informed user a different overall impression.

Dual protection

Legislative Decree No. 95 has repealed the principle of the prohibition of a dual protection, therefore it is now possible to enjoy protection under the Italian Design Law and the Italian Copyright Law.

The new law provides for the copyright protection combined with the design protection to be reserved only for industrial design works having a creative character artistic value.

Trade Marks

Registered trademarks

Trademarks in Italy are regulated under Royal Decree No. 929 of June 21, 1942 and subsequent amendments, Legislative Decree No. 480 of December 4, 1992, Legislative Decree No. 198 of March 19, 1996, and Legislative Decree No. 447 of October 8, 1999.

Registrability and the application procedure

The Italian Patent and Trademark Office does not conduct any novelty exam before registering a trademark application. In fact, the exam is merely related to formal requirements and to registrability with respect to distinctiveness and originality. The exam of the office is only related to the absolute grounds for refusal and not to the relative ones. Therefore, unless an objection is raised with respect to distinctiveness and originality, a trademark can be registered quite easily.

The Italian Patent and Trademark Office takes about three to four years to issue the relevant certificate of registration.

How long does trademark registration last?

A trademark lasts 10 years from the filing date and it is renewable for periods of ten years each.

A trademark lapses if, at five years from registration, it has not yet been used by the owner or with his consent for the products or services for which it has been registered, or if it has been withdrawn from current use for an uninterrupted period of five years, unless the non-use is legitimate and justified.

Italy

What rights does it give?

Rights of the registered trademark's owner consist in having the faculty of exclusive use of the trademark. The trademark's owner has the right to forbid third parties, subject to his consent, to use:

a) a sign identical to the trademark for products or services identical to those for which it was registered;

b) a sign identical or similar to the registered trademark for identical or similar products or services, if, owing to identicalness or similarity between the signs and identicalness or affinity between the products or services, a risk of confusion for the public may arise which can also involve the risk of association between the two signs;

c) a sign identical or similar to the registered trademark for products or services which are not alike if the registered trademark is of good reknown in Italy and if the use of the sign without a legitimate reason makes it possible to take undue advantage of the distinctive character or reknown of the trademark or is prejudicial to said character and reknown.

The trademark owner can in particular forbid third parties to affix said sign to the products or their packages; to offer the goods, to place them on the market or be in possession of them for these ends, or to offer or render services identified by said sign; to import or export goods identified by the sign itself; or to use the sign in business correspondence and advertising.

Advantages of registration

Only registration confers a right to the exclusive use of a trade mark. The trademark owner enjoys a high level of protection on the basis of the provisions related to unfair competition, slavish imitation and Italian Trademark Law.

Unregistered trademarks

Unregistered trademarks enjoy protection only on the basis of the provisions related to the unfair competition or slavish imitation.

However, under art. 9 of the Italian Trademark law, when prior use has been made by third parties of a non-registered trademark that is either little known, or known only locally, such third parties shall be entitled to continue using the trademark, also for advertising purposes, within its local diffusion limits, notwithstanding the granting of a registration for the trademark.

Copyright

How is copyright protected in Italy?

Copyright in Italy is regulated by the Law on the Protection of Copyright No. 633, April 1941, as amended by Law No. 406, July 1981, Decree Law No. 154, May

Italy

1997 and several laws on specific issues. The above Italian Law provides rules which refer principally to the protection of the original rights of the author who is always and only an individual. In addition, the above Law protects the works from the moment of its creation. Due to this fact, the appropriate term to define the above discipline is Author's Right instead of Copyright.

In order to qualify for protection under Italian copyright law, works must involve an intellectual effort and possess a creative character. In addition, the Law on the Protection of Copyright individuates some exemplifying categories to which the above works could belong in order to enjoy the above protection (literature, music, the figurative arts, architecture, theatre or cinematography). Software is protected since 1992. In addition, since 2001, industrial designs having creative character and artistic value are also protected.

Do I need to register copyright?

All published works protected by copyright may be filed with the Copyright Service of the Ministero dei Beni Culturali, while unpublished works may be filed in a separate register kept by S.I.A.E. (Public Entity for the Protection of Authors and Editors). However, under the above Italian copyright law, a work enjoys protection as an effect, and from the moment, of its creation. The above filing is therefore not a condition for protection, but it is advisable since it constitutes evidence of the authorship and existence of the work as from a specific date. For the same purposes, software may be registered as a published work with a Public Register.

What rights does copyright give?

Under the Italian law, the author enjoys the exclusive right to publish the work and to use it for economic purposes in any way, but respecting the limitation provided by Law. Furthermore, copyright protects the author against the actual copying of the author's creative idea as expressed in a particular work, while independent development of the same ideas are possible under certain circumstances. The above rights may be transferred or sold but, even in this case, the author maintains the moral rights to his work. In particular, the author maintains the right of "claiming authorship", the right to decide whether to remain anonymous or not, the right to withdraw the work from the market whenever serious moral reasons arise and the right to object to any distortion, mutilation or other modification of the work which could be prejudicial to the author's honour or reputation.

Term

The term of the exclusive economic rights in Italy is seventy years after the author's death. This is the general rule, but there are numerous exceptions—for example, the term is twenty-five years after the author's death for industrial designs and twenty years from the date of the creation for software. In contrast, moral rights may be always invoked by the author while alive, and by his heirs after his death.

Could a work already published abroad be qualified for protection under Italian copyright law?

Italy is a member of the Bern Convention for the protection of literary and artistic works as well as of the Universal Copyright Convention. Therefore, any work first published in a country belonging either to the Bern Convention or to the Universal Copyright Convention enjoys copyright protection in Italy.

Status of the last European Community Directive on copyright

Legislative Decree No. 68 of April 9, 2003 has implemented Community Directive No. 2001/29 on the harmonisation of certain aspects of copyright and related rights in the information society. The Decree, that came into force on April 29, 2003, amends Italian copyright law in order to harmonise its provisions on rights of reproduction, distribution, communication to the public, legal protection of anti-copying devices and rights management systems.

Competition

A specific provision about unfair competition is art. 2598 of the Italian Civil Code under which without prejudice to the rules governing the protection of distinctive signs and patent rights, acts of unfair competition are committed by anyone one who: 1) uses names or distinctive signs in a way apt to create confusion with respect to names or distinctive signs lawfully used by third parties, or slavishly copies the products of a competitor, or commits by any other means acts apt to create confusion with the products or the activity of a competitor; 2) gives news or evaluations on the products and on the activity of a competitor in a way to discredit or appropriate the merits of products or enterprise of a competitor; 3) uses directly or indirectly any other means not in accordance with the principles of fair competition and apt to create to other's enterprise.

Law No. 287 of October 10, 1990 prohibits anti-competitive agreements, in particular those preventing, limiting or restricting competition.

IP Special Judges

On July 1, 2003, the Italian Government approved the Decree Law as concerns the establishment of special sections for Intellectual Property issues. Said Decree

Italy

Law provides for the establishment of twelve sections at the Tribunals and Courts of Appeal of Bari, Bologna, Catania, Firenze, Genova, Milano, Napoli, Palermo, Roma, Torino, Trieste and Venezia specialised in Industrial and Intellectual Property. The panel of judges consists of three magistrates who have to decide collectively.

There were several reasons for shifting proceedings in intellectual and industrial property matters to the specialised sections. The most important one is the qualification of judges. In fact, the extreme technicality of the arguments requires specialised and professional magistrates to manage the underlying issues, as already happens in other European judicial systems which provide for "mixed panels" composed of experts.

The specialised sections have jurisdiction to hear matters relating to national and community trademarks, patents (both in general and for new plant varieties), utility models, models and designs, and copyright, as well as unfair competition interfering with the protection of industrial and intellectual property.

Italy

Chapter 17:
Latvia

Latvia

By Gatis Merzvinskis
(Petersona Patents)

Introduction

Latvia is a democratic, parliamentary republic initially founded on November 18, 1918. The Republic of Latvia has been continuously recognized as a state by other countries since 1920 despite occupation by the Soviet Union (1940-1941, 1945-1991). On August 21, 1991 Latvia declared the restoration of its *de facto* independence. The most prospective production sectors are information technologies, electronics and mechanical engineering, chemical and pharmaceutical industries, wood processing, food processing industries, and textile industries.

In the first 10 years of the transition from a centrally planned to a market economy following the political and economic changes which began in 1991, Latvia has established an appropriate legislative framework in many fields, including intellectual property.

Latvia is a member of the United Nations, Council of Europe, World Trade Organization, Organization for Security and Co-operation in Europe, Council of the Baltic Sea State, Euro-Atlantic Partnership Council, among others. A key foreign policy goal is full membership in the European Union and NATO. Latvia is also a member of most international treaties in the IP field (e.g. TRIPS Agreement, Paris Convention, Patent Cooperation Treaty) and its IP legislation has been harmonized and expanded according to the requirements and instructions of the European Union. Nevertheless, some work in this area remains.

Comparing the IP laws of Latvia with the IP laws of most European countries, one has to say that they are indeed very similar and the basic aspects of our IP legislation are in conformity with the respective laws and regulations of the EU to ensure adequate IP registration system, protection and enforcement of IP rights in the Republic of Latvia.

Gatis Merzvinskis is the head of the Legal and Licensing Departments at the patent agency, Petersona Patents. Petersona Patents is the leading and oldest Latvian consulting firm, providing assistance in the field of protection of intellectual property and in the process of technology transfer. Services cover the entire field of IP protection, i.e. patents, trademarks, utility models, designs, protection of appellations of origin and geographical indications, domain name registration and dispute resolution, copyright protection of computer programs and technical creations.

Latvia

Patents

Legislation

Rights to a patent in the Republic of Latvia are regulated under the Patent Law adopted on April 20, 1995 by the *Saeima* (the Parliament of the Republic of Latvia). An amended Patent Law is under procedure of approval which will be completely harmonized with the provisions of EPC (the joining is foreseen at the end of 2003) and of PLT (signed on 2 June 2000, not ratified yet).

Patentability of an invention and patent application /examination in Latvia

According to the Patent Law, a patent shall be granted for an invention that is new, possesses an invention level (inventive step) and is industrially applicable. Non-patentable objects among the traditionally excluded are the methods of treatment, business methods and software as such. A person (any natural or legal entity, foreign applicants must file through a registered patent attorney) who wishes to obtain a patent for an invention in Latvia has to file an application with the Latvian Patent Office. Patent application procedure in Latvia does not differ significantly from the procedure of other European countries.

It must be mentioned that the Latvian Patent Office does not conduct a substantive examination of patent applications and does not evaluate the conformity of an invention with the criteria of patentability, except the non-patentable objects and unity of inventions.

Patents in force in Latvia

In the Republic of Latvia a patent owner may be granted the rights to an invention:

- by filing a new patent application according to the national patent law of Latvia;
- with registration of a European patent (any European patent for which the application has been filed before the May 1, 1995 might be registered in Latvia within one year from the date of patent grant. This provision also applies to European patents resulting from PCT applications);
- with National entry of an International (PCT) patent application;
- with extension of European patent applications according to the agreement between the EPO and Latvia entered into force on May 1, 1995.

Period of patent validity in Latvia

Patents in force in Latvia are granted for a period of 20 years from the filing date of a patent application if annual renewals are made. Exclusive rights to registered European patents come into force to their full extent in the territory of Latvia as of the date a patent is applied and expire no later than 20 years from the filing date of the application for the registration of an European patent in Latvia. If the object of the patented invention is a pharmaceutical or a process for manufacturing such substance, or a new application of a known substance, the Latvian Patent Office may, at the request of the patent owner, extend the patent term beyond 20 years, but by no more than 5 years.

Patent infringements

Any person is responsible for direct or indirect infringement of a patent if he has performed the acts infringing exclusive rights without the consent of the owner of the patent valid in the Republic of Latvia, or without any other legal grounds. Responsibility for patent infringement may arise only in the event that the guilt of the infringer is proved. It is the obligation of the aggrieved party (the patent owner or the holder of the exclusive license) to prove the fact of the patent infringement and the guilt of the infringer. Disputes concerning exclusive rights, other rights related to patents or other disputes based on the Patent Law of Latvia, shall be reviewed by the Riga Regional Court in the same procedure as disputes for which civil liability is provided for in accordance with the provisions of the Civil Law of Latvia governing personal property.

Within the period of patent validity, if the dispute has arisen on the invalidation of granted patents and on the grant of licenses, an action may be instituted in court without any time limitation. In other cases of disputes, the term for instituting an action in court is limited to three years, unless the Patent Law or the legislative acts of Latvia in force provide for other terms.

Designs

Rights to a design in the Republic of Latvia are regulated under the Law on Industrial Design Protection enacted on May 4, 1993. This year a new industrial design law will be adopted in Latvia to confirm to the Community Designs Regulations (EC) No. 6/2002.

Trade Marks

Legislation

Trademarks in the Republic of Latvia are regulated by the Law on Trademarks and Indications of Geographical Origin adopted by the Saeima on June 16, 1999.

Trade mark application/ examination and registration aspects in Latvia

The Latvian Law on Trademarks contains provisions regulating legal relations as to trademark registration, as well as to the use and to the protection of

Latvia

trademarks, collective marks and indications of geographical origin. The following marks may be registered as trademarks in Latvia: verbal marks, graphic marks, three-dimensional marks, the shapes of goods or of their packaging, combined marks— consisting of a combination of the aforementioned elements (labels and the like), specific types of trademarks (sound or light signals and the like).

A person (any natural or legal entity, foreign applicants must file through a registered patent attorney), who desires to register a trademark in Latvia has to file a written application for trademark registration with the Patent Office of Latvia. Within three months from the date the application has been accepted for examination, the Patent Office of Latvia examines the compliance of the accepted application with the provisions of the Trademark Law and may refuse it on absolute grounds. The registration of a trademark is valid for a period of 10 years from the filing date of the trademark application in Latvia.

In addition, there are protected international trademark registrations territorially extended to Latvia according to the Madrid Agreement concerning the International Registration of Marks. Within three months from the date of the publication of a national trademark registration and within four months from the date of publication of a notice of trademark registration with respect to Latvia in the WIPO official gazette of international registration of trademarks, interested persons may, upon payment of the applicable fee, submit an opposition to the registration of a trademark. Where the opposition is fully or, inter alia, based on an earlier trademark that has been registered no less than five years previously, the owner of the opposed mark is entitled to request that the opponent provide obvious and sufficient (prima facie) evidence that this earlier trademark has been actually used in Latvia.

If the owner of the opposed trademark or the opponent is not satisfied with the decision of the Board of Appeal, they are entitled, within three months from the date of receipt of the copy of the decision of the Board of Appeal, to appeal the decision to the Regional Court of Riga. Lodging of a complaint with the court stays the execution (entry into force) of the decision of the Board of Appeal.

The owner of a trademark (or their successor in title) may bring an action in the Regional Court of Riga for any unlawful use of the trademark. Liability for unlawful use of a trademark shall arise where the fact of trademark infringement is proved. The burden of proof of the fact of infringement lies with the aggrieved party (the owner of the trademark or the licensee). A trademark registration may also be revoked by a judgment of the court if the trademark has not been actually used for a period of five successive years in connection with the goods and services with respect to which it is registered, and if there are no proper reasons for non-use.

Latvia

Copyright

Legislation

Copyright in Latvia is regulated by the Copyright law adopted by the Saeima on April 6, 2000.

Aspects of the Copyright protection in Latvia

According to the Copyright Law of Latvia, copyright belongs to the author as soon as a work is created, regardless of whether it has been completed, and applies to works of literature, science, art and other works, also unfinished works, regardless of the purpose of the work and the value, form or type of expression. Proof of copyright ownership does not require registration, special documentation for the work, or observance of any other formalities in Latvia.

Copyrights as well as neighbouring rights are governed by the same legal rights as personal property rights within the meaning of the Civil Law of Latvia, but it may not be an object of property claims. A work shall be deemed published simultaneously in a foreign state and in Latvia if it has been published in Latvia within 30 days after its first publication in a foreign state. An action whereby the moral or economic rights of a holder of copyright or neighbouring rights are infringed has to be considered as an infringement of copyright and neighbouring rights. Depending on the nature of the infringement of copyright or of neighbouring rights and the consequences thereof, the infringer will be held to liability in accordance with the law.

Latvian IP professionals as well as the court of Latvia have more experience in the field of the enforcement of trademarks than patents or other IP rights, as disputes have been more frequent in this field of law. In addition, it must be mentioned that in cases where trademark, patent, design or copyright infringement has been done deliberately or with malicious intent, according to the law of Latvia, the persons responsible may also be called to administrative or criminal liability.

Chapter 18: Lithuania

Lithuania

By Marius Jakulis Jason
(AAA Legal Services)

Introduction

The system of intellectual property in Lithuania functioned well until 1940, based on the Trademark Act of January 27, 1925, the Inventions and Improvements Protection Act of May 14, 1928, and the Industrial Models and Design Act.

After declaring its independence from the Soviet Union on March 11, 1990, Lithuania started reestablishing an independent national system for the protection of intellectual property. The Lithuanian Patent Bureau was established on April 12, 1991.

The main functions of the State Patent Bureau include protection of industrial property (inventions, designs, trademarks and service marks, firm names), drafting legal acts in the field of industrial property protection, and representation of the Republic of Lithuania in international organizations and international events related to industrial property protection.

Foreign natural and legal persons must be represented before the State Patent Bureau by patent attorneys registered in the Register of Patent Attorneys of the Republic of Lithuania.

Legal Acts

- The Resolution of the Government of the Republic of Lithuania on Legal Protection of Industrial Property Rights entered into force on May 20, 1992.
- A new version of the Law on Trademarks of the Republic of Lithuania came into effect on January 1, 2001.
- The Patent Law of the Republic of Lithuania came into force on February 1, 1994.
- The first Law on Designs of the Republic of Lithuania entered into force on September 1, 1995.
- A new version of the Law on Designs of the Republic of Lithuania entered into force on January 1, 2003.

Marius Jakulis Jason is the founder and senior patent attorney at AAA Legal Services in Vilnius. Mr. Jason has published extensively on IP law in Lithuania, Latvia and Estonia. The firm, which specialises in intellectual property law, has offices in Vilnius and Tallinn, and representatives in Riga.

Lithuania

- The Law on Legal Protection of Semiconductor Product Topographies of the Republic of Lithuania came into force on December 1, 1998.
- Firm Name Law of the Republic of Lithuania came into force on January 1, 2000.
- The Law on Fees for the Registration of Industrial Property Objects of the Republic of Lithuania came into force on July 1, 2001.
- The Law on Copyright and Related Rights of the Republic of Lithuania entered into force on March 5, 2003.
- The Competition Law entered into force on July 4, 1999.

International Agreements

Lithuania is a member of:

- Convention Establishing the World Intellectual Property Organization (WIPO), since April 30, 1992.
- Paris Convention for the Protection of Industrial Property, since May 22, 1994.
- Patent Cooperation Treaty (PCT), since July 5, 1994.
- Agreements with the European Patent Organization (EPO) for cooperation and for the extension of European patents to Lithuania, since July 5, 1994.
- Nice Agreement Concerning the International Classification of Goods and Services for the Purposes of the Registration of Marks, since February 22, 1997.
- Protocol relating to the Madrid Agreement Concerning the International Registration of Marks, since November 15, 1997.
- Trademark Law Treaty (TLT), since April 27, 1997.
- Budapest Treaty on the International Recognition of the Deposit of Microorganisms for the Purpose of Patent Procedure, since April 9, 1998.
- Bern Convention for the Protection of Literary and Artistic Works since May 28, 1996.
- Rome Convention for the Protection of Literary and Artistic Works since July 22, 1999.
- WIPO Copyright Treaty since March 6, 2003.

Patents

Under Lithuanian Patent Law, an invention is patentable if it is new (is not part of the prior art), involves an inventive step (is not obvious to one skilled in the art) and is industrially applicable (it can it be made and used in commerce, agriculture, health care or any other field).

The following are not considered patentable inventions:
1. discoveries, scientific theories and mathematical methods;
2. the appearance of articles of manufacture (industrial designs are protected under Lithuania's to-be-enacted Industrial Design Law);
3. games, methods of doing business, computer programs;
4. methods for presenting information.

Patents are not granted for methods of treating, diagnosing and preventing illness in humans and animals (except for apparatus and materials used in those methods), plants and animals (except microorganisms) and biological methods of their breeding (new breeds of animals to be protected under a separate law to be enacted) and inventions deemed to be contrary to public interests and morality.

If the patented invention is a method, patent protection is also granted for the product made by that method.

In Lithuania there is no examination of prior art to establish whether the invention is new, not obvious to one skilled in the art and/or has industrial applicability.

The patent term is 20 years from the filing date of the application. Prior to the third year term, and each year thereafter, an annual maintenance fee must be paid to keep the patent in force.

Industrial Designs

Lithuania's Industrial Design Law provides protection for the appearance of an article of manufacture. An industrial design is the appearance of an industrial product or part, created by its specific lines, contours, colors, forms and/or materials, made by machine or hand.

To register and protect an industrial design in Lithuania, the design must be new in Lithuania (no absolute novelty is required) and have distinctive characteristics (be distinctive in appearance).

Protection for a registered industrial design is valid for 5 years from the filing date of the application in Lithuania. The protection can be extended for 5 years, four times, for up to 25 years from the filing date of the design application in Lithuania.

A registered industrial design is protected like a registered trademark in Lithuania. One may not, without consent of the owner of the registration, use an industrial design identical or confusingly similar to a registered industrial design for the goods for which the design is registered.

Lithuania

Topographies of Semiconductor Products in Lithuania

The Law on Legal Protection of Semiconductor Product Topographies of the Republic of Lithuania came into force on December 1, 1998.

Legal protection provided by this Law shall apply only to such a topography which is original and is the result of its creator's intellectual effort and is not commonplace in the semiconductor industry.

The exclusive rights of the registered owner include the rights to authorise or to prohibit any of the following acts:

1) reproduction of a topography in any form and in any way;
2) commercial exploitation or the importation for that purpose of a topography or of a semiconductor product manufactured by using the topography.

There have been no applications for registration of topographies of semiconductor products in Lithuania since the Law on the Legal Protection of Topographies of Semiconductor Products entered into force.

License of the Industrial Property Rights

A license agreement is an agreement by which the owner of an industrial property rights, the licensor, permits another party, the licensee, under certain limitation of time, space and scope defined in the agreement to perform various production and distribution activities.

A license agreement regarding an industrial property (inventions, industrial designs, trademarks) must be recorded with the Lithuanian Patent Office in order for the license agreement to be valid and enforceable, and to have legal effect against the third parties. Information about the licensing of the industrial property is entered into the Official Register and published in the Official Bulletin of the Lithuanian Patent Office.

Register of Firm Names

Lithuania's Law on Firm Names provides that enterprises, companies and organizations (hereinafter firms) before registering their firms with the government, must first register their firm names with the patent bureau.

A firm name, apart from words defining the nature of the firm, must contain a proper word having a distinctive meaning (the name of a location, the name of a person, a symbolic name), combination of common words having distinctive meaning or a combination of symbols, containing at least 3 letters or numerals.

Firm names are not registerable if they:

- coincide with firm names registered or pending registration or names similar to these;
- contradict moral norms, public and human interest;

Lithuania

- define the quality, features, amount and value of the goods or services, or their production method and time;
- use anyone's surname without that person's permission;
- coincide with the name of states, national and international governmental bodies or names similar to these;
- are a cause of confusion to the public due to the location (address), the nature of the activity, the identical nature (or resemblance) of the firm bearing the name with foreign firm names, trade marks and service marks extending to the Lithuanian market and known to the public;
- are composed disregarding the norms of the Lithuanian language and the regulations approved by the State Commission of the Lithuanian Language of the Seimas of the Republic of Lithuania.

The firm name must sound Lithuanian but it does not have to mean something in the Lithuanian language. The requirement that firm names must be in the Lithuanian language does not apply to foreign firms and Lithuanian firms owned in whole or in part by foreign firms which register and use their entire foreign firm name or distinctive part of their foreign firm name.

The word "Lithuania" may only be used with the permission of the Government of the Lithuanian Republic.

An application for the registration of the firm name is submitted to the State Patent Bureau, in which the name, location (address) and nature of the firm's activity is indicated.

A firm name registration is valid for the life of the firm. If the firm is not registered, the firm name registration expires one year after the registration of the firm name. Upon expiration of a firm name registration, the firm name cannot be registered by another firm for three years after the expiration of the firm name registration. Firm name conflicts are investigated by the State Competition Board and decided by the courts.

Trade Marks

Under Lithuanian trade mark law, a mark subject to registration in Lithuania shall be any sign which distinguishes the goods or services of one person from the goods or services of another person and which can be represented graphically.

A mark may constitute words, personal names, slogans, letters, numerals, pictures, emblems, three-dimensional forms, products, packaging, containers, colors and any combination of the above signs.

The application to register a trademark shall be for one mark for goods and services in one or more International Classes. Paris Convention priority may be

Lithuania

obtained. The application shall be filed through a person registered to practice before the Lithuanian Patent Office.

There is no examination for prior conflicting marks in Lithuania. The prior trademark owner must oppose the registration or seek cancellation of the registration in order to protect his rights.

The term of the trademark registration is 10 years from the date the application was filed in Lithuania and may be renewed for additional like terms indefinitely without proof of use.

Only registered marks shall be subject to protection in Lithuania. The holder of the registration shall have the right to prevent third parties from using, importing or exporting without authorization any sign identical or confusingly similar to the registered mark for the same or similar goods or services.

Copyright and Related Rights

Copyright is regulated by the Law on Copyright and Related Rights of the Republic of Lithuania, which entered into force in 2003.

Copyrights are applied to original literary, scientific and artistic works, which are the result of intellectual activity of an author expressed in any objective form.

Thus, a work must meet three criteria (originality, result of intellectual activity and form of objective expression), so that it would be applied copyright as well as copyright protection.

The Law on Copyright and Related Rights of the Republic of Lithuania also regulates the rights (related rights) of performers, producers of phonograms, broadcasting organizations and producers of the first fixation of an audiovisual work as well as sui generis rights of makers of databases. Registration for legal protection of copyright is not obligatory.

Under the Law on Copyright and Related Rights of the Republic of Lithuania the duration of protection of the author's economic rights run for the life of the author and 70 years after his death, regardless of the date of the lawful communication of a work to the public.

Lithuania

Chapter 19: Luxembourg

Luxembourg

By Sophie Wagner-Charles and Heloise Bock
(Arendt & Medernach)

Introduction

This chapter describes Luxembourg's intellectual property law only to the extent that it differs from the provisions outlined in the Belgian and Dutch chapters concerning intellectual property legislation (please refer in particular to the developments on trademark and design law in the Belgian and Dutch chapters).

Country Overview

Major issues affecting intellectual property

Luxembourg's intellectual property legislation has changed substantially in recent years. New laws have been adopted in matters of copyright, trademark law, patent law and design law in order to put Luxembourg legislation in compliance with the most recent European directives, namely Directive 96/9/EC of March 11, 1996 on the legal protection of databases, Directive 2001/84/EC of September 27, 2001 on the resale right for the benefit of the author of an original work of art and Directive 98/71/EC of October 13, 1998 on the legal protection of designs.

Relevant treaties

The treaties to which Luxembourg is a party are listed according to their subject matter in the various sections of this chapter.

Current legislative climate

The Luxembourg legislature has not yet implemented all European directives. However, several bills concerning such directives have been tabled with Parliament.

Thus, Luxembourg has not implemented Directive 2001/29/EC of May 22, 2001 on the harmonisation of certain aspects of copyright and related rights in the information society. However, a bill (no. 5128), which is due to implement the above-mentioned directive, has been tabled with Parliament.

Another bill (no. 4673A) has been tabled with Parliament in order to implement Directive 98/44/EC of July 6, 1998 on the legal protection of biotechnological inventions.

Sophie Wagner-Charles and Heloise Bock are attorneys with Arendt & Medernach in Luxembourg.

Luxembourg

Since January 2003, it is possible to file for registration of a Community design with the Office for Harmonization in the Internal Market (OHIM) on the basis of the provisions of the Council regulation 6/2002 of December 12, 2001 on community designs.

Patents

Relevant legislation

The applicable law is the law of July 20, 1992, as amended by the laws of May 24, 1998 and of August 11, 2001 (the "Patent Law").

Luxembourg is also a party to the following conventions: the Convention of Strasbourg of November 27, 1963, the Washington Treaty of June 19, 1970, the Arrangement of Strasbourg of March 24, 1971, the Convention of Munich of October 5, 1973, the Convention concerning the European Patent for the Internal Market of December 15, 1975 and the Agreement concerning Community Patents of December 15, 1989.

What can be patented

The Patent Law determines the conditions of what is patentable and lists a number of subject matters which may not be considered as inventions: discoveries, scientific theories and mathematical methods; esthetical creations; maps, principles and methods in the exercise of intellectual activities in relation to games or economic activities as well as computer programmes; and presentations of information.

The Patent Law sets out that methods of surgical or therapeutic treatment of the human or animal body and diagnostic methods applied on the human or animal body may not be used industrially and are thus not patentable. However, such provision does not concern the products, in particular substances or compositions, used to apply any such method.

Moreover, the Patent Law provides for an exception to patentability for inventions, the publication or application of which would be contrary to public order or morality. The Patent Law specifies that an invention may not be considered contrary to public order or morality only because it is prohibited by a legal provision.

Plant varieties, animal breeds as well as the essentially biological processes of obtaining plants and animals are also excluded from the protection of the Patent Law. This latter exclusion from the scope of patentability does not apply to microbiological processes and to the products obtained from such processes.

Luxembourg

Even though Directive 98/44/EC clearly establishes the patentability of biological material and sets out the scope of protection of biotechnological inventions, including gene sequences, the Patent Law has not yet been modified in order to take into account the provisions of such directive.

Patentability criteria

A patent is granted for new inventions that imply an inventive step which may be used industrially.

Novelty means that the invention is not part of the current state of technology, such state being everything that has been made available to the public before the date of application for the patent by way of a written or oral description, a use or any other way. Equally, the Patent Law considers as forming part of the state of technology the content of applications for a Luxembourg patent, a European patent or an international patent designating Luxembourg, which have been filed before the date of the filing of the application for registration of a patent and which have not been published at such date or only at a later date.

An invention is considered as implying an inventive step if an expert in the field concerned does not regard it as resulting in an obvious manner from the state of technology.

An invention is considered to have a possible industrial use if its object may be built or be used in any kind of industry, including agriculture.

The above-mentioned conditions of patentability are not examined ex ante. A Luxembourg patent is delivered on the sole condition of compliance with the applicable registration formalities. However, in a subsequent court action, a patent may be challenged if it does not comply with the patentability criteria set out above.

Duration

Protection is given for a maximum of twenty years from the date of filing of the application for registration of the patent, subject to the payment of the annual fees.

The Patent Law also provides for the right of the patent holder, under certain conditions, to the payment of a reasonable indemnity from any third party for the time preceding the delivery of the patent, if such third party has commercially used the invention in a manner that would have been prohibited if the patent had already been delivered, between the date when the application was made available to the public or the date of the notification of a copy of the application to such third party and the date of delivery of the patent, if such date is prior to the first date.

Luxembourg

Cost and timing

The deposit fee of fourteen euros and the applicable publication fee have to be paid within a month following the deposit. For any subsequent modification of the submitted data or any other inscription in the patent registry, an administrative fee of seven euros is charged.

The most expensive part of the patent application is the establishment of a search report which costs approximately nine hundred euros.

The annual fees required to maintain the registration of the patent increase progressively and range from twenty nine euros, for the third year after the filing of an application for registration of a patent, to two hundred and seventy euros, for the twentieth year after the filing of such application.

The search report or at least a request for its establishment must be filed by the patent applicant within eighteen months following the date of application for registration of the patent, or, if a priority is claimed, from the date of priority. If the applicant does not provide or request a search report within the above-mentioned time limit, the Patent Law provides that a patent certificate is issued for a reduced six year period, starting from the date of filing of the patent application.

The application must be made available to the public, at the latest, eighteen months after the filing of the patent application, or if a priority is invoked, after the date of priority. Third parties may make written observations from the date of publication of the patent application until the date of the delivery of the patent.

Patent notices

The Patent Law does not provide for any obligation to indicate the existence of a patent on a patented product.

Challenges to validity

A Luxembourg patent certificate is delivered without any prior patentability examination. The result of the search report does not affect the decision on the delivery of a patent.

Therefore, the validity of a patent may only be challenged before a court.

According to the Patent Law, a third party may bring a nullity claim before a court, alleging that:

- the subject matter of the patent applied for is not patentable;
- the patent does not describe the invention in a sufficiently clear and complete manner in order for an expert to be able to apply such invention;
- the object of the patent exceeds the content of the application or, under certain circumstances, if it exceeds the content of an initial application;

- the protection granted by the patent has been extended;
- the patent holder had no right to obtain the patent because he is neither the inventor nor the entitled party.

The competent court is the court of the elected domicile of the entitled patent holder. In order to be valid, any claim must be entered in the patent register and all parties entitled, as indicated in the register, must be involved in such action.

Infringement

The Patent Law provides that any infringement of the rights of the patent holder, as defined by the Patent Law, constitutes counterfeiting. The author of the counterfeit shall be held liable under civil law.

A person other than the manufacturer of the counterfeit product shall also be liable for the offering, the marketing, or the use of a counterfeit product as well as the possession in order to use or market a counterfeit product if such person acted in full knowledge.

An action in counterfeiting may be brought by the owner of the patent. The beneficiary of an exclusive right of exploitation of the patent may also bring such an action, unless the license contract provides otherwise and if the patent holder, after a formal notice, does not engage legal proceedings. Certain licensees may also file an action in counterfeiting if the patent holder, after a formal notice, does not bring such an action. An intervention in the legal proceedings concerning patent counterfeiting by a licensee for the compensation of damages suffered by him is also possible.

The Patent Law provides that the president of the *Tribunal d'arrondissement* may order the confiscation of the counterfeited goods and of the instruments that served to commit counterfeiting. An injunction may also be taken against any person in the case where there are serious clues concerning possible counterfeiting.

The competent court for a counterfeiting action and for an action in damages relating to counterfeiting is the *Tribunal d'arrondissement*. The rules relating to summary proceedings apply to such action.

It is possible for the alleged counterfeiter to file a counterclaim in nullity against the patent holder.

Impending changes to the law

A bill (no. 4673B), which provides for the implementation of Directive 98/44/EC concerning the patentability of biotechnological inventions, was tabled with Parliament on January 25, 2001.

Moreover, a bill (no. 5128) providing for the abolition of the requirement,

Luxembourg

that the representative of a patent applicant must reside in Luxembourg (set out in the Patent Law) was tabled with Parliament on May 14, 2003.

The protection by patents of computer-implemented inventions is the subject of a proposal for a directive by the Commission dated February 20, 2002. The proposed directive would harmonise the way in which national patent laws deal with inventions using software.

Copyright

Relevant legislation

The rules regarding copyright are set out in the law of April 18, 2001 on author's rights, neighbouring rights and databases (the "Copyright Law").

International conventions

Luxembourg is a party to the following international conventions on copyright: the Berne Convention of September 9, 1886, as amended (the "Berne Convention") the Universal Convention on Copyright of September 6, 1952 (the "Universal Copyright Convention"), the Rome International Convention for the Protection of Performers, Producers of Phonograms and Broadcasting Organisations of October 26, 1961, the Convention for the Protection of Producers of Phonograms against Unauthorised Duplication of October 29, 1971, the WIPO Copyright Treaty (the "WCT") and the WIPO Performances and Phonograms Treaty (the "WPPT"), both ratified by two laws dated January 14, 2000. As a member of the WTO, Luxembourg is also bound by the 1994 TRIPS Agreement.

What can be protected

Protection is granted to any original artistic or literary work of art, of whatever type, form or expression, including photographies, databases and computer programmes. The Copyright Law does not, as such, protect mere ideas, functioning methods, concepts or information.

Ownership

According to the Copyright Law, the author of a work is, except if otherwise proven, the person under whose name the work is publicly disclosed.

In case a work of art is the joint work of two or more persons and the contribution of each author cannot be distinguished, the authors' rights are inseparable and the exercise of such rights must be regulated by contract. In the absence of such contract, none of the authors may exercise the rights attached to the collective work individually, unless a court holds otherwise.

However, each co-author is free to bring an action, in his name and without the intervention of others, against a copyright infringement and to claim damages for damages suffered by him in relation to his contribution, if he summons his co-authors to appear in such a case.

If the contribution of the authors to the joint work is distinguishable, each co-author may, unless otherwise provided by contract, commercially exploit his personal contribution if such exploitation is not made with that of another co-author and does not prejudice the common work.

When a work is created by several authors, upon the initiative and under the control of a physical or moral person who publishes or produces the work and discloses it under his/its own name and where the contribution of the authors is designed to be integrated in the work as a whole, such physical or moral person is granted the moral and economic rights in the work, unless otherwise provided by contract.

Nationality requirements

As Luxembourg is a party to the Berne Convention, every author from a country which is party to the Berne Convention is granted the same rights in Luxembourg as an author of Luxembourg nationality.

Term

The duration of protection has been harmonized throughout the European Union with Directive 93/98/EEC of October 29, 1993 harmonising the term of protection of copyright and certain related rights.

The Copyright Law provides for the European standard protection of the author's life plus seventy years for literary and artistic works and for computer programmes.

Concerning related rights, the Copyright Law provides that the rights of performers, of producers of phonograms and of producers of the first fixation of a film, expire fifty years after the date of the relevant performance. However, if the fixation of the performance is the object of a lawful publication or communication to the public, the rights expire 50 years after the date of occurrence of the first of these acts.

The Copyright Law provides that *sui generis* databases are protected for a period of fifteen years from the first of January of the year that follows the date of completion of the database or the date of making the database available to the public. However, if a substantial modification to the content of the database is made, a new period of protection of fifteen years is granted.

Luxembourg

Copyright notices

No provision of the Copyright Law explicitly provides for copyright notices. The author of a work is not obliged to affix a copyright notice on his work in order to be able to invoke his rights in Luxembourg.

Nevertheless, it is recommended to affix a copyright to the work as article III (1) of the Universal Copyright Convention considers that if a work, which first published outside the territory of a Member State and whose author is not a national of such Member State, bears a copyright sign as from the first publication of such work, the national formalities such as deposit, registration, notice, publication, etc., are considered as being fulfilled.

Licensing, assignment and security

The Copyright Law provides that the author has the exclusive right to authorise the reproduction of his work, in any manner and in any form. This reproduction right includes the right of adaptation, arrangement and translation of the work as well as the rental and lending of the original work and of copies of the work.

According to the Copyright Law, economic rights may be freely licensed or assigned. The Copyright Law provides for the requirement that the licensing and assignment of economic rights must be proven by a written contract which must be interpreted narrowly in the author's interest.

Some restrictions apply regarding the assignment of moral rights. According to the Copyright Law, the author retains the right to claim the paternity of the work and to object to any deformation, mutilation or other modification or any other act that might prejudice his honour or reputation, independently of the economic rights and even after the assignment of such rights.

The assignment of exploitation means which are unknown at the date of the contract is only authorised if such assignment is specifically remunerated.

Infringement

Remedies against copyright infringement are available to the author of a work under civil and criminal law.

Concerning remedies under civil law, the Copyright Law provides that the president of the *Tribunal d'arrondissement* may order the cessation of any act infringing the author's rights.

The copyright owners, the neighbouring rights' owners, the database rights' owners or any interested party may also file a request with the president of the *Tribunal d'arrondissement* for an authorisation to proceed to the description of the allegedly counterfeit goods or of the acts of counterfeiting and of the objects that are in direct relation to the perpetration of the infringing acts. The president of such court may also prohibit the holder of the counterfeit objects to discard such goods or he may decide to have the goods put under seal. He may also order the seizure of the counterfeit goods.

The Copyright Law also provides for remedies under criminal law, which consist of fines and/or the sentencing to a term of imprisonment. The seizure of the counterfeit goods is ordered by the court if the counterfeiter is held guilty. An order for the destruction of the counterfeit goods may also be handed down.

Moral rights

The author has certain moral rights provided for by Copyright Law. Thus, the author of a copyright work has a paternity right, a right to oppose any modification, deformation or mutilation that prejudices his reputation and he may decide solely about the divulgence of his work. The Copyright Law also provides for the non-assignable resale right of authors of works of plastic arts.

The Copyright Law provides that authors may assign all or part of their moral rights as far as their reputation or honour are not prejudiced.

Moral rights are protected during the author's life and for seventy years following his death. After the death of the author, such rights may be exercised by the author's heirs or any other entitled person.

Database rights

Apart from databases which, by reason of the selection or arrangement of their contents, constitute the author's own intellectual creation and which are, as such, protected by copyright, a *sui generis* protection is provided for by the Copyright Law in relation to all labour intensive databases.

The Copyright Law provides for a *sui generis* right in a database if a substantial, qualitative or quantitative investment has been made concerning the obtention, the verification or the presentation of the content of the database. A fifteen year extension of the protection period may be granted if the content of the database has been substantially modified.

Software

Software is listed by the Copyright Law as works of literary and artistic art that may be protected by copyright. The protection of a computer programme includes the protection of the preparatory material of conception.

The Copyright Law protects the expression, in any form, of a computer programme, but not the underlying concept or idea.

Luxembourg

Recent developments

A bill (no. 5128) has been tabled with Parliament in order to amend the Copyright Law. The main objectives of such bill are the implementation of the provisions of Directive 2001/29/EC of May 22, 2001 on the harmonisation of certain aspects of copyright and related rights in the information society as well as the implementation of the provisions of the WCT and the WPPT.

Designs

Designs and models are protected under the Benelux Convention on Designs and Models, signed in Brussels on October 25, 1966. The Uniform Benelux Law for the Protection of Designs and Models (the "Design Law") came into effect on January 1, 1975. On the basis of the Benelux Convention on Designs and Models, various Protocols have been adopted on the following dates: November 21, 1974, November 6, 1981, May 31, 1989, March 28, 1995 and August 7, 1996.

The law of August 12, 2003 approving the Protocol amending the Uniform Benelux law on designs and models, signed in Brussels on June 20, 2002, was published on September 16, 2003. The purpose of such Protocol is to implement Directive 98/71/EC of October 13, 1998 on the legal protection of designs.

The Protocol will enter into force the first day of the third month following the deposit of the ratification instruments of Belgium, the Netherlands and Luxembourg with the Belgian Government. The planned date of entry into force is January 1, 2004.

For the purposes of registration of designs and models, the three Benelux countries are considered as forming one territory.

The procedure of registration and the rights of the owner of a design or model are set out in the Belgian and Dutch chapters. In fact, the uniform legislation concerning designs and models is the same in the three countries.

Trade Marks

The basic rules on trademarks are set out in the Uniform Benelux law on trademarks, as amended, which approved the Benelux Convention on trademarks of March 19, 1962 (the "Trademark Law").

On the basis of the Benelux Convention on trademarks, various Protocols have been adopted on the following dates: July 31, 1970, May 11, 1974, November 6, 1981, November 10, 1983, December 2, 1992, November 20, 1995, August 7, 1996, and August 3, 1998.

A law of August 11, 2003, approving the Protocol modifying the uniform Benelux law on trademarks, signed in Brussels on December 11, 2001, was published on September 3, 2003. The law of 2003 substantially adapts the current Trademark Law.

Luxembourg

The most important development is the introduction of opposition proceedings. Luxembourg is a party to the Madrid Agreement on the Registration of Trademarks of April 14, 1891, as last modified on June 27, 1989, and to the Madrid Protocol signed in Madrid on June 28, 1989, which entered into force on April 1, 1998.

Furthermore, since March 25, 1975, Luxembourg is a party to the Nice Agreement concerning the International Classification of Goods and Services for the Purposes of the Registration of Marks of June 15, 1957, as amended on September 28, 1979 (Nice Union).

Finally, Luxembourg is a party to the Vienna Agreement Establishing an International Classification of the Figurative Elements of Marks since August 5, 1985.

Regarding the procedure of registration of trademarks and the rights of the owner of a trademark, please refer to the Belgian or Dutch chapters. In fact, the Benelux countries are considered as forming one territory in relation to trademarks and the applicable legal provisions are identical in the three countries.

Geographical Indicators

As a member of the WTO, Luxembourg is bound by the provisions concerning geographical indications of origin in part II, section 3 of the 1994 TRIPS Agreement. However, Luxembourg is not a member of the Lisbon Agreement for the Protection of Appellations of Origin and their International Registration of October 31, 1958, as amended.

As a Member State of the European Union, Luxembourg is bound by Council Regulation 2081/92 of July 14, 1992 on the protection of geographical indications and designations of origin for agricultural products and foodstuffs, as amended.

On the basis of the above-mentioned regulation, two grand-ducal regulations of December 19, 2000 have established the conditions of the allocation of the "marque nationale" geographical indication of origin for pork meat and smoked ham.

Specific regulations are in force concerning the description and presentation of wines and grape musts, following Commission Regulation 3201/90 of October 16, 1990, as amended, laying down detailed rules for the description and presentation of wines and grape musts.

The grand-ducal regulation of January 30, 2001 determines the conditions of the allocation of the "marque nationale" geographical indication of origin for wines.

Domain Names

Restena Foundation, the Luxembourg network for education and research, manages the domain name services for the Luxembourg national top level do-

Luxembourg

main ".lu". The registration of a domain name is governed by the Domain Name Charter, which is in force since November 1, 2001, and the terms and conditions, both established by Restena Foundation.

The registration of a domain name is made on a first-come first-served basis, without any prior examination. According to the Domain Name Charter, the registration of a domain name by Restena Foundation does not constitute an endorsement by the Restena Foundation that the applicant has a right to use the domain name in question, for instance with regard to names of natural persons, legal entities, trade names, trademarks, etc.

The initial registration fee for a ".lu" domain name is 50 euros. This fee covers the registration of one active or inactive ".lu" domain name. A recurring fee of 40 euros covers the lease of one registered active or inactive ".lu" domain name. This fee is charged on a yearly basis.

Although domain names may be registered by any natural or legal person, without taking into account such person's domicile or place of establishment, the administrative contact must be established in Luxembourg. Domain name holders established outside Luxembourg must therefore give a valid power of attorney to an agent who is established in Luxembourg for the registration and management of their domain name.

Restena Foundation's Domain Name Charter acknowledges that international guidelines have been or are currently published by international organizations and provides for the right for the Restena Foundation to refer to such guidelines when defining its registration policy for national top level ".lu" domain names.

Recent developments

During a meeting of the Domain Name Working Group in June 2001, which is composed of governmental representatives and private representatives of the national Internet community, the Domain Name Charter was modified. It was decided that registrations of domain names containing only numbers are allowed as from June 15, 2003.

Confidential information

Trade secrets and know-how may be protected by contractual provisions. However, certain legal provisions also provide for the protection of trade secrets.

The unauthorised divulgence or use of trade secrets is prohibited by article 309 of the Criminal Code, according to which any employee who uses or discloses any trade secret during the course of his employment or within the two years following termination of his employment, either to compete with the employer, to cause damages to the employer or to get an illicit advantage from the employer, is liable to imprisonment of three months to three years and a fine of 251 euros to 12,500 euros. The same liability applies to a person who, having had the knowledge of trade secrets and secret processes, obtained from an employee, worker, or apprentice, acting in violation of the above provisions, by an act contrary to the law or to good customs, uses such secrets or divulges them, either for purposes of competition, or with the intent to be prejudicial to the owner or to procure himself an illicit advantage. The person who either for purposes of competition, or with the intent to be prejudicial to the owner or to procure himself an illicit advantage uses or communicates, without such right, models or designs which have been entrusted to him in order to execute commercial or industrial orders, incurs the same liability.

A specific legal obligation of confidentiality is provided for by the law of July 8, 1961 concerning the divulgence and execution of inventions and trade secrets interesting the defense of the territory or the security of the State.

Even in the absence of any specific contractual provision, a Luxembourg judge may consider that the disclosure of a trade secret or of know-how constitutes an act of unfair competition, as defined in the Unfair Competition Law, as set out below.

Unfair Competition

The law of July 30, 2002 regulating certain commercial practices, sanctioning unfair competition and implementing directive 97/55/EC of October 6, 1997 amending directive 84/450/EEC concerning misleading advertising so as to include comparative advertising (the "Unfair Competition Law",) is applicable in matters of unfair competition.

According to the Unfair Competition Law, any retailer, manufacturer, craftsman or member of a liberal profession may be held liable for having committed an act of unfair competition when, by an act contrary to honest practices in trade and industry or contrary to a contractual engagement, he deprives, or attempts to deprive, his competitors, or one of them, of part of his customers or undermines, or attempts to undermine, the competitive capacity of his competitors.

One important change in the new law on unfair competition is the suppression of the prohibition of a sale with a gift. It is possible under the Unfair Competition Law to make joint sales provided such sales do not constitute sales at a loss.

The Law also introduces a regulation of commercial lotteries, publicity-games and advertising tombolas. In fact, according to the Unfair Competition Law, the organisation of such lotteries, publicity-games and advertising tombolas is legal and authorised by the law if they comply with the following conditions:

Luxembourg

a) the advertiser of a lottery, a publicity-game or an advertising tombola shall establish, prior to any dissemination of the advertising message, a regulation which indicates the conditions and the procedure of the commercial operation. This regulation and a copy of the documents addressed to the consumers must be filed before a ministerial authority who verifies their regularity. The full text of the regulation is sent free of charge by the advertiser to any person who requests such document;

b) the advertising documents shall neither cause a confusion of whichever nature in the mind of the addressee nor deceive as to the number and the value of the prizes and on their condition of allocation;

c) the entry form shall be distinct of the order form of the goods or the service;

d) the participation to the drawing of the lots, whichever the rules or details, cannot be subject to any financial counterpart of whichever nature nor to a purchase duty;

e) the advertiser who by the conception or the presentation of the communication gives the impression that the consumer has won a prize, shall deliver this prize to the consumer.

The Unfair Competition Law also introduces a new section on the prohibition of misleading advertising, which is now expressly defined, and sets out criteria concerning the lawfulness of comparative advertising.

Finally, under certain circumstances, it is also now possible to bring a criminal action against the perpetrator of an act of unfair competition, even in the absence of the breach of an initial order of the judge to cease an act of unfair competition. The violation of such order is not a condition for the filing of a criminal action under the new law on unfair competition.

Other Intellectual Property Rights

The law of December 29, 1988 implemented Directive 87/54/EEC of December 16, 1986 on the legal protection of topographies of semiconductor products. According to such law, the semiconductor topography is protected insofar as it results from an intellectual effort on the part of the creator and is not common in the semiconductor industry.

Luxembourg

Chapter 20:
Malta

Malta

By Austin Sammut
(Gando Sammut)

Introduction

Intellectual property in Malta is regulated by a number of laws which are largely in line with the EU regime. Malta is also a member of the WIPO and WTO and a Party to the Universal Copyright Convention, the Berne Convention, the Paris Convention and the WTO Agreement on Trade Related Aspects of Intellectual Property Rights (TRIPS).

The Maltese Industrial Property Registration Directorate is responsible for the registration of trademarks as well as for the registration of Industrial Designs and Patents. This Directorate is also involved in the updating and upgrading of the law on copyright. All applications for the registration of Trademarks, Industrial Designs and Patents are processed by this office.

Copyright

Copyright is regulated by the Copyright Act (Act No. XIII of 2000). This Act, besides being in line with the TRIPS Convention, also transposes the relevant EU Community Directives into Maltese law.

Trade Marks

Trademarks are regulated by the Trademarks Act (Act No. XVI of 2000). This Act transposes the EU's Council Directive 89/104 on the approximation of the laws of the Member States relating to trademarks into Maltese law and is also in line with TRIPS.

Below is a brief outline of the Maltese Trademarks Act.

Definition of trademark

Trademark means any sign capable of being represented graphically, and of distinguishing goods and services of one undertaking from those of another. A trademark may consist of words (including personal names), figurative elements, letters, numerals or the shape of goods or their packaging.

Austin Sammut is the Managing Partner of Gando Sammut. Gando Sammut is a commercial law firm with a general practice covering European law, litigation, intellectual property, financial services and trust management, corporate law and conveyancing. In the area of IP it provides a range of services in patent and trade mark registration, competition law and enforcement of IP rights.

Malta

Implication of registration

When a proprietor registers his trademark, he acquires a property right, benefiting from specific remedies.

Application for registration of a trademark

An application for registration of a trademark must be made to the Comptroller of Industrial Property ("Comptroller"), who examines the application, asserting whether all requirements for registration of such application are met.

An application for the registration of a trademark must be filed on the appropriate form and should contain a number of specified details though it is not necessary for all the details to be furnished all at once together with the application.

Rights conferred by a registered trademark

The proprietor of a registered trademark has exclusive rights in the trademark. Such rights are infringed by such use of the trademark in Malta when:
- the use in the course of trade is made of a sign which is identical with or similar to the trademark in relation to goods or services which are identical with or similar to those for which it is registered, and there is the likelihood of confusion on the part of the public, including the likelihood of association with the trademark;
- the use in the course of trade is made of a sign which is identical with or similar to a trademark in relation to goods or services which are not similar to those for which the trademark is registered, but the trademark has a reputation in Malta and such use takes unfair advantage of or is detrimental to the distinctive character or the repute of the trademark.

Classification

If the applicant wishes to apply for a trademark in respect of different goods and services he must make a different application for each category. Goods and services are classified by the office according to the International Classification of Goods and Services for the Purposes of the Registration of Marks under the Nice Agreement.

Claim to priority of Convention application

A person who has filed an application for the protection of a trademark in a country, which is a member of the World Trade Organisation or a member of the Paris Convention for the Protection of Industrial Property, he or his successor in title has the right to claim priority in registering the same trademark in any member country for any or all of the same goods or services for which the application has been filed. Such claim to priority is applicable for a period of six months from the date of filing of the first application.

Absolute grounds for refusal of registration of a trademark

Once the formalities are fulfilled, the application is then checked for substantive requirements. A sign, which does not fall within the definition of trademarks, shall not be registered as a trademark.

Registration of trademark is refused if the trademark:
- Lacks distinctive character.
- Is made up entirely of signs or indications which may serve, in trade, to designate the kind, quality, intended purpose, value, geographical origin, the time of production of goods or of rendering of services, or other characteristics of goods or services.
- Consists entirely of signs or indications which have become customary in the current language or in the bona fide and established practices of the trade.

Not withstanding these last three exceptions, the registration of a trademark is not to be refused if it can be shown that before the date of application for registration, the trademark has acquired a distinctive character as a result of the use made of it in Malta.

In addition a trademark shall not be registered if it consists exclusively of:
- The shape which results from the nature of the goods themselves;
- The shape of goods; and
- The shape which gives substantial value to the goods.

Finally a trademark shall not be registered if:
- It is contrary to public policy or morality;
- It is of such a nature as to deceive the public as to the nature, quality or geographical origin of the goods or services;
- Its use is prohibited in Malta by any enactment or rule of law;
- It consists of or contains any signs, arms, armorial bearing on flags as listed in Article 5 of the law; or
- It is made in bad faith.

Relative grounds for refusal of registration of a trademark

Registration of a trademark is also refused if:
a) it is identical with or similar to an earlier trademark and the goods or

services for which the trademark is applied for are identical with or similar to the goods or services for which the earlier trademark is protected;

b) it is identical with or similar to an earlier trademark, and although the goods or services are not similar to those in the earlier trademark, yet the registration would take unfair advantage of the distinctive character or repute of the earlier mark;

c) its use in Malta is liable to be prevented by virtue of any rule of law protecting an unregistered trademark or other sign used in the course of trade or by virtue of an earlier right.

An application for a trademark shall not be refused where the proprietor of the earlier mark or right consents to the registration of the application.

Limitation of registration

The applicant or the proprietor of a registered trademark may:

- Disclaim any right to the exclusive use of any specified element of the trademark, or
- Agree that the rights conferred by the registration are subject to a specified territorial or other limitation.

Alternatively, the Comptroller may refuse any right to the exclusive use of any specified element of the trademark.

Publication and issuing of certificates

When a trademark is registered, the Comptroller publishes the registration and issues a certificate of registration to the applicant.

Duration and renewal of registered trademark

The duration of registration of a trademark is ten years, which starts running from the date of registration.

The trademark may be renewed for further periods of ten years at the request of the proprietor, after the payment of the renewal fee within not more than six months before the date of expiry.

The renewal takes effect from the expiry of the previous registration. If the registration of a trademark is not renewed, then the Comptroller removes the trademark from the register.

Revocation and surrender

The proprietor may surrender a registered trademark in respect of some or all of the goods or services for which the trademark is registered.

The registration of a trademark may be revoked when:
- In consequence of acts or inactivity of the proprietor, it has become the common name in the trade for a product or service for which it is registered, or
- In consequence of the use made of it by the proprietor or with his consent, it is liable to mislead the public in relation to the goods or service for which it is registered, particularly as to the nature, quality or geographical origin of those goods or services.

Licensing of a registered trademark

A license to use a registered trademark may be general or limited; and it may be exclusive or non-exclusive.

The license is binding on a successor in title to the grantor's interest, unless the license provides otherwise. Where the license so provides, the licensee may grant a sub-license.

Transmission of a registered trademark

A registered trademark is transmissible by assignment, testamentary disposition or operation of law in the same way as other personal or moveable property.

Collective marks and certification marks

Besides trademarks the industrial property office also receives applications for collective and certification marks.
- A *collective mark* is a mark distinguishing the goods or services of members of an association from those of other undertakings.
- A *certification mark* is a mark indicating that the goods or services in connection with which it is used are certified by the proprietor of the mark in respect of origin, material, mode of manufacture of goods or performance of services, quality, accuracy or other characteristics.

Criminal offenses

It is a criminal offense for any person to make unauthorised use of a trademark. A person guilty of such an offense shall be liable on conviction to imprisonment for a term not exceeding three years or to a fine not more than LM10,000 or to both such fine and imprisonment.

The Trademarks Act also makes provision for regulations to be made to extend the effect of the Community trademark regime to Malta upon accession. In fact, all Community trademarks that have been registered or applied for before the date of Malta's accession will be automatically extended to Malta. Obviously,

Malta

it has been envisaged that a number of problems relating to conflict between trademarks may arise in this respect.

To this end, Malta has accepted that in exceptional cases of conflict between extended Community trademarks and earlier national trademarks which have been registered or applied for before accession, or other earlier rights referred to in Articles 8 and 52 of the Community Trademark regulation, holders of earlier national trademarks or "earlier rights" acquired in good faith before the registration of the Community trademark should be allowed to oppose the use of a given extended Community trademark in the Maltese territory through an action before a national court.

Furthermore, Malta has also accepted that pending Community trademark applications which have been filed before the date of accession shall not be examined on absolute grounds for refusal vis-a-vis new Member States. On absolute grounds for refusal, there will be the possibility for the holders of national trademarks to prevent the use of certain Community trademarks on the grounds of Article 106 of Council Regulation 40/94 which provides for the possibility to prohibit the use of a Community trademark to the extent that the use of a national trademark may be prohibited under the law of that member state or under Community law. Insofar as relative grounds for refusal are concerned, there will be the possibility for holders of national trademarks to oppose pending applications which are filed within a period of six months before the accession of Malta to the EU, insofar as the period for the filing of oppositions is still running.

Patents

Patents are regulated by the Patents Act (Act No. XVII of 2000). This Act incorporates the principal substantive provisions of the European Patent Convention (EPC) and is in line with TRIPS. Legislation has also been adopted which has transposed the European Parliament and Council Directive 98/44 on the Legal Protection of Biotechnological Inventions and Council Regulations 1768/28 and 1610/96 regarding supplementary protection certificates for medicinal and plant protection products into Maltese law.

The following is a brief outline of the Maltese legal position insofar as patents are concerned:

Patentable inventions

An invention shall be patentable if it is novel, involves an inventive step and is industrially applicable.

Malta

What may not be patented?
- (a) discoveries, scientific theories and mathematical methods;
- (b) aesthetic creations;
- (c) schemes, rules and methods for performing mental acts, playing games or doing business and programs for computers;
- (d) presentations of information
- (e) a method for the treatment of the human or animal body by surgery or therapy and a diagnostic method practiced on the human or animal body;
- (f) an invention the exploitation of which would be contrary to public order or morality.

Requirements of application

An application for a patent shall be made in duplicate and shall be accompanied by:
- (a) a request for the grant of a patent;
- (b) a description of the invention;
- (c) one or more claims;
- (d) any drawings referred to in the description or the claims;
- (e) an abstract of the invention.

Disclosure of the invention

The application shall disclose the invention in a manner sufficiently clear and complete for the invention to be carried out by a person skilled in the area.

Inspection of files

After a patent application or the patent granted thereon has been published, any person may inspect the files of the application.

Rights of priority

The application may contain a declaration claiming priority pursuant to the Paris Convention for the Protection of Industrial Property, of one or more earlier national, regional or international applications filed by the applicant or his predecessor in title in or for any State party to the said Convention or the World Trade Organisation or for any State with which Malta has made an international arrangement for mutual protection of inventions.

Examination and grant or refusal

The application shall be examined in order to determine whether the application complies with the requirements laid down in the Act and in the regulations.

Malta

The applicant shall be given the opportunity to amend the application in order to comply with the requirements. If the applicant fails to make such amendments the Comptroller may refuse the application.

If the application as originally filed or as amended complies with all the formal requirements, the Comptroller shall grant a patent on the application.

Terms of patents

The term of a patent shall be 20 years from the filing date of the application. The maintenance of a patent shall be subject to the payment of the prescribed fee in respect of the third year and each subsequent year thereafter.

Rights conferred by a patent

The proprietor of the Patent shall have the right to prevent third parties from performing without his authorisation:

a) the making of a product or the use of a process, which is the subject-matter of the patent;

b) the offering on the market of a product incorporating the subject-matter of a patent; and

c) the inducing of third parties to perform any of these acts.

A patent application which has been published shall provisionally confer upon the applicant the same rights as mentioned above.

Assignment of patents

A change in the ownership of a patent application or a patent shall be recorded in the patent register on payment of the prescribed fee. The new proprietor of the application or patent shall be entitled to institute any legal proceedings concerning the patent only if he has been recorded in the patent register as the new proprietor.

License contract

A patent application or patent may be licensed in whole or in part for the whole or part of Malta. A license may be exclusive or non-exclusive.

Non-voluntary licenses

The Civil Court, First Hall, may, on a writ of summons filed by any person who proves his ability to work the patented invention in Malta, made after the expiration of a period of four years from the date of filing the application for the patent or three years from the grant of the patent, whichever is later, direct the Comptroller to grant a non-exclusive, non-voluntary license if the patented invention is not worked or is insufficiently worked in Malta.

Exploitation by the government or by third parties authorized by the government

Where the national security or public safety so requires, the Minister may authorize, even without the agreement of the proprietor of the patent or the patent application, by notice published in the prescribed form, a government agency or a person designated in the said notice to make, use or sell an invention to which a patent or an application for a patent relates, subject to payment of equitable remuneration to the proprietor of the patent or the application for the patent.

Right of appeal

An appeal shall lie from any decision of the Comptroller refusing the grant of a patent, an application for the re-establishment of rights or any other request of the applicant for, or proprietor of, a patent.

Notice of appeal and a statement setting out the grounds of appeal shall be filed in writing at the Office of the Comptroller by the applicant or the proprietor of a patent within two months of being informed of the decision, and if the Comptroller considers the appeal to be admissible and well founded, he shall rectify his decision within three months from receiving the appeal.

Criminal offenses

Whoever puts into circulation or sells any article falsely representing that it is a patented article shall, on conviction, be liable to a fine of not less than one hundred liri and not more than five thousand liri.

Designs

Designs are currently protected in Malta under the Industrial Property (Protection) Ordinance of 1900. Nonetheless, legislation transposing European Parliament and Council Directive 98/71 on the legal protection of designs has already been drafted and should imminently come into force.

Chapter 21:
The Netherlands

The Netherlands

By Albert P. Ploeger
(Houthoff Buruma)

Introduction

In addition to a brief general description, this chapter describes Dutch intellectual property law only where it differs from European intellectual property law as outlined in chapter 3.

Patents

The scope of this section will be limited to patents obtained through the national procedure. Under the European Patent Convention, patents can also be applied for from the European Patent Office. If the Netherlands is chosen as the designated country, the centralized application procedure that leads to a bundle of national patents, will result in a Netherlands national patent. The Netherlands is also a member of the Patent Co-operation Treaty, through which a national patent can be obtained. For more information on European patents and international applications, we refer to chapter 3.

Legislation

Patents in the Netherlands are protected under the 1995 Patents Act ("the Act"). At present, the previous 1910 Patents Act is still in force for a transitional period with respect to patents filed before the enactment of the Act on April 1, 1995.

Object of protection

Inventions that are new, that involve an inventive step and that are susceptible to industrial application are protected under the Act. Discoveries, as well as scientific theories and mathematical methods, aesthetic creations, schemes, rules and methods for performing mental acts, playing games or doing business, as well as computer programs are not protected. This implies that business methods cannot be patented as in the United States. Notwithstanding the exclusion of computer programmes *per se*, software patents are generally granted (by describing its function).

Albert P. Ploeger is a partner in the Intellectual Property practice group of Houthoff Buruma in Amsterdam. Houthoff Buruma is one of the largest law firms in the Netherlands, with some three hundred highly qualified specialists providing made-to-measure legal services to both Dutch and international clients. In addition to its offices in Amsterdam, Rotterdam and The Hague, Houthoff Buruma has independent offices in Brussels and London.

The Netherlands

The invention must be new, which means that the invention must not form part of the state of the art at the time of filing. The state of the art comprises everything made available to the public both within and outside the Netherlands, by means of a written or oral description, by use or in any other way before the date of filing the application.

Application procedure

An application for a Dutch patent must be submitted to the Industrial Property Office in The Hague.

The patent application must contain the name of the applicant, the name of the inventor, a clear and full description of the invention and one or more claims describing the right for which protection is requested. The description should, if necessary, be accompanied by drawings and enable a person skilled in the art to understand and perform the invention on the basis of that description.

Search of the state of the art

After filing a patent application, the applicant has 13 months to decide whether or not it wishes the Industrial Property Office to conduct a search of the state of the art with respect to the subject matter of the patent application.

The applicant can choose between a national or an international search of the state of the art. The national search of the state of the art is carried out by the Industrial Property Office. The international search of the state of the art is carried out by the European Patent Office, and can also be used for the application of patents under the European Patent Convention (EPC) or the Patent Cooperation Treaty (PCT).

Although the Industrial Property Office conducts a search of the state of the art, it does not check whether the patent application fulfills the requirements of novelty, innovation and/or industrial applicability of the patent application. In the event of a patent dispute, these requirements will be judged by the courts.

Six-year patent

In the event the applicant does not request the Industrial Property Office to conduct a search of the state of the art within 13 months of the patent application, or informs the Industrial Property Office earlier in writing that it does not wish to have such a search carried out, a six-year patent will be granted 18 months after the date of application.

If the holder of a six-year patent wishes to initiate legal proceedings based on its patent, it needs to submit the results of a search into the state of the art relating to the patent into the proceedings. This search into the state of the art, to be conducted after the six-year patent has been granted, is performed by the Industrial Property Office upon request.

Twenty-year patent

If the applicant requests the Industrial Property Office to conduct a search of the state of the art with respect to the subject matter of the patent application, a patent with a maximum validity of 20 years can be granted. Based on the results of the search, the applicant may choose to amend the patent application.

The patent application will be published 18 months after the date of application, regardless of whether the search into the state of the art has been performed or the applicant wishes to amend the patent application.

The twenty-year patent can only be registered after the search into the state of the art has been conducted.

Registration

Registered patents are published in the Industrial Property Journal.

The application procedure for a six-year patent takes 18 months, after which the patent is automatically registered. At the request of the applicant, the six-year patent may be registered earlier.

The length of the application procedure for a twenty-year patent depends on when the results of the search into the state of the art become available.

Exclusive rights

Exclusive rights to a patent are acquired by registration of the patent. A registered patent gives the registrant exclusive rights to manufacture and use the patented product or patented process. The use covers, in particular, the making, using, putting on the market or reselling, hiring out, offering, importing or stocking a patented product or product obtained directly as a result of the use of the patented process, in the course of trade or for commercial purposes.

Exclusive rights can be subject to a license or an assignment. A patent right cannot be assigned divided into parts, but can be jointly owned. An assignment or license is only binding on third parties after registration with the Industrial Property Office.

The District Court of The Hague has exclusive jurisdiction in most patent matters (enforcement, infringement, legal effect, invalidation).

Duration

The registered patent will be protected for a maximum period of twenty years, subject to payment of an annual fee as from the fifth year after the date of applica-

The Netherlands

tion of the patent. A six-year patent will have maximum protection period of six years.

Qualification

Any 'legal person' can apply for a patent registration. In the event the applicant wishes to file its patent through a representative, such representative should be either a registered patent agent or a lawyer admitted to the Netherlands bar.

Ownership

The Act operates on a "first to file" principle. The applicant does not need to be the inventor ("first to invent"), as required in the United States. Rights are granted to the first applicant.

If the applicant by filing a patent is acting unlawfully against the original inventor, the inventor can claim the rights to the patent within two years of the date of publication of the registration.

If the invention is made by an employee, the employer has the right to apply for a patent. The employee is entitled to be named as the inventor and to fair compensation (normally deemed included in the employee's remuneration.)

Future developments

The 1910 Patents Act is still in force for a transition period with respect to patents filed (or, with respect to European patents, granted) prior to April 1, 1995, and is expected to be abolished within a few years.

Contacts

Industrial Property Office: www.bie.nl

Designs

Legislation

Designs in the Netherlands are regulated under the Uniform Benelux Designs Law ("the Act"). It is not possible to obtain protection in just one Benelux country, as the Benelux is considered as a single entity for the purpose of this law.

Unregistered designs are not protected under the Act. The concept of unregistered design rights was unknown until the introduction of the Community unregistered design right on March 6, 2003.

The Act contains several controversial provisions: the obligation to file a "maintenance declaration" upon the expiry of a registered design in order to avoid the lapse of any concurring copyrights and the limitation of action under legislation against unfair competition (tort). These provisions and related protection under

The Netherlands

copyright law that also applies to products with a utilitarian function in the Netherlands, have caused registered designs to play a marginal role in practice in the Netherlands.

Object of protection

The new appearance of a product having a utilitarian function can be protected under the Act. The object can be two-dimensional (a pattern on wallpaper) or three-dimensional (electric appliances). The elements that are necessary for obtaining a technical effect are excluded from protection.

Application procedure

An application must be submitted via the Netherlands Industrial Property Office or directly to the Benelux Designs Office (the "Office").

The design must be new, which means that the product must not be identical or largely similar in appearance to any product in the relevant industrial or trade circle in the Benelux for 50 years prior to the application for a registered design. There is one important exception to this rule: the novelty of a design is not harmed if the applicant (or a related third person) made the design available to the public within a grace period of 12 months prior to the application.

The application must clearly show the characteristics of the product.

In a multiple application, a single design can be deposited for different objects creating as many separate design rights as there are objects (*e.g.* a design applied to clothing and wallpaper) or various designs which form part of a single object can be combined.

The Office will invite the applicant to withdraw an application if the Office considers the application contrary to morality or the public order. Should the applicant refuse to withdraw the application, the Benelux Designs Office can start a nullification action with respect to the application.

Registered designs are published in the Benelux Industrial Designs Gazette. The application procedure takes about four to six months.

Exclusive rights

Exclusive rights to a design are acquired by the applicant of the first application. The applicant does not need to be the creator of the design. The designer may claim the rights to a registered design within 5 years from the publication thereof. A registered design gives the proprietor exclusive rights to prevent others from using a product with an identical or similar appearance as the registered design. The use covers, in particular, the producing, importing, exporting, selling,

The Netherlands

offering for sale, lending, offering for lending, exposing, delivering, or the stocking of an article for those purposes, in the course of trade or for commercial purposes.

Exclusive rights can be the subject of a license or an assignment. An assignment must apply to the entire Benelux. Failure to comply with the terms of a license qualifies as a breach of contract. Only when the licensee uses a design beyond the duration of the license is there infringement under the Act. An assignment or license is only binding on third parties after registration with the Office.

Duration

The registered design will be protected for one or more periods of five years, up to a total term of 15 years from the date of filing. Design registrations that had not lapsed on or before October 28, 2001 are granted renewal up to a total term of 25 years by the Office in anticipation of the implementation of the EC Directive described under future developments below. It is important to pay renewal fees in time to avoid a premature expiry of the registered design right.

Qualification

Any 'legal person' can apply for a design registration. There is no territorial restriction on a foreign company or resident being the proprietor of a design registration. Foreign applicants must, however, make use of a Benelux correspondent, which may be a design attorney or any person or company with a postal address in the Benelux.

Future developments

The October 28, 2001 deadline for the implementation of the changes imposed by the European Community for the harmonisation of design laws across the Community[1] has not been met by the Benelux countries. The pending protocol to amend the Benelux Designs Act[2] will bring some important changes to the existing legislation in line with legislation in other EU countries. The most important changes are:

- the definition changes: the design must have an "individual character" (the overall impression it produces must differ from the overall impression produced by a design which has already been made available to the public) in order to qualify for registration. This requirement raises the criteria for new design applications;
- the restriction that only products with a utility function qualify for design registration will no longer apply;
- exclusive rights to a design are only acquired by registration and no longer upon application;

- a right of prior use by third parties limiting the proprietor's exclusive rights is introduced;
- the maximum term of protection is extended to 25 years;
- the registered design right concerning a component part can no longer be invoked against a third party making use thereof for the purpose of repair of the product of which the component is a part;
- general action under the legislation against unfair competition in respect of designs is no longer excluded;
- the novelty requirement will not be linked to a 50 year period.

The amendments need to be approved by all the Benelux countries and are expected to come into force in 2004. Based on case law, the changes in the protocol to the extent prescribed by the EC Directive can be applied directly by Dutch courts as from the required date of implementation, October 28, 2001.

Contacts

Benelux Designs Office: www.bbtm-bbdm.org
Industrial Property Office: www.bie.nl

Trade Marks

Legislation

Trademarks in the Netherlands are protected under the Uniform Benelux Trade Marks Act ("the Act"). It is not possible to obtain protection in just one Benelux country, as the Benelux is considered a single entity. Unregistered trademarks are not protected under the Act.

Object of protection

Any sign that is capable of graphic representation and is used to distinguish a product or service of a company can in principle be registered as a trademark.

Application procedure

An application must be submitted via the Netherlands Industrial Property Office or directly to the Benelux Trademarks Office (the "Office").

The Office can only reject an application on absolute grounds. For the purposes of the Act, a mark filed is not considered suitable for a trademark if one of the following events occurs:

1. It has no distinctive power
2. It is contrary to morality or public order
3. It could deceive the public
4. It is a flag or an emblem protected by the Paris Convention.

The Netherlands

Although the required search for availability may reveal identical or similar existing trademarks, the Office cannot reject an application on "relative grounds", *i.e.* for the reason that an identical or similar trademark is already registered.

Currently, the Benelux Trademark Act does not provide for an opposition procedure for rejecting a trademark on "relative grounds" (see *Future developments* below). Claims for nullification or cancellation must be brought before the competent District Court.

In general, the application will be registered within eight months of being filed. Registered trademarks are published in the Benelux Trademarks Gazette.

The use of the symbol Æ for a registered trademark and ™ for a pending trademark application are without legal basis in the Netherlands. The use thereof is not obligatory, nor does it guarantee that any trademark is registered or applied for.

Exclusive rights

A registered trademark gives the registrant exclusive rights to prevent others from using in the course of business:

(a) any identical sign in relation to identical goods or services;

(b) any identical or similar sign in relation to similar goods or services, where there is a likelihood of confusion;

(c) any identical or similar sign in relation to dissimilar or similar goods or services, where the use without due cause takes unfair advantage of or is detrimental to the distinctive character or the repute of the trademark;

(d) use of an identical or similar sign not in relation to goods or services, where the use of that sign without due cause takes unfair advantage of, or is detrimental to, the distinctive character or the repute of the trademark.

Exclusive rights to a trademark are acquired by the first application. However, case law tends to anticipate future amendments of the Act and deny protection until registration has occurred.

The trademark rights can be subject to a license or an assignment. An assignment must apply to the entire Benelux. An assignment or license is only binding on third parties after registration with the Office.

Duration

An application filed for a trademark and followed by registration, is valid for a period of 10 years. It can be renewed indefinitely, for successive periods of 10 years. Payment of renewal fees should be made in time to avoid expiry. Although a trademark can be re-filed upon expiry, it will have lost its first date of filing.

The Netherlands

Qualification

Any 'legal person' can apply for a trademark registration. There is no territorial restriction on a foreign company or resident being the proprietor of a trademark registration. Foreign applicants must, however, make use of a Benelux correspondent, which may be a trademark attorney or any person or company with a postal address in the Benelux.

Future developments

The protocol to amend the Benelux Trademarks Act[3] contains some important changes to the existing legislation, some of which were made in order to conform to the EU Trademark Directive (89/104/EEC) more closely. The most important changes are:

- the notion of a likelihood of confusion will be amended to bring it in line with the directive and the judgment of the European Court of Justice in the case Puma/Sabel: "likelihood of confusion including the likelihood of association between the sign and the trade mark";
- exclusive rights to a trademark are only acquired by registration;
- introduction of an opposition procedure.

The amendments are expected to come into force in 2004.

Contacts

Benelux Trademarks Office: www.bmb-bbm.org
Industrial Property Office: www.bie.nl

Copyright

Legislation

Copyright in the Netherlands is regulated by the Copyright Act 1912 ("the Act"). Currently, the proposed bill implementing the EU Copyright Directive is before parliament (see *Future developments*).

Object of protection

The Act protects original works embodied in books, pamphlets, newspapers, periodicals, etc; dramatic and musical works; recitations; choreographed works and mime; drawings, paintings, works of architecture and sculpture, lithographs, engravings; geographical maps; drafts, sketches and three-dimensional works relating to architecture, geography, topography or other sciences; photographic works; cinematographic works; works of applied art and industrial designs and models; computer programs and preparatory material; and, under certain condition, databases. Although the Act refers to a 'literary, scientific or artistic work', case law has established that almost any work that meets the originality criteria

The Netherlands

qualifies for copyright protection, including the appearance of products with a utilitarian function (*e.g.* furniture, kitchenware).

No registration

Copyright arises when an original work is created. No formality, such as registration or the use of a copyright notice ©, is required. A copyright register does not exist.

To obtain evidence that a work was created before a certain date, a copy thereof can be date-stamped by the registrations office with the Netherlands tax department or a copy could be deposited with a civil-law notary. To indicate that a work is protected by copyright, it is commonplace in written works to use a copyright notice, giving the proprietor's name and year of first publication.

Exclusive rights

The exclusive rights that are granted to the copyright owner are:
- the right to communicate the work to the public (in whole or in part) which also means the right to distribute, rent, lend, recite, perform, present the work (in whole or in part) and to broadcast the work incorporated in a radio or television programme;
- the reproduction right, including the translation, arrangement of music, cinematographic adaptation or dramatization and generally any partial or total adaptation or imitation of the work in a modified form, which cannot be regarded as a new, original work; including the fixation of the whole or part of the work on an object which is intended to play a work or to show it.

Limited protection is granted to writings that do not qualify as original works. This stems from the inclusion of "all other writings" in the definition of a copyright work. This *geschriftenbescherming* only protects against proven derivation (direct copying) from writings.

The exclusive rights can be subject to a license or an assignment. Assignment must be effected by a written deed of assignment. The assignment comprises only such rights as are recorded in the deed or necessarily derive from the nature or purpose of the title. The license is not regulated in the Act. A license can be granted by verbal agreement. It will also be deemed to include only the rights of use explicitly referred to or necessarily implied.

Even after assignment of copyright, the author maintains certain rights, such as to be named as author and to oppose changes to the work, known as the "droit moral".

The Netherlands

Duration

The copyright of a work will be protected for seventy years after the death of the author of the work.

Ownership

The author owns the copyright of a work. If a work has been made under the guidance and supervision of another person, that person will be deemed the author of the work. Where labour carried out by an employee consists in the making of certain "literary, scientific or artistic works", the employer will be deemed the author of the work, unless otherwise agreed between the parties. Freelance personnel are not considered employees under the Act. A common misconception is that a paid commission leads to assignment of copyrights: unless assignment of ownership is explicitly agreed and effected by a written instrument, only the principal holds a license.

Future developments

The Netherlands has not yet implemented the European Copyright Directive (2001/29/EC). The draft bill implementing the directive was submitted to the Dutch parliament in 2002.

The main proposed amendments to the Act are:
- community exhaustion of the distribution right. Copyright is currently based on a system of universal exhaustion;
- an exception for temporary copying;
- private copying: must be restricted to a few copies;
- an exception is made for the incidental inclusion of a work of minor importance in a component of another work;
- an exception is made for communication to the public or reproduction of a work in the context of a caricature, parody or pastiche;
- provisions relating to the circumvention of technological measures.

Neighbouring Rights Act

The efforts of performing artists, phonogram and film producers and broadcasting organisations are protected by the Neighbouring Rights Act. The word "neighbouring" refers to copyright, to which these rights are related.

A performing artist has exclusive right with respect to the recording and reproduction of a performance (including the distribution of copies and broadcasting thereof). The performing artist has also been granted "droit moral".

The Act further grants exclusive rights to producers of phonograms and films and broadcasting organisations on the reproduction of their works.

Intellectual Property Law in the European Community

The Netherlands

As with copyright, neighbouring rights arise when the performance is given or work is created. No formalities are required. For phonograms, it is common to use the ownership notice ℗ listing the proprietor's name and year of first publication. The duration of a neighbouring right is 50 years following the creation of the work.

An important restriction on the exclusive rights of a performing artist and phonogram producer of a commercially released phonogram or reproduction is the conversion of their exclusive right to broadcast or otherwise make public into a right to fair compensation only for such use made by third parties.

Information is available on the organisation that administers the collection of these fair compensations: www.sena.nl

Database Act

The Database Act, implementing the European Database Directive[4], protects databases where there has been a substantial investment in obtaining, verifying or presenting the contents of the database.

The right to a database arises with the creation thereof. It is acquired by the producer, *i.e.* the 'legal person' that made the investment.

The producer of a database has the right to prevent the extraction or re-utilization of all or a substantial part of the content of the database and to prevent the repeated and systematic extraction or re-utilization of insubstantial parts of the content of a database where this does not conflict with the normal exploitation of that database or unreasonably prejudice legitimate interests of the producer of the database. The duration of a database right is 15 years.

A database right concurs with other rights on the database, *e.g.* copyrights or claims for unfair competition (tort). If there has not been a substantial investment, the database may still be protected under the Copyright Act if it qualifies as an original work.

Databases that qualify under the Database Act are explicitly excluded from the limited protection for all writings (*geschriftenbescherming*) under the Copyright Act.

Confidential Information

In the Netherlands, the protection of confidential information is not a separate legal concept. No specific legislation exists with respect to the protection of confidential information, other than two provisions in the Criminal Code.

It is advisable to have the disclosure and use of confidential information governed by a non-disclosure agreement or confidentiality agreement. In the event the receiving party uses or discloses the confidential information in a manner other than agreed upon, the receiving party will be in breach of its obligations under such agreement.

If no non-disclosure agreement exists between the disclosing and receiving party, the disclosing party may act against the use of its confidential information by claiming that such use constitutes unfair competition (tort) or is otherwise wrongful (*onrechtmatig*).

Trade Names

Trade names are names under which a company conducts its business (*e.g.* Koninklijke Luchtvaart Maatschappij N.V. is better known under its trade name KLM). A company can have several trade names (*e.g.* Transavia Airlines C.V. also operates under the trade name Basiq Air). The Trade Name Act offers protection against misleading use by third parties. It does not create an exclusive right *per se*. The scope of protection depends on the nature of the business and the place of establishment of the company (*i.e.* the territory where the trade name is commonly known). The trade name right arises through use thereof. The first user has the oldest rights. No formalities are required. The trade name right cannot be assigned separately from the business (or a part thereof) to which it is connected. In practice, a trade name right is nevertheless most of the times treated as a regular intellectual property right. Trade names often coincide with identical trademarks.

Domain Names

Domain names are not regulated by law. Although not an intellectual property right as such, domain names are often considered equal.

Domain names can be held by any 'legal person', including foreign persons provided they have a chosen domicile in the Netherlands.

A domain name can coincide with or infringe on trademark, trade name or copyrights.

Disputes involving domain names can be brought before the relevant court. In 2003, alternative dispute resolution became available by constitution of an arbitration regulation.

Information is available on the website of the organisation that issues and registers .nl domain names: www.sidn.nl

Practical Tips

Attachment of counterfeited goods or goods otherwise infringing or even allegedly infringing copyrights, trademarks, designs and/or patents is relatively easy under Dutch procedural law. It can be arranged for and effected within a

The Netherlands

matter of days. Permission from the President of the competent District Court can be obtained *ex parte* by written request, unless the defendant anticipated attachment and filed a prior request to be heard in the event of a request for permission to attach goods. An attachment of goods must be followed by court proceedings. Such proceedings can be preliminary injunction proceedings, which can take place in a matter of weeks. Often parties accept the resulting preliminary decisions as 'final' to avoid full-length civil proceedings.

Footnotes

[1] EC Directive 98/71/EC of the European Parliament and of the Council of 13 October 1998 on the legal protection of designs (L289/28, 28 October 1998)

[2] Protocol containing amendments to the Uniform Benelux Design Act as agreed by the governments of Belgium, the Netherlands and Luxembourg on 20 June 2002 (Tractatenblad 2002, no. 129)

[3] Protocol containing amendments to the Uniform Benelux Trademark Act as agreed by the governments of Belgium, the Netherlands and Luxemburg on 11 December 2001 (Tractatenblad 2002 no. 37)

[4] EC Directive 96/9/EC of the European Parliament and of the Council dated 11 March 1996 concerning the protection of databases (Pb EG 1996 L77/20)

The Netherlands

Chapter 22:
Poland

Poland

By Monika Chimiak
(Kulikowska & Kulikowski)

Introduction

On June 30, 2000 the Polish Parliament passed the new Industrial Property Law. It came into force on August 22, 2001, resulting in the harmonisation of Polish law with European Community law in this area. The obligation of harmonisation arose from articles 66-68 of the European Agreement of December 16, 1991, which established the association between Poland and the European Communities and their member states.

The new Industrial Property Law is the act which regulates all the industrial property rights and replaces several previous regulations regarding trademarks, inventions and utility models, designs and topography of electronic circuits. The Copyright Law and regulations regarding unfair competition are regulated in separate acts.

In preparation for Poland's accession into the European Community, IP Law in Poland has been largely harmonised with IP law in the European Community, such that the protection of individual IP rights under both regimes is comparable.

The recent amendment of the Industrial property Law introduces special provisions regarding protection of biotechnological inventions. This amendment was based on the Directive 98/44/EC of the European Parliament and of the Council on the legal protection of biotechnological inventions.

Patents

Legislation

The issues regarding filing of inventions and granting of patents are regulated by the Industrial Property Law of June 30, 2000 and the Regulation on Filing and Considering of Patent Applications and Utility Models Applications of Sep-

---

Monika Chimiak is a trademark and patent attorney with Kulikowska & Kulikowski in Warsaw. Kulikowska & Kulikowski is one of the first private firms in Poland dealing with protection of intellectual property. The firm provides complete legal services to national and international companies with respect to all areas of intellectual property. It is a member of INTA (International Tradmark Association), ECTA (European Community TradeMark Association), PTMG (Pharmaceutical Trade Mark Group) and the AIPPI (Association Internationale pour la protection de la Propriété Industriale).

Poland

tember 17, 2001. Poland is also a member of the Patent Co-operation Treaty, the Paris Convention and TRIPS.

Patent and procedures

The definition of a patent and the prerequisites of granting patents are the same for the European Community, the United Kingdom and Poland.

The application procedure is similar to that presented in the United Kingdom chapter. The patent application must include a request, a specification, claims and an abstract plus drawings if necessary. Afterthe publication of the patent application, there is a six-month period of time when anyone may file observations citing obstacles for granting a patent for the invention. The Patent Office has to take this observation into account while conducting a substantial search.

The application procedure is quite long in Poland due to the backlog of applications at the Patent Office. The procedure, from filing application to granting the patent, may take up to 5 years.

After conducting a substantial search, the Patent Office issues a decision in which the Office refuses to grant the patent or grants the patent for the whole invention or for some part of it. When the decision is not satisfactory for an applicant, he may file a request for reconsideration of the matter to the Appellate Division of the Patent Office. The final decision of the Polish Patent Office may be appealed at the District Administrative Court, and finally, at the Supreme Administrative Court.

It is also possible in Poland to convert an invention into a utility model if the invention fulfills all the prerequisites required for utility models.

Patents are granted for a period of 20 years from the filing date and this period is divided into eight periods: five years, three years and six periods of two years each. The fee for the first five years of protection is paid after the patent has been granted. A patent may expire after the lapse of 20 years, or earlier if the fee for the next period of protection is not paid before the previous period is ended or within a subsequent six-month grace period.

The granted patent may be opposed by any person during six months after its publication in the Official Journal of the Polish Patent Office. The opposition is filed with the Department of Registers and forwarded to the owner of the patent. When the patent's owner recognises the opposition as groundless, the opposition is transferred to the litigation procedure before the Patent Office.

A patent may also be invalidated if a person who has a legal interest proves that, at the time of filing an invention, he did not possess patentability. The invalidation procedure is conducted through the litigation procedure before the Patent Office.

Poland

A patent may be granted to an inventor or any other natural or legal person who is legally entitled to ownership.

The exclusive right conferred by a patent may be limited by the right of a user who, in good faith, was already exploiting an invention to an inconsiderable extent before the date according to which the priority for the granting of a patent is determined. The user can exploit a patent free of charge only in his business and to the extent to which he previously exploited the invention before the priority date.

Patent infringements are recognised in the first instance by the Commercial Division of the Regional Court. If a judgement is not satisfactory to the patent's owner, he may appeal against it to the Court of Appeal as a court of the second instance. The Supreme Court is the final instance.

In Poland, an exploitation of an invention to the extent necessary to obtain registration or authorisation to market certain products, in particular pharmaceutical products, is not regarded as an infringement of a patent.

Designs

Legislation

Regulations regarding industrial designs are included in the Industrial Property Law of June 30, 2000 and the Regulation on Filing and Considering Design Applications of January 30, 2002.

In Poland, only registered designs are protected by the provisions of the Industrial Property Law. Unregistered designs are protected under the Copyright Law if they fulfill the prerequisites of that law.

Definition, criteria of registration and scope of protection

The definition of an industrial design as well as the criteria of registration and scope of protection is the same as in the European Community and United Kingdom.

Procedures

A design application must include a request, a specification and a drawing. If the subject of the design is texture or material of the product, a design application may also contain photographs or samples of a textile fabric. One industrial design application may relate to individual appearances of a product having common essential features (variants of an industrial design). One application may contain no more than ten variants of an industrial design, unless the said variants taken together constitute a complete set of products, e.g. table set. All the variants of an industrial design contained in one application shall be presented in the form of figures of the drawing.

The Patent Office does not conduct a substantial search. The right of registration is granted after verifying that all formal conditions are fulfilled and if there are no absolute grounds to refuse registration of the design. If the Patent Office refuses to grant the registration right for the design, an applicant may file a request for reconsideration of the matter with the Appellate Division of the Patent Office. He may then appeal against the final decision of the Polish Patent Office at the District Administrative Court, and finally at the Supreme Administrative Court.

The right deriving from a design registration lasts 25 years and is divided into five separate periods. Renewal fees are paid every five years before the previous period is ended or within a six-month grace period.

The provisions regarding observations, opposition, invalidation and persons legally entitled to the ownership set out under Patents above, apply equally to designs. Any infringements of the design are considered through court proceedings.

Trade Marks

Registered trademarks

Legislation

Regulations regarding trademarks are included in the Industrial Property Law of June 30, 2000 and in the Regulation on Filing and Considering of Trademark Applications of July 8, 2002. Poland is also a member of both the Madrid Agreement and the Madrid Protocol.

Definition and procedures

The types of trademarks that can be registered in Poland are as discussed in the European Community chapter.

The Polish Industrial Property Law also provides for a joint right of protection. This right may be granted in the name of several undertakings who intend to use the mark concurrently and have jointly applied for the protection, provided that such use is not contrary to the public interest and is not intended to mislead the public, in particular as to the nature, intended purpose, quality, properties or origin of the goods. Along with the application for granting joint right of protection, the regulation governing the use of the trademark adopted by the undertakings has to be filed.

It is also possible in Poland to grant protection rights for collective trademarks and collective guarantee trademarks.

After the lapse of six months from the filing date, the Patent Office publishes information about the trademark application in the Bulletin of the Patent Office.

Poland

Until this time, trademark applications do not appear in searches.

With trademarks, as with patents and designs, Polish law provides for a six-month period from the date of publication about filing application for filing observations by any third person who can submit obstacles for granting protection right for the trademark.

Rights of protection will not be granted for an indication which cannot constitute a trademark and which is devoid of a sufficient distinctive character. The right of protection will not be granted for an indication, the use of which constitutes an infringement of personal or economic rights of third parties, which is contrary to law, public order or morality or which may mislead the public, in particular as to the nature, quality, properties or origin of the goods.

The decision of the Patent Office with respect to the granting or not granting of the protection right for the trademark, which is not satisfactory to an applicant, may be the subject of a request for reconsideration of the matter. An applicant may file the request for reconsideration of the matter regarding the decision to the Appellate Division of the Patent Office. The final decision of the PPO may be appealed at the District Administrative Court, and finally, at the Supreme Administrative Court.

Information about the granting of the protection right for a trademark is published in the Official Journal of the Patent Office. During the six-month period starting from the date of publication, any third person may file an opposition against the decision of the Patent Office granting the protection right for the trademark.

A trademark may be invalidated in full or in part, or lapsed. A request for invalidation as well as a request for lapse may be filed by a person who has a legal interest. The bases of the request for invalidation are relative or absolute grounds. The request for lapse may be filed if the trademark has not been used for a continuous period of five years for goods covered by the registration or if the trademark lost its distinctive character.

A request for invalidation of the trademark will not be admissible:
- on the grounds that it conflicts with an earlier trademark or if the personal or economic rights of the requesting party have been infringed, where the requesting party has acquiesced, for a period of five successive years, in the use of the registered trademark while being aware of such use;
- after the expiration of a period of five years from the granting of the right of protection, where the right in question was granted in breach of the provisions regarding distinctiveness, however in consequence of its use the trademark has acquired a distinctive character;

Poland

- on the grounds that it conflicts with a well-known trademark, where the party using the well-known trademark has acquiesced, for a period of five successive years of the use of the registered trademark, in the use of the latter while being aware of such use.

If, however, the holder of the right of protection has acquired his right in bad faith, the request for invalidation may be filed at any time. Infringements of trademarks are considered by the court.

Unregistered trademarks

Unregistered trademarks may be protected under the Act on suppression of unfair competition of April 16, 1994. They may also seek protection under the Polish Industrial Property Law. However, some conditions have to be fulfilled:
- the trademark has to be well-known and its owner has to prove the well-known character of his trademark, e.g. through conducting an opinion poll;
- use of an identical or similar trademark by another entrepreneur may bring him unfair advantage without due cause or is detrimental to the distinctive character of the trademark.

Geographical Indications

Legislation

Geographical indications are regulated in the Industrial Property Law of June 30, 2000 and in the Regulation on Filing and Considering Geographical Indications of April 25, 2002.

Definition and procedures

In the meaning of the above mentioned Law, geographical indications will be word indications which in an explicit or implicit manner designate the name of a place, locality, region or country (territory), which identify a good as originating in that territory, where a given quality, reputation or other characteristic of the good is essentially attributable to the geographical origin of that good.

A foreign geographical indication may only be granted protection in Poland if it enjoys protection in the country of its origin.

An application may be filed by an organization entitled to represent interests of the producers running their business activities in a given territory. An application may also be filed by a state or local administration agency competent in respect of the territory to which the geographical indication relates.

A geographical indication, the use of which would encroach upon a right of protection for a trademark, shall only be eligible for registration if the holder of the right of protection surrenders his right. Such surrender shall not be required where, in the application of the geographical indication for registration, filed in agreement with the holder of the trademark registration, the latter is mentioned among the parties authorized to use that indication and the maintenance of his right is not seen to entail excessive restrictions on freedom to use the geographical indication by other authorized parties.

The Patent Office does not publish any information about filing application for registration of a geographical indication. After formal search, it issues a decision regarding registration.

A right in registration for a geographical indication may be invalidated at the request of any party having a legitimate interest therein if he is able to prove that the statutory requirements for the granting of that right have not been satisfied.

Any party having a legitimate interest may demand that a decision be made on the lapse of the right in registration for the geographical indication which ceased to satisfy the requirements for the granting of protection or has not been used for a period of five years and there are no serious reasons for non-use thereof. However, this does not apply to indications which follow from an international agreement.

Copyright and Related Rights

Legislation

Copyright in Poland is regulated by the Law on Copyright and Neighboring Rights of February 4, 1994. Poland is also a member of the Berne Convention.

Definition

The subject matter of copyright is any and all manifestation of creative activity of individual nature, established in any form irrespective of its value, designation or manner of expression. In particular, the subject matter of copyright is: work expressed in words, mathematical symbols, graphic signs (literary, journalistic, scientific and cartographic works and computer programs), artistic works, photographic works, string musical instruments, industrial design works, architectural works, architectural and town planning works and town planning works, musical works and textual and musical works, stage works, stage and musical works, choreographic and pantomime works, and audiovisual works (including films).

The protection covers only the manner of expression. The author shall not enjoy copyright protection irrespective of complying with any formalities.

Term of protection

The author of a work possesses personal and economic rights to his work. The personal rights last until the author's death and they are inalienable, contrary to the economic rights.

Poland

Copyright

The author's economic rights expire after the lapse of seventy years:

- from the death of the author, and in the case of joint works, from the death of the coauthor who has survived the others;
- if the author of the work is unknown, from the date of the first publication, unless a pseudonym does not leave any doubt as to the identity of the author or if the author discloses his identity;
- with respect to works whose economic rights belong to a person other than the author, from the date of publication, and if the work has not been published, from the time of its establishment;
- with respect to audiovisual works, after the death of the last of the following persons: the principal director, the author of the screenplay, the author of the dialogues, the composer of the music created for use in the audiovisual work.

Neighboring rights

The rights of artistic performer to exploit the artistic performance expire after the fifty years following the year in which the artistic performance was established. If, however, the performance has been published or reproduced in public in this time, the term of protection is counted from that event, and if both of the events has taken place, from the earlier.

The producer's rights to use and dispose of the phonograms and videograms on the specific fields of exploitation expire after fifty years following the year in which the phonogram or videogram was made.

The rights of radio or television organizations to dispose of and use their programs on the specific fields of exploitation expire after fifty years following the year of the first broadcast of the program.

An editor who has published or in some other way propagated a work which has not previously been made available to the public and in which protection has expired, possesses the exclusive rights to exploit the work for a period of twenty five years from the date of the first publication or propagation.

The person who has prepared a critical or scientific edition of the work whose protection has expired, and the edition is not a work, possesses the exclusive right to use and dispose in a specific way through a period of thirty years form the publication date.

Computer programs

Computer programs possess special provisions within the framework of the Copyright Law. The provisions of this regulation are based on the Council Directive on the Legal Protection of Computer Programs of May 14, 1991.

Poland

Database rights

In Poland, databases are protected under the Copyright Law and under the Act on the Protection of Databases of July 27, 2001. Under the Copyright Law, only those databases which are simultaneously a work are protected. If a database is not a work, it is protected under the aforementioned Act.

The scope of protection of databases is the same as described in the European Community chapter.

The database is protected fifteen years from the following year of its creation. If any substantial changes are made to the database, the protection period starts again. If, however, the database is made available to the public within the fifteen year protection period, the period of protection expires after fifteen years following the year of the first publication.

Confidential Information

Protection of business secrets and know-how is mainly regulated in the Act on Suppression of Unfair Competition of April 16, 1994 and in the Labor Code of June 26, 1974.

Definition

A business secret is any technical, technological, trade or organizational information not disclosed to the public concerning the enterprise in respect of which the entrepreneur has taken appropriate measures to preserve its confidentiality. Therefore, patentable or impatentable inventions, utility and industrial designs as technical and technological information are protected under this Law.

Unfair competition

Disclosure of a business secret is treated as an act of unfair competition. The Act on Suppression of Unfair Competition provides that: 'A transfer, disclosure or use by other persons of business secrets or the acquisition thereof from unauthorized persons if such acquisition endangers material interest of the entrepreneur is considered as an act of unfair competition.'

Liability

Any person who commits an act of unfair competition as described above is subject to civil and penal liability.

Civil and penal liability under the above Act also refers to a person who worked under an employment contract or within the scope of another legal relationship for a period of three years of termination thereof, unless such contract provides otherwise or the requirement for secrecy has ceased.

Poland

Employment relationship

Similar to the United Kingdom, an employment contract in Poland may include an obligation to maintain the confidendiality of business secrets.

However, as in the United Kingdom, the main way to protect confidential information is executed by individual bilateral or multilateral commercial contracts.

Competition

Polish antimonopoly law is mainly regulated by the Law on Protection of Consumers and Competition of December 15, 2000. This Law is the result of the harmonisation of the Polish competition law with the standards of the European Community. This Law prohibits anticompetitive agreements which may limit fair competition on the market and provides that the provisions of the antimonopoly law do not infringe rights adjudicated according to the provisions regarding the Intellectual and Industrial Property Law.

Another act, which also refers to competition, is the Law of Suppression on Unfair Competition of April 16, 1994. Moreover, many individual acts contain their own provisions in the field of competition.

Poland

Chapter 23: Portugal

Portugal

By Isabel Franco
(J.E. Dias Costa, Lda.)

Introduction

In Portugal, all industrial property rights, such as patents, designs or models and trade/service marks, are ruled by the Industrial Property Code (Decree-Law No. 36/2003, dated March 5, 2003) which entered into force on July 1, 2003. This Code is an improved version of the previous Code (of 1995) with several significant changes. The present Code brings the Portuguese legislation closer to the European Community legislation, namely as regards patents, designs and marks.

Any application for registration of an IP right should be filed in Portugal before the official body called *"Instituto Nacional da Propriedade Industrial"* (INPI).

For all IP rights, there exists a system of provisional protection as from the date of their publication in the Industrial Property Bulletin. There is also the possibility of arbitration appeal for every IP right.

The aforesaid Code clearly determines that the sole competent Court for judicially appealing a final administrative decision is the *"Tribunal de Comércio de Lisboa"*. Furthermore, there is also only one competent Court at the second instance level, which is the *"Tribunal da Relação de Lisboa"* (also located in Lisbon).

The principle of Community exhaustion of rights has been maintained, although there is a slight change in the wording of the law, replacing the word "Community" with a reference to the European Economic Area, or EEA, which includes (in addition to the European Union member states) Iceland, Liechtenstein and Norway.

Any IP right granted covers all the continental territory of Portugal as well as the Azores Archipelago and the Madeira Island.

Patents and Utility Models

According to Portuguese Industrial Property Code (Decree-law No. 36/2003, dated March 5, 2003, which entered into force on July 1, 2003), the procedure of a

---

Isabel Franco is a lawyer and Official Industrial Property Attorney with J.E. Dias Costa, Lda. in Lisbon. Ms. Franco is a European Representative before the "EPO" (European Patent Office) and the OHIM (The Office for Harmonisation in the Internal Market). J.E. Dias Costa, Lda. provides filing, maintenance, prosecution, advisory and technical services related to the protection of intellectual property rights.

Portugal

national Patent Application has been simplified. Once applied for, the Application shall be published for opposition purposes, without any pre-examination.

The following European Union legislation has already been implemented in Portugal:

- Directive No. 98/44/CE, on the legal protection of biotechnological inventions;
- Council Regulation EEC No. 1768/92, concerning the creation of a supplementary protection certificate for medicinal products;
- Regulation (EC) No. 1610/96, concerning the creation of a supplementary protection certificate for plant protection products.

Regarding biotechnology, it is worthwhile noting that the following, *inter alia*, is patentable:

- biological material which is isolated from its natural environment (or produced by means of a technical process), even if it previously occurred in nature;
- an element isolated from the human body (or otherwise produced by means of a technical process), including the sequence (or partial sequence) of a gene, even if the structure of that element is identical to that of a natural element provided that novelty, inventive step and industrial applicability are clearly shown.

The same invention may be the object, simultaneously or successively, of a patent or utility model application. However, utility models protection is not obtainable for a chemical or pharmaceutical product or process, nor for biological matter.

Designs or Models

Directive 98/71/CE regarding the protection of designs has already been implemented.

The validity of a design or model registration is 5 years as from the respective application date, with the possibility of renewal for the same period, up to a limit of 25 years. Presently, the owner of a design or model has to pay a quinquennial fee (and no longer an annuity).

A special 6 months prior protection for models or designs of textiles and clothing can be applied for.

Trade and Service Marks

Portugal is a so-called "registration country". Thus, marks need to be registered to confer rights. There is no use or intent to use requirement for the filing of a mark application in this country.

Portugal

Any new mark application is published in the Official Bulletin for opposition purposes, prior to the examination by the Portuguese Industrial Property Institute. There is examination by the Portuguese Industrial Property Institute of absolute and relative grounds for refusal of mark applications.

As regards absolute grounds for refusal, colours cannot be registered unless there is a combination of colours, or the colours are accompanied by words or other elements, provided they are distinctive.

It should also be mentioned that the registration of a mark application might be refused if there is clear infringement of the trade dress (unregistered) of another party's container or label.

An administrative formality called "Declaration of Intent to Use" ("DIU") has to be submitted every five years, except when a renewal is due, for national Portuguese marks and international mark registrations extended to Portugal. This is a mere administrative statement and it is not required to join any proof of use. Whether or not the marks are being used in the Portuguese market is irrelevant, since the "Declaration" to be submitted is not a declaration of use but simply a declaration of intent to use. In fact, what the trade mark owner declares is that he/she is *still* interested in the mark.

However, a Portuguese national mark registration (or an international mark registration valid in Portugal) must be used in Portugal within 5 years counted from the respective registration date, otherwise the registration may risk a declaration of cancellation (partial or total) on the grounds of non-use at the request of any interested party.

Copyright and Related Rights

Portugal is a member of the Berne Convention. Although Copyright registration is not required, it is highly recommended for enforcing rights more easily.

Confidential Information

Confidential information and trade secrets are protected.

Chapter 24:
Slovak Republic

Slovak Republic

By Marta Majlingová, Mária Fajnorová, Magdaléna Bachratá,
Katarína Sepeláková, Baya Nikolajová and Katarína Majlingová
(Majlingová Fajnorová Bachratá)

Introduction
Major issues affecting intellectual property

Issues of industrial legal protection in the independent Slovak Republic arose and were addressed in the latter half of 1992, together with other state legal questions related to the split of the Czech and Slovak Federal Republic. The Slovak Republic accepted all statutory regulations of the former Czech and Slovak Federal Republic regarding industrial property protection.

Patent, design and trade mark protections were provided in the territory of Slovakia in 19th century. Similar to other territories, protection of results of technical creativity in the Slovak territory emanated from privileges and patent laws vested by sovereigns. Slovak pioneers of technical progress hold an important position in the world history of science and technology.

After the Czechoslovak Republic was constituted in the year 1918, the Austrian Patent Act No. 30/1897 of Austrian Law of January 11, 1897 remained valid in the territories of Bohemia, Moravia and Silesia. The Hungarian Act (section XXXVI) on Inventional Patents of July 14, 1895 remained valid in Slovakia and Transcarpatho-Ukraine. Act. No. 305/1919 of Digest of May 25, 1919 ended this ambiguity. However, being only a partial amendment to Austrian Patent Act. No. 30/1897 of Austrian Law, it was also extended to the territory of Slovakia. The Hungarian Act was abrogated for the whole of Czechoslovakia. Contemporaneously, the Patent Office as well as the Patent Court seated in Prague were established.

In the year 1919, the Czechoslovak Republic also accepted Austrian Act No. 19/1890 of Austrian Law with its amendments of 1895 and 1913 for the whole territory, and it became valid for Slovakia then as well.

Marta Majlingová, Mária Fajnorová, Magdaléna Bachratá, Katerína Sepeláková, Baya Nikolajová and Katarína Majlingová are partners with Majlingová Fajnorová Bachratá Patent Attorneys and Trademark Agents in Bratislava. The firm is one of the first patent agencies established in the Slovak Republic after the breakup of Czechoslovakia. All partners are competent to represent clients in all areas of industrial property rights and are qualified to prepare professional reports on these matters for judicial purposes.

Slovak Republic

The first self-contained branch of the previous patent offices of former Czechoslovakia was established in 1957 in Bratislava (branch of the State Office for Inventions and Normalisation). From 1972, an inner-directed office of the Office for Inventions and Discoveries (from January 1, 1989 the Federal Office for Inventions) operated in Bratislava.

Establishment of the Industrial Property Office as a central administrative authority in industrial property law (based on the Act of the National Council of the Slovak Republic No. 2/1993 January 1, 1993) is a part of the most recent history.

Treaties and conventions

The Slovak Republic is a member of the following Conventions/Treaties:
- Berne Convention (Literary and Artistic Works)
- PCT (Patent Cooperation Treaty)
- European Patent Convention
- Madrid Agreement (International Registration of Marks)
- Madrid Agreement (False or Deceptive Indications of Source on Goods)
- Madrid Protocol (International Registration of Marks)
- Nice Agreement (International Classification of Goods and Services)
- Lisbon Agreement (Appellations of Origin)
- Rome Convention (Performers, Producers of Phonograms and Broadcasting Organizations)
- Locarno Agreement (International Classification for Industrial Designs)
- Strasbourg Agreement (International Patent Classification)
- Geneva Convention (Unauthorised Duplication of Phonograms)
- Budapest Treaty (Deposit of Microorganisms)
- TLT (Trade marks)
- WCT (WIPO Copyright Treaty)
- WPPT (WIPO Performances and Phonograms Treaty)
- WTO
- CEFTA (Central European Free Trade Agreement)
- UCC
- UPOV

Current legislative climate

Back in 1989, the Slovak Republic (then part of Czechoslovakia) started the process of harmonisation with the laws and directives of the European Union. At present, when the negotiation on acceding Slovakia to the EU has been completed, it can be stated that the majority of the laws regarding industrial property is wholly

Slovak Republic

compatible with the EU regulations. Others are in the process of approval and shall be passed by the time Slovakia accedes to the European Union (May 1, 2004).

Recent trends

After Slovakia becomes part of the European Union (May 1, 2004), implementation of further related European law into the law of the Slovak Republic is expected, as is the approximation of the practice of the Slovakian authorities in the industrial property and related law with that of the European Union.

Patents

Patent law in the Slovak Republic is regulated by Act No. 435/2001 and has been harmonised according to the terms of EU Accession Documents.

Wording of patent claims and description

Generally, requirements of the Industrial Property Office of the Slovak Republic are similar to the requirements of the EPO. However, there are some exceptions. The Slovak Office considers the following combination of categories of patent claims as lacking the unity of the patent application: a compound; a pharmaceutical composition comprising said compound; a method for producing of said pharmaceutical composition. Examiners usually request the exclusion of claims for production of such pharmaceutical composition.

If a pharmaceutical composition for treatment or prophylaxis is claimed, the specification has to comprise tests of effectiveness and harmlessness of the active ingredient.

The insertion of additional examples into the specification to support claims during the proceedings is not allowed. Such examples are only taken into the file.

Substantive examination

The Office conducts substantive examinations upon a request of the applicant, of any third party or in a special case in ex officio procedure. The request is subject to the examination fee. The request for substantive examination has to be filed within 36 months of the filing date. In the case of national phase of a PCT application, the request for substantive examination has to be filed within 36 months of the international filing date. If the request for substantive examination was not properly filed within the above stated time limit, the Office shall terminate the application procedure.

Observations

After publication of the patent application, any person may file observations with the Office on the patentability of its subject matter; the Office shall take ob-

Slovak Republic

servations into consideration during substantive examination of the application. Persons who have filed observations shall not become parties to the application proceedings. However, the applicant has to be notified about the observations and they have the right to respond.

Opposition

Opposition procedure, which allows anyone to file opposition against the granted patent within the set time limit after granting can be found in jurisdictions of many European countries as well as in the EPC, but not in the Slovak Patent law. The only possibility to contest a patent is to file a request for its revocation.

Patent rights

The owner of the patent has an exclusive right to exploit the invention, to grant consent for exploitation of the invention, assign the patent to another person or establish lien to the patent. The said exclusive rights belong also to the applicant, starting from the day of publication of the patent application in the Slovak language in the Official Journal, provided that a patent has been granted for the invention which is the subject matter of the application. However, execution of the right vis-a-vis third parties is possible only as from the day on which announcement on grant of the patent is published in the Official Journal (Vestník). The same applies for European patent applications designating the Slovak Republic.

Upon request, the court is entitled to grant a compulsory license to any person who can demonstrate the ability to exploit the invention, provided that the patent owner does not himself exploit the invention on the territory of the Slovak Republic without a proper reason.

Rights of the patent owner are not infringed if the invention is used for specifically defined activities on board vessels or aircrafts which temporarily or accidentally enter the territory of the Slovak Republic, in individual preparation of a medicine in a pharmacy, in activity being conducted privately or for non-commercial purposes, and in activity being conducted for experimental purposes. Clinical trials are considered experimental purposes.

Disputes on infringement of patent rights are heard and ruled on by courts. They also deal with disputes on the right to file a patent application.

Cancellation proceedings

The Industrial Property Office shall cancel a patent if the proceedings started on a third party's request or ex officio prove that requirements for patentability were not met, the invention is not explained clearly and fully, the scope of protection was extended, or the owner does not have the right to the patent.

Slovak Republic

Payment of maintenance fees

Validity of the patent is twenty years from the filing date of the patent application. There is no requirement to pay annual renewal fees during the proceedings. After granting of a patent, accumulated annuities have to be paid. For each following year a maintenance fee has to be paid. The Slovak Industrial Property Office does not remind the patent owner to pay an annuity.

Further processing

If a party to the proceedings before the Office has failed to comply with the time limit set by the Office for performing an act, they are entitled to ask the Office for further processing and at the same time perform the omitted act no later than two months from the service of the official decision issued as a consequence of failure to comply with the time limit.

Restitutio in integrum

If the party to the proceedings before the Office unintentionally has failed to comply with the statutory time limit or the time limit set by the Office for performing an action, they are entitled to request of the Office *restitutio in integrum* and at the same time perform the omitted action. Both actions are due within two months as from the removal of the cause for which they could not act, however, no later than twelve months from the expiry of the non-complied time limit.

Supplementary Protection Certificates

It is possible to obtain a patent term extension in the form of a Supplementary Protection Certificate (SPC). The SPC can be granted for medicinal products and for plant protection products. It can be granted for any medicinal product, which is the ingredient of a medicine approved by the Slovak authority for registration of medicinal products (State Institute for Drugs Control). An application for a certificate has to be filed within six months of the date on which the first Slovak marketing authorisation for the medicinal product was granted. If the marketing authorisation is granted before the grant of the basic patent, the application for the SPC has to be lodged within six months as of the date of the patent granting.

The SPC is only granted for the products covered by the marketing authorisation.

The SPC takes effect from the end of the basic patent term. It takes effect for a period equal to the period which elapsed between the filing date of the application for the basic patent and the date of the granting of the marketing approval for the medicine, reduced by a period of five years. However, the duration of the SPC may not exceed five years from the date on which it takes effect.

Slovak Republic

Utility Models

Protection in the form of a utility model (handled in accordance with Act No. 478/1992) is generally suitable for technical solutions of lower level of inventive capacity, or of lesser economic importance. It is mainly intended for the activities of small- and medium-sized businesses as it provides them with the option of a simple, swift and, above all, financially less demanding protection of results of their technical creative activity.

The utility model proceedings are based on a registration principle. Only formal and legal examinations are accomplished before registration of the utility model. The average time limit for decisions on applications concerning utility models is now less than six months. On the request of a third party, the Office will cancel the utility model from the register if the technical solution is not novel, industrially applicable, or if it does not go beyond the basic professional skills.

In contrast with the patent protection, neither production methods nor operations or biological reproductive materials are eligible for protection by the utility model. An applicant of the utility model can claim priority from the earlier patent application.

Protection by the utility model lasts for four years from the filing date of the application and can be extended upon request twice, each time for three years.

Designs

Designs are regulated by Design Act No. 444/2002, which has been harmonised in accordance with the Directive 98/71/EC of the European Parliament and of the Council of October 13, 1998 on the legal protection of designs. Therefore all substantial features and principals of the design protection in the Slovak Republic are in compliance with the above Directive. There are no differences in registrability requirements, definitions of relevant terms, formal requirements, or scope of the owner's rights or cancellation procedures.

Ownership

A designer has a right to a design registration. If the design was created in the course of employment, the right to the design registration is transferred to the employer. In such case a formal assignment from the designer to employer is required.

The design owner can assign or license the design right. It is also possible to establish a lien on the design. The applicant can request deferment of the publication for a period not exceeding 30 months from the priority date.

Slovak Republic

Duration

Design registrations are valid for a maximum of twenty-five years with the need to request their renewal every five years (and pay appropriate fees). However, designs that were registered in accordance with the previous Design Act remain in force for a maximum of fifteen years (two five-year extensions are possible).

Unregistered design rights

The Slovak legal system does not provide unregistered design rights. After May 2004 (accession of the Slovak Republic to the European Union), however, rights from the unregistered Community designs will be automatically effective in the Slovak Republic. There is a possibility that some conflicts with the Slovak design registration provisions will occur.

Trade Marks

Trade mark provisions have been amended and are now fully harmonised with the law of the European Union. Below are important features and interesting aspects of trade mark protection in Slovakia.

Registered trade marks

Trade marks in the Slovak Republic are regulated under Act No. 55/1997 of Digest on Trade Marks amended by Act No. 577/2001 of Digest.

Registrability and the application procedure

In Slovakia, the use or intent to use the mark before or after filing is not required. The claimed specification shall correspond to the registered business activities of the applicant.

Any mark can be registered if it can be represented graphically and is capable of distinguishing goods or services of one undertaking from those of another. The Slovakian IPO has not dealt with any application for an unusual trade mark, e.g. smell, sound or moving mark. Accordingly, there is not proof these marks would be registrable under the Slovakian law. The only colour registered as a trade mark is Kraft lilac for chocolate confectionery.

An examiner will examine each application and will reject any mark which:
- Has no distinctive capacity;
- Consists exclusively of indications or elements that serve in the trade to designate the kind, quality, quantity, purpose, value, geographical origin or other characteristics of goods or services, or, if appropriate, time of production of goods or of rendering of services;
- Consists exclusively of signs or indications which have become custom-

Slovak Republic

ary in current language or have been used in established practices of trade, or consists exclusively of the shapes of goods or of their packaging which results from the nature of the goods themselves or is necessary to obtain a technical result, or gives substantial value to the goods;

- Is of such a nature as to deceive the public, particularly with regard to the nature, quality or geographical origin of the goods or services;
- Is contrary to public order or principles of morality,
- Use would be contrary to the obligations of the Slovak Republic under international treaties;
- Contains a sign of a high symbolic value, particularly a religious symbol;
- Sign applied for wines or spirits containing a geographical indication identifying wines or spirits with respect to such wines or spirits not having that origin.

The examiner will also search the Register for any identical or confusingly similar prior applications or registrations registered or filed in respect of identical or similar goods and/or services and will object to the application if such earlier mark exists. The objection can be overcome if the applicant can show that the owner of the earlier mark consents to concurrent use by the applicant of its similar or identical mark.

If the examination procedure of the trade mark application is successfully completed it will be advertised in the Office Journal (Vestník), thereby giving third parties the opportunity to oppose the application on relative grounds before registration is finally granted.

A straightforward trade mark application should be registered within 12 months of filing.

Wine products and spirit beverages are protectable under the Slovakian law unless unless they are misleading as to the origin of the goods covered by a trade mark or address of the trade mark proprietor. Such registration, however, does not bar the use of the geographical indication by any other competitor manufacturing or producing goods in the same territory.

The Slovakian law does not allow registration of the marks that apply for wines or spirits containing a geographical indication identifying wines or spirits with respect to such wines or spirits not having that origin.

How long does trade mark registration last?

Trade marks can be registered indefinitely. Initially the trade mark is valid for ten years from the filing date. Thereafter it is renewable in perpetuity for further ten-year periods upon filing a renewal application and payment of renewal fees.

Slovak Republic

Unless used for a period of five years, a trade mark registration may be cancelled, in full or in part if challenged by a third party.

What rights does it give?

A registered trade mark gives the trade mark proprietor rights to prevent others from using a mark identical with or confusingly similar to the registrant's mark in relation to identical or similar goods and/or services.

The trade mark proprietor is entitled to require information about the origin of goods or documents accompanying the goods or services from everybody offering on the market goods or services which are marked with a mark identical with or confusingly similar to registrant's trade mark.

Advantages of registration

Although the holder of the unregistered mark possesses certain rights, rights in the trade mark are easier to be defended and infringement or unfair competition challenged/banned if the mark is registered.

Unregistered trade marks

Trade marks do not need to be registered to confer rights to legal protection on their owners. The owner of an unregistered trade mark can file opposition or cancellation action against the registered trade mark.

However, due to practical difficulties and costs involved in obtaining the necessary evidence to sustain an action for passing off (proving reputation and goodwill is notoriously difficult) many traders prefer to register their names, marks and logos at the Trade Marks Registry.

Slovak law does not recognise passing off. Unregistered marks are protected under the unfair competition law.

Domain names and brand protection on the Internet

.sk is the top-level domain in Slovakia for both commercial and non-commercial purposes. An applicant for registration of the .sk domain name shall be domiciled or operate a business in Slovakia. A foreign applicant can request the registration of the domain name through a proxy.

There is not any law in the Slovak Republic regulating relationship between trade marks and domain names. All disputes, such as registering the domain by a distributor of branded goods, cybersquatting, using metatags of competitor's or any other kinds of trade mark infringement, shall be resolved amicably or by the courts.

There exist rules for registration and maintenance of the .sk domains developed by ccTLD Registrar (SK-NIC). The rules have been massively amended re-

Slovak Republic

cently. The new regulations have introduced the following main changes:
- A .sk domain can be registered on behalf of an individual not involved in business activities;
- Domains shall be maintained on annual basis and the maintenance fee shall be paid by the local proxy;
- Use of the domain is not mandatory, the non-use of the registered domain cannot result in its cancellation for non-use;
- Domains that consist of a dominant element of a registered trade mark valid in the Slovak Republic or a trade mark well-known in Slovakia, regardless of the country of its origin, cannot be registered and used by an entity other than the trade mark owner or its subsidiary;
- Any dispute as to the registration or use of the domain shall be decided only by the civil courts, ccTLD Registrar does not serve as the arbitrator and cannot be liable for any damage;
- Termination of the general agreement with the domain name holder or proxy shall result in cancellation of the domain.

In addition, under the new rules, all previously registered domains shall be re-registered. The deadline for re-registration is October 1, 2003; otherwise the domains will be cancelled as of January 5, 2004 and left free for a third-party registration. The re-registration procedure is analogous to the registration.

Copyright and Related Rights

Copyright in the Slovak Republic is regulated by Copyright Act No. 383/1997 of Digest of December 5, 1997 as subsequently amended.

The subject of the Act is regulation of relations arising in connection with creation, use and dissemination of literary works, scientific works and artistic works in a manner to protect the rights and legitimate interests of authors of works, including the authors of computer programmes and databases, performing artists, phonogram producers, producers of audiovisual fixations, radio broadcasters and television broadcasters.

The provisions of the Act apply to:
a) Works of authors who are nationals of the Slovak Republic or who have their permanent residence within the territory of the Slovak Republic; the same shall apply for the works of authors to whom the legal status of refugee, according to the respective legislation, is granted in the territory of the Slovak Republic;
b) Works made public for the first time in the Slovak Republic, irrespective of nationality or permanent residence of their authors, including works

Slovak Republic

made public for the first time in another country but simultaneously published in the Slovak Republic within the term of 30 days;
c) Performing artists who are nationals of the Slovak Republic;
d) Performing artists who are not nationals of the Slovak Republic but whose performances took place in the territory of the Slovak Republic or which are incorporated in phonograms that are protected under the Act, or performances which have not been fixed in phonograms but which were communicated by broadcast or by original programmes communicated by wire and due to this they fulfill the conditions for protection under the Act;
e) Phonograms or audiovisual fixations of the producers who are nationals of the Slovak Republic or who have their permanent residence or seat in the Slovak Republic;
f) Phonograms or audiovisual fixations, the first fixation of which was made in the Slovak Republic;
g) Phonograms or audiovisual fixations, that were made public for the first time in the Slovak Republic;
h) Radio broadcast and television broadcast of broadcasters and programmes of organisations communicating to the public their own programmes, if their seat is in the territory of the Slovak Republic;
i) Radio broadcast and television broadcast by broadcasters and to original programmes communicated to the public from the place within the territory of the Slovak Republic.

The provisions of the Act also apply to works to which protection in the Slovak Republic is granted by virtue of international agreements or conventions by which Slovakia is bound.

Duration of copyright relating to the work of foreign nationals cannot be longer than in the country of origin of the work.

The provisions of international agreements by which Slovakia is bound shall not be affected by the Act.

The subject of copyright

Literary, scientific and artistic works that are the result of the author's own creative intellectual activity, are subject to copyright. They are in particular the following:
a) Literary work and computer programme,
b) Work delivered orally, declaimed or otherwise performed literary work, in particular the speech and the lecture,
c) Theatre work, in particular dramatic work, dramatico-musical work, pan-

Slovak Republic

tomimic work and choreographic work as well as any other work created for its making public or public performance,
d) Musical work with or without lyrics,
e) Audiovisual work, in particular film work,
f) Painting, drawing, sketch, illustration, sculpture and other work of visual art,
g) Photographic work,
h) Work of architecture, work of building architecture and urbanism, work of garden and interior architecture and the work of building design,
i) Work of applied art,
j) Work of cartography in analogue or any other form.

A database, irrespective of its form, is also subject to copyright, under the sole condition it is original from the point of view of creative selection or arrangement of its contents.

<u>No protection shall extend to:</u>
a) Any idea, procedure, system, method, concept, principle, discovery or information, which was expressed, described, explained, illustrated or embodied in a work;
b) Any text of legislation, decision of administration and legal nature, public document, official document, daily news and speeches delivered in the course of public events and their translation; however, the publication of a collection of such speeches or their inclusion into annals requires consent of the person who delivered them.

Work of co-authors, combined work, collective work, collected work

A work of co-authors is a work that was created by the own creative intellectual activity of two or more authors as a single work, rights to which belong to all authors jointly and inseparably.

A combined work is a work created by combination of several single works with the permission of their authors for the agreed purpose. The combined work is disposed of by all the authors jointly. The rights of authors to dispose works, which were combined in that manner in any other manner different from the disposes in such combination shall be without prejudice. In case of performance of musical work with lyrics this requires only the permission of the author of the musical part alone.

A collective work is a work which was created by the joint activity of two or more authors who agreed with the use of their own creative intellectual activity for its creation. The work thus created can be distributed under the name of physical person or legal entity who or which undertook the initiative for the creation of the work or otherwise facilitated the creation of that work.

A collected work is a collection, periodical, review, exhibition or another collected work, provided that their arrangement is a result of the own creative intellectual activity of the author. A work can be included into a collected work only with the preceding permission of the author.

Copyright to the collected work as a whole shall belong to the person who arranged it; this shall not prejudice the rights of authors of works included in the collection. Copyright to published collections, cartography work and periodical is exercised by the publisher.

Establishment of copyright to work

Copyright to a work is established in the moment the work is expressed in a form perceptible by senses, irrespective of its form, content, quality, purpose or form of its expression. Copyright to a work relates to the work as a whole as well as to its parts.

It is not possible to register Copyright in the Slovak Republic. However, because of this, proving ownership of copyright can be difficult unless proper written records are kept.

The content of copyright

The author has the right to protect his/her authorship, in particular the right to:

a) Sign his/her work by his/her name; his/her name shall be indicated on all copies of work in appropriate manner, within any public use of that work, the manner of this indication depending on the nature of this use,

b) Sign his/her work by a pseudonym; his/her pseudonym shall be indicated on all copies of work in appropriate manner, within any public use, depending on the nature of this use,

c) Not to sign his/her work,

d) Inviolability of his/her work, in particular to protection against any interference in a work or against any derogatory disposal with his/her work which would cause the distortion of his/her honour or good reputation,

e) Decide on making public his/her work.

The author also has the right to make corrections in the proofs of his/her work. In the case of works of architecture, the supervision of the author over the construction of building is a form of checking the proofs.

Slovak Republic

The above-mentioned rights of the author are untransferable and unlimited in time.

Furthermore the author of the work has an exclusive right to authorise any use of the work, in particular:

a) Any reproduction of the work,
b) Translation of the work,
c) Adaptation, arrangement or other transformation of the work,
d) Use of the work or its part for creation of another work,
e) Distribution of the work or its copy into the public by sale, rental, lending or any other form of distribution of the work or transfer of ownership,
f) Public display of the work or its copy,
g) Public performance of the work,
h) Broadcasting of the work,
i) Cable retransmission of the work,
j) Communication of the work by any other method.

The author has the right for remuneration for any use of his/her work. The rights of the author cannot be contractually limited or excluded.

Duration of copyright

Copyright shall last throughout the life of the author and seventy years after his/her death. In case of the work of co-authors and combined work created for purpose of use of that work in that combination, copyright shall last throughout the life of the last of the authors and seventy years after his/her death.

In the case of a collective work, other than work of applied art, copyright shall last 70 years from the moment when the work was first time lawfully presented in public. In the case the work has been signed by the names of authors who created the work, copyright shall last throughout the life of the last of the authors and seventy years after his/her death.

In the case of an audiovisual work copyright shall last throughout the life of the co-authors and seventy years after the death of the last one of them.

In the case of a work made public under a pseudonym or anonymous work, copyright shall last seventy years after first publication of such work; however, when there are no doubts as to an identity of the author, it shall last seventy years after his/her death.

In the case of work published in volumes, the duration of copyright shall be calculated from the moment when the work was made public; it shall be calculated for each volume separately.

In the case of a database, copyright shall last seventy years from the moment of its making. In the case of a work of applied art, copyright shall last twenty years from the making of the work.

The calculation of duration of copyright shall start from the first day of the year following the year in which the event decisive for the calculation occurred.

Transfer of copyright

The author can transfer only the right to use the work.

The acquirer can transfer the acquired right to another person only with the permission of the author.

If a legal entity or a physical person to which or whom the right to use the work has been transferred ceased to exist or dies without a successor-in-title, the author shall re-acquire the right to decide on further use of the work.

Passage of copyright

Copyright shall pass on to heirs. The provisions of the Act concerning the author shall apply to his/her heirs, unless the nature of the provisions implies otherwise.

Imperilment and violation of copyright

The author whose copyright has been violated may demand in particular that further violation be prohibited, the consequences of the violation be removed, and that he/she be given appropriate satisfaction. If a considerable detriment of non-proprietary nature has resulted from a violation of copyright, the author has the right to satisfaction in money on condition other satisfaction appears insufficient. The value of the satisfaction in money shall be determined by the court which, in particular, takes into account the extent of the suffered detriment as well as the circumstances of the violation.

The provisions of Civil Code shall apply to the claim of the author for coverage of damages suffered by violation.

The author can make the same claims of imperilment or violation of his/her rights against persons who or which import, manufacture or exploit the equipment exclusively or partly designed for removal, termination of operation or limitation of the functioning of technological devices used for protection of work against unauthorised use.

Rights similar but distinct from copyright
    1. Rights of performing artists

The subject of the rights of performing artists are their artistic performances, in particular the performances of the actors, singers, musicians, dancers and other persons who perform, sing, act, recite or otherwise interpret literary, musical or other artistic works.

Slovak Republic

Duration of rights of performing artists shall be fifty years and it shall start from the first day of the year following the year in which the fixation of the artistic performance has been made. However, if the fixation of the performance is made public or communicated to the public within this term, the protection shall last fifty years from the first day of the year following the year when the fixation has been made or the communication to the public took place; the term shall be calculated from the earlier event.

2. Rights of producers of phonograms

The subject of rights of producers of phonograms are aural fixations of performances of performing artists or other sounds irrespective of the method by which or medium on which these performances or sounds are fixed.

Duration of rights of phonogram producers shall be fifty years and it shall start on the first day of the year following the year in which the phonogram has been produced. However, if a phonogram has been made public or communicated within this term, the right of producer shall last for 50 years and it shall start on the first day of the year following the year in which it has been made public or in which communication of the phonogram took place; the term shall be calculated from the earlier event.

3. Rights of producers of audiovisual fixations

Duration of the rights shall be fifty years and it shall start on the first day of the year following the year in which the audiovisual fixation has been made. However, if the fixation has been made public or communicated within this term, the right of producer shall last fifty years and it shall start on the first day of the year following the year in which it has been made public or in which communication took place; the term shall be calculated from the earlier event.

4. Rights of radio and television broadcasters and broadcasters communicating their own programmes by wire

Duration of rights shall be fifty years and it shall start on the first day of the year following the year in which the first broadcasting or communication by wire took place.

5. Database right

Database right exists where there has been a substantial investment of financial, human or technical resources in obtaining, verifying or presenting the material constituting the database.

The database right arises automatically, and gives the owner the right to prevent anyone from extracting or re-utilising all or a substantial part of the contents of the database. Duration of the database right is fifteen years from its creation. The term recommences upon any substantial modification made to the database, which results in creation of a "new" database.

6. Rights of publishers of previously unpublished works that are protected by virtue of international agreements or conventions by which the Slovak Republic is bound

Any person who, after expiry of copyright, for the first time makes public or communicates to the public a previously unpublished work shall have copyright to it. The right shall last for twenty-five years from the publication or communication to the public.

Confidential Information

To be protected by law, business information shall be kept secret and confidential and it has to be identifiable and of some potential commercial interest.

Trade secrets

Trade secrets are dealt with in the Commercial Code. Trade secrets consist of all business, manufacturing and technological facts related to the enterprise with actual, or at least potential, tangible or intangible value. Trade secrets are not commonly available in the respective industry and should not be disclosed without the entrepreneur's consent, providing the entrepreneur adequately ensures such non-disclosure. Unless otherwise stipulated by a special Act, the entrepreneur running the enterprise subject to the applicable provisions on trade secrets enjoys the exclusive right to dispose of their enterprise's trade secrets, in particular to authorise its use by a third party and determine the terms and conditions of such use.

Competition

Individuals and legal entities involved in economic competition are entitled both to engage freely in competition for the purpose of economic gain, and to associate in performance of their activities. However, they are obliged to respect legally binding rules of economic competition and shall not be allowed to abuse their involvement in economic competition. An unfair competition conduct and unlawful restrictions on economic competition are regarded as an illegal restriction of economic competition. Illegal restrictions of economic competition are involved in Competition Act No. 136/2001 of Digest, which prohibits anti-competitive agreements (agreements which have the effect of preventing, restricting or distorting competition) unless they have received an individual exemption from the Antimonopoly Office of the Slovak Republic, or are subject to a block exemption which exempts whole categories of agreements.

Unfair competition is regulated by Article 44 to 52 of the Commercial Code under which persons whose rights have been impaired or endangered by unfair

Slovak Republic

competition may demand that the perpetrator abstain from their conduct and remedy the objectionable state of affairs. They may further demand appropriate relief that may be granted in cash, indemnities and the forfeit of the unjustified gains.

Unfair competition shall be such competitive conduct that is contrary to the standard practices of competition and that may be detrimental to other competitors or consumers. The following conduct is mainly regarded as unfair competition:

a) Deceptive advertising;
b) Deceptive description of goods and services;
c) Misrepresentation;
d) Benefiting from the exploitation of a competitor's reputation;
e) Bribery;
f) Defamation;
g) Breach of trade secrets;
h) Endangering of health and the enviroment.

Unfair competition is prohibited.

All other issues are governed by the regime outlined in the European Community chapter.

Useful Industry Contacts

Industrial Property Office of the Slovak Republic is a central state administration body, which has been operating in the field of granting protection on subjects of industrial property.
www.upv.sk/

Chamber of Patent Agents of the Slovak Republic is a self-administered organisation, which protects and enforces the interests of patent attorneys and it supervises the proper practising of their industrial property profession.
www.patentattorneys.sk/

Slovak Bar Association is an independent self-administrative professional organisation currently associating more than 2186 advocates.
www.sak.sk/

Council for Broadcasting and Retransmission
www.rada-rtv.sk

LITA – Society of Authors is a Slovak Literary Agency
www.ifrro.org/members/lita.html

IFPI – International Federation of Phonogram Industry is an organisation representing the international fixation industry.
www.ifpi.sk
www.ifpi.org

Slovak Republic

SLOVGRAM - Joint collecting society for performers and audio video producers.
www.slovgram.sk

SOZA – Society of authors and composers
www.soza.sk

Chapter 25: Slovenia

Slovenia

By Tomaz Ilesic
(Colja, Rojs & Partnerji)

Introduction

Since its birth as an independent country in 1991, Slovenia has been making its best effort to efficiently protect intellectual property rights. Although many important pieces of legislation remained unchanged until very recently, the Law on Industrial Property adopted in 1992 was one of the first new acts to supersede old Yugoslav legislation. The regulation of the field of intellectual property continued in 1995, when the Copyright and Related Rights Act and the Law on Protection of Topographies of Integrated Circuits were adopted. Additional changes were made in 2001 when the new Industrial Property Act was adopted and the Copyright and Related Rights Act was amended. The Act Regulating Customs Measures Relating to Infringements of Intellectual Property Rights was also adopted in 2001. In 2002, the Slovenian Parliament ratified the European Patent Convention and the Patent Law Treaty.

Apart from its own regulatory activities, Slovenia declared itself to be bound by several international treaties to which the former Yugoslavia had acceded prior to its dissolution (Paris Convention, WIPO Convention, Berne Convention, Madrid Agreement, Locarno Agreement, Nice Agreement, etc.)

Since obtaining its status as an independent country, Slovenia has become party to the numerous treaties inter alia to the Patent Cooperation Treaty, TRIPs, European Patent Convention, etc. A full list of applicable legislation may be found on the website of the Slovene Intellectual Property Office (established in 1994, http://www.uil-sipo.si/dok_eng.htm).

Patents

As mentioned in the introduction, Slovenia adopted a new Industrial Property Act ("IPA") in 2001. The enactment of this law was made in order to comply with EU Law and numerous international treaties which bind upon Slovenia. The IPA protects all the categories of industrial property.

Tomaz Ilesic is an attorney with the law firm Colja, Rojs & Partnerji in Ljubljana. Mr. Ilesic specialises in competition law, EU law and international commercial law. Colja, Rojs and Partnerji is one of the largest law firms in Slovenia, specialising in business and commercial law and providing services to both local and foreign clients. The firm also has an office in Belgrade.

Slovenia

Since the Slovene legislation is to a great extent harmonized with international rules, the application made according to provisions of PCT or EPT would satisfy the formalities. Foreign natural and legal persons shall be represented by a patent agent. However, foreign applicants may file applications, perform acts relating to the establishment of the filing date, pay fees, file copies of first applications when claiming the right of priority and receive notifications by the Office relating to those proceedings, without a representative, provided that they communicate to the Office an address for correspondence which is in the territory of Slovenia.

The application made according to the Regulations under the Patent Cooperation Treaty or Implementing Regulations to the European Patent Convention, fulfills all formal requirements. Both systems enable the applications to enter the national phase in Slovenia once the European patent has been granted. SPC is provided for patents applied for after January 1, 1993.

The IPA also provides for a specific type of protection called a "short-term patent" which basically corresponds to utility model protection (known for example in Germany). With the exception of processes, plant varieties or animal breeds, a short-term patent may be granted for inventions which are new, susceptible of industrial application and are the result of a creative effort. The maximum term of a short-term patent is ten years as from the date of filing the application[1].

Trade Marks

According to the IPA, any sign, or any combination of signs, capable of distinguishing the goods or services of one undertaking from those of another undertaking and capable of being graphically represented, in particular words, including personal names, letters, numerals, figurative elements, three dimensional images, including the shape of goods or of their packaging, combination of colours as well as any combination of such signs, shall be eligible for registration as marks.

Slovenia is a member state of the Madrid Agreement and the Madrid Protocol. Therefore, an application for the registration of a trademark in Slovenia can also be filed under Madrid Agreement and Madrid Protocol. International applications are subject to the same procedure (examination on absolute grounds for refusal and the possibility of filing the opposition) as if they had been filed nationally.

Registering a trademark with the Slovenian Intellectual Property Office protects one's rights in Slovenia only. But the filing date of a Slovenian national application can be used as a priority date for the application when applying up to six months later for protection abroad. It can also be used as the basis of an application for an international registration under conditions set up by the Madrid Agreement or Madrid Protocol[2].

Slovenia

Copyright

The Copyright and Related Rights Act ("CRRA") enacted in 1995 already includes quite modern features of copyright protection (computer software, cable TV). It is based on the legal framework of the EU, the Council of Europe, WIPO, WTO, etc. In order to ensure one of its main goals—prevention of counterfeiting—severe penal provisions related to this matter have been included in the Criminal Code. An extensive amendment to the CRRA has been prepared but has not yet been adopted. A draft is available at the Slovenian Intellectual Property Office web site (http://www.uil-sipo.si/dok_eng.htm).

Industrial Design

An industrial design[3] shall be registered for a design to the extent that it is new and has an individual character. A design shall be considered new if no identical design has been made available to the public before the date of filing of the industrial design application or, if priority is claimed, the date of priority. A design shall be considered to have individual character if the overall impression it produces on the informed user differs from the overall impression produced on such a user by any design which has been made available to the public before the date of filing of the application or, if priority is claimed, the date of priority.

The industrial design shall confer on its owner the exclusive right to use it and to prevent any third party not having his consent from using it. The aforementioned use shall cover, in particular, the making, offering, putting on the market, importing, exporting or using of a product to which the design is applied, or stocking such a product for those purposes. An industrial design shall be eligible for copyright protection as from the date on which the design was created or fixed in any form if it fulfills the conditions under which such a protection is conferred under the Act regulating copyright and related rights.

The term of an industrial design shall be one or more periods of five years as from the date of filing up to a total term of 25 years from the date of filing of the application.

An application for the registration of an industrial design in Slovenia can also be filed under the Hague Agreement Concerning the International Deposit of Industrial Designs (Act 1960) to enjoy the same protection in Slovenia as generally conferred on industrial designs by the Slovenian Act. Registering an industrial design with the Slovenian Intellectual Property Office protects your rights in Slovenia only. However the filing date of a Slovenian national application can be used as a priority date for the application when applying up to six months later for protection abroad[4].

Slovenia

Footnotes

[1] Information from SIPO web site, for detailed information see http://www.uil-sipo.si).

[2] For more detailed information see http://www.uil-sipo.si).

[3] ªDesign´ means the appearance of the whole or a part of a product resulting from the features of, in particular, the lines, contours, colours, shape, texture and/or materials of the product itself and/or its ornamentation.

[4] Information from SIPO web site, for detailed information see http://www.uil-sipo.si).

Slovenia

Chapter 26: Spain

Spain

By Hugo Ecija Bernal and Emilio Hurtado
(Ecija Abogados)

Introduction

This report provides a general overview of Spanish Law on intellectual and industrial property law. It gives a brief description of Spanish Law on patents, industrial designs, trademarks and copyright, which are the most important intellectual and industrial property rights.

Topographies of semiconductor products, utility models, biotechnological inventions and plant varieties, as well as other forms of intellectual and industrial property rights, are not covered by this report.

Patents

Legislation

Patent law in Spain is regulated by Law 11/1986 of March 20, on Patents.

Subject matter and patentability

Novelty, inventive step and industrial application are the three requisites for the patentability of inventions. Accordingly, new inventions involving an inventive step and susceptible of industrial application shall be patentable even when the subject-matter is a product consisting of or containing biological material, or a process for producing, processing or using biological material.

Following the provisions of the European Patent Convention, Law 11/1996, the following shall not be regarded as inventions to the extent to which the subject matter of a patent application comprises any of them:

a) Discoveries, scientific theories and mathematical methods.
b) Literary or artistic works or any other aesthetic creation whatsoever, and scientific works.

Hugo Ecija Bernal and Emilio Hurtado are attorneys with Ecija Abogados in Madrid. Ecija Abogados is one of the leading Spanish TMT law firms as recognised by one of Europe's leading legal publications. It is a full service law firm which focuses on the TMT industries, providing services to national and international clients in the public and private sectors. The intellectual property and media departments led by Hugo Ecija have developed a particualrly strong reputation; Mr. Ecija is often named as one of the leading Spanish experts in this field.

Spain

c) Schemes, rules and methods for performing intellectual acts, playing games or doing business, and programs for computers.

d) Presentations of information.

Additionally, methods for treatment of the human or animal body by surgery or therapy and diagnostic methods practised on the human or animal body shall not be regarded as inventions which are susceptible of industrial application.

In any case, the following subject matters shall not be patentable:

1. Inventions, where their commercial exploitation would be contrary to public policy or accepted principles of morality; however, exploitation shall not be deemed to be so contrary merely because it is prohibited by law or regulation. This prohibition includes in particular the following:

   e) Processes for cloning human beings.

   f) Processes for modifying the germ line genetic identity of human beings.

   g) The use of human embryos for industrial or commercial purposes.

   h) Processes for modifying the genetic identity of animals which are likely to cause them suffering without any substantial benefit to mankind or animal, and also animals resulting from those processes.

2. Plant and animal varieties, provided that inventions concerning plants or animals shall however be patentable where the technical feasibility of the invention is not confined to a particular plant or animal variety.

3. Essentially biological processes for obtaining plants or animals[1].

4. The human body, at the various stages of its formation and development, and the simple discovery of one of its elements, including the sequence or partial sequence of a gene[2].

Novelty

An invention shall be deemed to be new if it does not form part of the state of the art, which comprises everything that has been made available to the public in Spain or abroad, before the date of filing of the patent application, by written or oral description, by use or in any other way.

The state of the art shall also be taken to comprise the contents of any Spanish patent or utility model applications, as originally filed, the date of filing of which is prior to that mentioned in the foregoing paragraph, and which were published on or after that date.

Thus, in order to secure its patentability, an invention shall not be disclosed before the filing of a patent application. However, for the purposes of determining the state of the art, disclosures shall be disregarded if occurring within the six months preceding the filing of the application with the Patent Office and as a direct or indirect consequence of:

    a) An obvious breach of confidence towards the applicant or his predecessor in title.

    b) The applicant or his predecessor in title having displayed the invention at official or officially-recognized exhibitions.

    In this case it will be necessary for the applicant, when filing the application, to declare that the invention has actually been exhibited and to produce in support of his declaration a certificate within such term and subject to such conditions as shall be determined in the regulations.

    c) Tests conducted by the applicant or by his predecessor in title, providing they do not involve the exploitation or commercial offering of the invention.

Inventive step

An invention shall be deemed to involve an inventive step if it does not result from the state of the art (excluding the contents of any Spanish patent or utility model applications whose filing date is prior to the date of filing of the patent application) in a manner obvious to a person skilled in the art.

Industrial application

An invention shall be deemed to be capable of industrial application if its object may be manufactured or used in any kind of industry, including agriculture.

Procedure for the grant of a patent

In order to obtain a patent it is necessary to fill in an application including the following information:

    a) A formal petition addressed to the Director of the Patent Office.

    b) A description of the invention for which the patent is sought.

    c) One or more claims.

    d) The drawings referred to in the description or claims, and

    e) An abstract of the invention.

There are two different procedures for the grant of a patent: (a) a general procedure where a report on the state of the art is drafted for the purpose of giving knowledge of the background of the invention necessary to evaluate the novelty and inventive step thereof, and (b) a procedure with prior examination, where the Patent Office performs a deep analysis of the novelty and inventive step requisites as well as of the description of the invention. The latter procedure is voluntary, so that once the report on the state of the art has been published,

Spain

the applicant may opt between the general procedure or the performance of the deep examination.

In the general procedure, once its different steps have been fulfilled, the patent shall be granted regardless of the contents of the report on the state of the art. However, in the procedure with prior examination, the grant or denial of the patent shall depend upon the result of the thorough analysis and the remedy of the objections raised therein.

Both procedures have a common phase until the publication of the report on the state of the art, which comprises the following steps:

1. Within 10 days of receipt of the application the Patent Office performs an examination as to the requirements for the grant of a filing date. This examination comprises formal requirements and patentability requirements, except novelty and inventive step (although novelty is not examined, the Patent office may refuse the patent on the grounds of notorious lack of novelty).

2. If the application does not contain errors or if the relevant errors have been remedied, the Patent Office notifies the applicant that he shall formally request the issue of the report on the state of the art. The request shall be made in writing to the Patent Office and the applicant shall pay the relevant fees. Both the request and the payment of the fees can be made from the beginning of the file, within a term of 15 months since the date of filling the application or, if it had not been done within said term, the Patent Office would notify the applicant of the need to request the report on the state of the art within a term of one month.

3. Publication, comprising the description, the claims and any drawing as filed, shall take place within eighteen months from the date of filing or from the date of priority, if a priority has been claimed. The novelty search report shall be notified to the applicant and laid open to public inspection.

4. A notice on the publication of the report on the state of the art is posted in the Official Industrial Property Bulletin whereupon the procedure is stayed for a term of 6 months within which the applicant may request either the continuance of the general grant procedure or the performance of a prior examination. If the applicant does not expressly elect between the prior examination or the general procedure, the Patent Office shall automatically resolve to continue the general procedure.

Resumption by the General Procedure
Continuance of the general procedure: Remarks by third parties

Both in the case that the applicant has expressly requested the continuance of the general procedure and in the case that there has not been an express election for the general procedure or the procedure with prior examination, the Patent

Office publishes a notice in the Official Industrial Property Bulletin stating that the general grant procedure shall be resumed. Upon such notice there is a two-month term within which any person may file remarks to the novelty and inventive step of the invention based on the report on the state of the art.

Notice of the remarks: Amendment of the claims

At the end of the two-month term referred to above, the Patent Office notifies the applicant of remarks filed by third parties so that within a two-month term he may make observations to the report on the state of the art, comments to the remarks filed by third parties or amendments to the claims in order to avoid a lack of novelty or inventive step.

Grant of the Patent

Upon the end of the two-month term mentioned above, the Patent Office shall examine any amendment to the claims. If the new claims could not be admitted for being an increase or amendment of the object of the invention, the Patent Office shall notify the applicant and grant him a 10-day term to make the allegations he may deem applicable.

Finally, the patent shall be granted whatever the contents of the report on the state of the art or the remarks filed by third parties, but the documents concerning the report on the state of the art and the remarks shall remain open to public inspection.

Resumption by the Procedure with Prior Examination
Continuance of the grant procedure with prior examination

If the applicant makes a request for the performance of a prior examination and pays the applicable fee, the Patent Office will publish the resumption of the grant procedure with prior examination in the Official Industrial Property Bulletin.

Opposition by third parties

Any interested party may, within two months of the examination request being published, oppose the grant of the patent, arguing the failure to satisfy any of the requirements for such a grant. The written opposition shall enclose all appropriate supporting documents.

Thorough examination

Upon the end of the term for filing oppositions, the Patent Office shall carry out a thorough examination of the application including the sufficiency of disclosure, novelty and inventive merit of the subject matter of the patent application.

Spain

If no oppositions have been filed and the examination does not reveal the lack of any requirement which would prevent it, the Patent Office shall grant the patent applied for.

Notice of the result of the examination and of the oppositions

If there are any oppositions, or from the examination performed there arises the lack of any requisite preventing the grant of the patent, the Patent Office shall inform the applicant of the existing objections and shall notify him of the oppositions filed. Within a term of two months from receipt of the notice, the applicant may amend the description and the claims upon the result of the examination as well as reply to the filed oppositions.

Examination of the amendments

Upon the end of the abovementioned term, the Patent Office shall examine the amendments made by the applicant and/or his reply to any opposition filed by third parties.

If there continue to be objections preventing the grant of the patent, the Patent Office shall notify the applicant of the objections and grant him a one-month term to remedy them.

Grant

The Patent Office shall grant the patent when the reply to the objections filed both as a result of the examination and/or of third parties' oppositions, as well as, where applicable, of the examination of the amendments, have been duly remedied.

The notice on the grant of the patent at the Official Industrial Property Bulletin shall include a reference stating that it has been made with prior examination of the novelty and inventive step of the patent's subject matter.

Refusal

The Patent Office shall refuse the patent application if the applicant does not reply to the notices made or if the objections filed are not remedied.

Term of protection

A patent shall have a non-extendible life of twenty years from the date of filing of the application, and shall take effect from the date on which a statement that it has been granted is published, subject to the payment of the applicable renewal fees.

Spain

To whom can a patent be granted: employees' inventions

The right to obtain a patent is vested in the inventor or his successors in title, and it is transferable by all the means recognized by Law.

Where the invention has been made jointly by several persons, the right to obtain a patent shall be held by all of them in common.

Where the same invention has been made by different persons independently, the right to obtain a patent shall belong to the person whose application has the earliest date of filing in Spain, provided that such application is published in accordance with the provisions of Law 11/1986.

The inventor shall have, with respect to the proprietor of the application for the patent or of the patent, the right to be mentioned as such inventor in the patent.

As regards employees' inventions, Law 11/1986 provides that inventions made by an employee during the term of his contract, work or service with a company, and which are the result of research that is explicitly or implicitly the object of his contract, shall belong to the employer. An employee responsible as an inventor shall have no right to additional remuneration for his achievement, except where his personal contribution to the invention and its importance to the company obviously go beyond the explicit or implicit terms of his contract or work.

Inventions made otherwise than in accordance with the conditions referred above belong to the employee making them, provided that where the employee makes an invention related to his professional activity and the knowledge gained within the company has had a decisive influence thereon or he has used means provided by the company, the employer shall have the right to claim ownership of the invention or to reserve a right to its use.

Where the employer claims ownership of an invention or reserves a right to its use, the employee shall have the right to equitable financial remuneration fixed in relation to the invention's industrial and commercial importance and taking into account the value of the means or knowledge provided by the company and the contribution made by the employee himself.

An employee who makes any of the inventions mentioned above, shall duly inform the employer in writing, setting out the necessary data and information so that the latter may, within a period of three months, exercise the relevant rights. Failure to fulfill this obligation shall lead to loss of the rights of the employee.

Inventions for which a patent application or other title of exclusive protection has been filed within a year following expiry of the work or service relationship may be claimed by the employer. Any advance renunciation of the rights granted to the employee by Law 11/1986 shall be null and void.

Spain

Scope of protection

Publication of the patent application in the Official Industrial Property Bulletin, once the applicant has requested the Patent Office to establish the report on the state of the art, confers a provisional protection until the patent is finally granted. Said provisional protection consists of the right to require reasonable remuneration appropriate to the circumstances from any third party who, between the date of that publication and that of the announcement that the patent has been granted, has made use of the invention in a manner that would have been prohibited had the patent already been granted.

A patent shall give its owner the right to prevent any third party from undertaking the following acts without his consent:

a) manufacturing, offering for sale, putting on the market or using the product that is the subject matter of the patent or importing or possessing the product for one of the above-mentioned purposes;

b) making use of a process that is the subject matter of a patent or offering such use when the third party is aware, or the circumstances make it obvious, that use of the process without the consent of the patent's owner is prohibited;

c) offering for sale, putting on the market or using the product directly obtained by the process that is the subject matter of the patent or importing or possessing the said product for any of the above-mentioned purposes.

A patent shall also entitle its owner to prevent a third party from handing over or offering to hand over to unauthorized persons without his consent, elements related to an essential part of the invention to be used for putting the invention into effect, when the third party knows, or the circumstances make it obvious, that such elements are capable of putting the invention into effect and are to be used for that purpose.

The rights conferred by the patent shall not extend to:

a) acts carried out in private and not for any commercial purpose;

b) acts carried out for experimental purposes related to the subject matter of the patented invention;

c) the extemporaneous preparation of medicines in pharmacies carried out singly in making up a prescription and acts related to the medicines thus prepared;

d) use of the subject matter of the patented invention on board vessels of countries of the Paris Union, in the body of the vessel, in the machinery, tackle, gear and other accessories, when such vessels temporarily or accidentally enter Spanish waters, provided that the subject matter of the patent is used exclusively for the needs of the vessel;

e) use of the subject matter of the patented invention in the construction or operation of aircraft or land vehicles of country members of the Paris Union, or of accessories of such aircraft or land vehicles, when those aircraft or land vehicles temporarily or accidentally enter Spanish territory;

f) acts provided for in Article 27 of the Convention of December 7, 1944, on international civil aviation, when such acts relate to aircraft of a State to which the provisions of the said Article apply.

The rights conferred by the patent shall not extend to acts relating to a product protected by that patent once that product has been placed on the market in the territory of a European Union Member State by the holder of the patent or with his consent.

The proprietor of a patent shall not be entitled to prevent persons who, in good faith and before the date of priority, exploited in Spain what proves to constitute the subject of such patent, or made serious and effective preparations to do so, from continuing or commencing the exploitation thereof in the same manner as they had been doing up to then, or for which they had made the preparations, and to an extent adequate to satisfy the reasonable needs of their business.

Designs

Legislation

Industrial designs are regulated by Law 20/2003, of July 7, on the Legal Protection of the Industrial Design.

Registration requisites: novelty and individual character

According to Law 20/2003 a design is defined as the appearance of the whole or a part of a product resulting from the features, in particular the lines, contours, colors, shape, texture or materials, of the product itself or its ornamentation.

A design shall be protected to the extent that it is new and has individual character. For legal purposes, a design shall be considered to be new if no identical design has been made available to the public before the date of filing of the application for registration of the design for which protection is claimed, or, if priority is claimed, the date of priority.

Designs shall be deemed to be identical if their features differ only in immaterial details.

A design shall be considered to have individual character if the overall impression it produces on the informed user differs from the overall impression produced on such a user by any design which has been made available to the public before the date of filing the application for registration or, if a priority is claimed, the date of priority.

Spain

In order to assess the novelty and individual character of the relevant design, a design shall be deemed to have been made available to the public if it has been published, exhibited, used in trade or disclosed, before the date of filing the application for registration or, if a priority is claimed, the date of priority, except where these events could not reasonably have become known in the normal course of business to the circles specialized in the sector.

A disclosure shall not be taken into consideration for these purposes if the disclosure has been made:

a) by the designer, his successor in title, or a third person as a result of information provided or action taken by the designer or his successor in title; and

b) during the 12-month period preceding the date of filing of the application or, if a priority is claimed, the date of priority.

The same shall also be applicable if the design has been made available to the public as a consequence of an abuse in relation to the designer or his successor in title.

Right to the registered design

The right to the design vests in the designer or his successor in title. If two or more persons have jointly developed a design, the right to the design shall vest in them jointly absent any agreement to the contrary.

Where the same design has been created by different persons independently, the right to register the design shall belong to the person whose application has the earliest date of filing in Spain, provided that such registration is published in accordance with the provisions of Law 20/2003.

Where a design is developed by an employee in the execution of his duties or following the instructions given by his employer, or on commission within the framework of a services relationship, the right to register the design shall vest in the employer or the party that commissioned the making of the design, unless otherwise agreed in the relevant employment or services contract.

Registration procedure

The author of the design shall have the right to be mentioned as such in the application, the Registry and in the publication of the registered design.

In order to register an industrial design it is necessary to fill in an application with the identity and signature of the applicant or his representative, a description reproducing the design, and a certificate of having paid the applicable registration fees.

The Patent Office will examine if the application has any formal defects in which case it shall notify them to the applicant and grant him a term of one month to remedy the defects. If the defects are remedied, the application shall be published in the Official Industrial Property Bulletin. If the defects are not remedied, the application shall be regarded void.

Once the application has been published, there is a two-month term for any interested party to file an opposition deed to the registration application. The applicant shall be notified of any opposition granting him a 15-day term to reply if he so chooses.

If the application has not received any opposition or if they are deemed ungrounded, registration shall be granted. If the opposition is sustained, the registration shall be refused. The applicant shall be notified of the final decision so that within 15 days he can pay the applicable fees or file an administrative appellation against the refusal.

Term of protection

Registration of the design shall be granted for a period of five years as from the date of the filing of the application. The right holder may have the term of protection renewed for one or more successive periods of five years each, up to a total term of 25 years from the date of filing.

Scope of protection

Registration of the design shall confer on its holder the exclusive right to use it and to prevent any third party not having his consent from using it. The aforementioned use shall cover, in particular, the making, offering, putting on the market, importing and exporting or using of a product in which the design is incorporated or to which it is applied or stocking such a product for those purposes.

The rights conferred by the registered design are effective upon its publication, but the registration application confers a provisional protection until the registered design is published, against any third party to whom, even before the date of publication of the registration, the registration application and its contents had been notified. Such provisional protection consists of a right to require reasonable remuneration from any third party who, between the date of the registration application and that of publication of the registered design, has made use of the design that would have been prohibited after that date. This provisional protection can be claimed only after the publication of the registered design.

The protection conferred by the registered design shall extend to any design which does not produce on the informed user a different overall impression. In

Spain

assessing the scope of protection, the degree of freedom of the designer in developing his design shall be taken into consideration.

The rights conferred by a registered design shall not be exercised in respect of:

a) acts done privately and for non-commercial purposes;
b) acts done for experimental purposes;
c) acts of reproduction for the purpose of making citations or of teaching, provided that such acts are compatible with fair trade practice and do not unduly prejudice the normal exploitation of the design, and that mention is made of the source.
d) the equipment and repair of ships and aircraft registered in a third country when these temporarily enter the Spanish territory or the importation of spare parts and accessories for the purpose of repairing such craft.

The rights conferred by a registered design shall not extend to acts relating to a product in which a design included within its scope of protection, when the product has been put on the market in the European Economic Area by the holder of the design or with his consent.

Additionally, the holder of a registered design shall not be entitled to prevent third parties who can establish that before the date of filing of the application, or, if a priority is claimed, before the date of priority, have in good faith commenced to use in Spain, or have made serious and effective preparations to that end, of a design included within the scope of protection of a registered design, from continuing or commencing the exploitation thereof in the same manner as they had been doing up to then, or for which they had made the preparations.

Trade Marks

Legislation

Trade marks in Spain are regulated by the Trademark Law 17/2001, of December 7, and Royal Decree 687/2002, of July 12, approving the Regulations for the implementation of Law 17/2001.

Definition and requisites

Under Spanish Trademark Law, a trade mark is defined as any sign capable of being represented graphically and capable of distinguishing in the market the goods or services of one undertaking from those of other undertakings.

Such signs include without limitation the following:

a) Words or words combinations, including those used to identify persons;
b) Images, forms, symbols and drawings;
c) Letters, numbers and any combination thereof;
d) Three dimensional forms including wrappings, packaging and the form

of the product or its presentation;
e) Sound signs; and
f) Any combination of the above.

Law 17/2001 provides certain prohibitions for the registration of trademarks, which are known as absolute and relative prohibitions.

Under the absolute prohibitions, the following signs shall not be registered as a trade mark:

a) Signs which are not capable of being represented graphically and capable of distinguishing in the market the goods or services of one undertaking from those of other undertakings.
b) Signs which are devoid of distinctive character.
c) Signs which consist exclusively of signs or indications which may serve, in trade, to designate the kind, quality, quantity, intended purpose, value, geographical origin, the time of production of the goods or of rendering of the service, or other characteristics of the goods or services.
d) Signs which consist exclusively of signs or indications which have become customary to designate goods or services in the current language or in the bona fide and established practices of the trade.
e) Signs which consist exclusively of the shape which results from the nature of the goods themselves or the shape of goods which is necessary to obtain a technical result, or the shape which gives substantial value to the goods.
f) Signs which are contrary to the Law, public policy or accepted principles of morality.
g) Signs which may deceive the public, for instance as to the nature, quality or geographical origin of the goods or service.
h) Signs which are applied to identify wines or spirits and containing or consisting of geographical indications of origin identifying wines or spirits with no such geographical origin, even when the true origin of the goods is indicated or the geographical indication is used translated or along with such expressions as "kind", "type", "style", "imitation" and the like.
i) Signs which introduce or imitate the escutcheon, flag, decorations and other emblems of Spain, its Autonomous Communities, its towns, provinces or other local entities, unless the appropriate consent has been given.
j) Signs which have not been authorized by the competent authorities and are to be refused pursuant to Article 6ter of the Paris Convention.
k) Signs which include badges, emblems or escutcheons other than those

Spain

covered by Article 6ter of the Paris Convention and which are of particular public interest, unless the consent of the appropriate authorities to their registration has been given.

Under the relative prohibitions the following shall not be registered as trade marks:

1. Earlier trade marks.
   a) Signs which are identical with an earlier trade mark designating identical goods, services, or activities.
   b) Signs where, because of their identity with or similarity to an earlier trade mark and the identity or similarity of the goods or services they designate, there exists a likelihood of confusion on the part of the public; the likelihood of confusion includes the likelihood of association with the earlier trade mark.

2. Earlier trade names.
   a) Signs which are identical with an earlier trade name designating activities which are identical with the goods or services for which the trade mark is applied for.
   b) Signs where, because of their identity with or similarity to an earlier trade name and the identity or similarity of the designated activities with or to the goods or services for which the trade mark is applied for, there exists a likelihood of confusion on the part of the public; the likelihood of confusion includes the likelihood of association with the earlier trade mark.

3. Registered trade marks and trade names that are well known and have a reputation.

A sign shall not be registered as a trade mark where it is identical with or similar to an earlier trade mark or trade name although it is applied for to be registered for goods or services which are not similar to those protected by said earlier signs, where, because the same are well known or have a reputation in Spain, the use of that trade mark may indicate a connection between the goods or services covered thereby and the proprietor of those signs or, in general, where that use, without due cause, would take unfair advantage of, or be detrimental to, the distinctive or well-known character or the reputation of those earlier signs.

4. Other earlier rights.

The following shall not be registered as trade marks without due consent:
   a) A personal name or a portrayal identifying a person other than the applicant for the trade mark.
   b) The name, surname, pseudonym or any other sign identifying a person other than the applicant to the public at large.

c) Signs reproducing, copying or transforming creations protected by a copyright or other industrial property right

d) The trade name or designation, business or company name of a legal person used before the filing or priority date of the trade mark applied for to identify in the course of trade a person other than the applicant if, because it is identical with or similar to those signs and because its scope of application is identical or similar, there exists a likelihood of confusion on the part of the public.

Trademarks may be classified depending on the signs or devices composing them, and their function.

According to their composition, trademarks may be: (a) denominative (words or combined words), (b) graphic or emblematic (images, shapes, symbols or graphics), (c) mixed (combining denominative and graphic signs), and (d) three-dimensional (packaging).

According to their function, trademarks may be: (a) product or service trademarks (distinguishing products or services), (b) derivative (which is a non-substantial variation of another trademark also registered), (c) collective (distinguishing in the marketplace products and services produced or rendered either by an association or by its members), (d) of warranty (certifying the common characteristics—source, quality and composition—of products and services produced or rendered by people duly authorized and controlled by the trademark owner).

Procedure for the grant of a trademark
<u>Application</u>

The application for trade mark registration shall contain at least the following:

a) A request for the registration of a trade mark.
b) An identification of the applicant.
c) A representation of the trade mark.
d) A list of the goods or services in respect of which the registration is requested.

The application shall be subject to the payment of a fee, which shall be determined by the number of classes of goods or services in the international classification established under the Nice Agreement, of June 15, 1957.

The date of filing of an application shall be the date on which the competent body, as provided in Law 17/2001, receives the documents containing the elements referred above.

Spain

Formal examination

The competent body for receiving the application shall examine whether: the trade mark application satisfies the requirements for the accordance of a date of filing; the application fee has been paid; the trade mark application complies with all other formal requirements laid down in the implementing regulations; the applicant has capacity to apply for a trade mark.

If it follows from the examination that the application has any irregularity or deficiency, the application proceeding shall be stayed and the applicant will be given a one-month term (two months for those domiciled abroad when the irregularities refer to the minimum requisites to obtain a filing date) to remedy the same or submit all appropriate arguments, as the case may be.

When the competent body examining the trade mark application is an Autonomous Community it shall transmit to the Spanish Patent and Trade Mark Office, along with all process, applications that passed the formal examination or remedied the deficiencies noted.

Lawfulness examination

Upon receiving the trade mark application, the Spanish Patent and Trade Mark Office shall examine whether the application is contrary to public policy or accepted principles of morality. If the Spanish Patent and Trade Mark Office identifies any legal defect, it shall notify the interested party so that within a one-month term he may file the arguments he deems fit. If the application does not pass this examination it shall be refused.

Publication of application and notice to holders of earlier rights

If the lawfulness examination is passed, the application shall be published in the Official Industrial Property Bulletin for a term of two months, so that anyone considering that a grievance exists may oppose the trade mark registration.

The Spanish Patent and Trade Mark Office shall notify the publication of the application, purely for informative purposes, to the proprietors of earlier registered or applied for signs so that they may file an opposition to the registration of the new application.

Thorough examination

Upon expiry of the term for filing oppositions, the application is examined to assess whether it falls within any of the absolute prohibitions referred to above (as set out in section. 5.1 of Law 17/2001) and whether it consists of the name, surname, pseudonym, image or any other sign that the general public identifies with a person other than the applicant (according to section 9.1.b) of Law 17/2002).

Spain

When oppositions or third-party observations are filed, or it follows from the examination that the application falls within any of the abovementioned prohibitions, the proceeding shall be stayed and the applicant shall be notified of the oppositions or observations made and the objections noted ex officio in order that arguments may be filed within a 1 month term from the date of publication of the stay.

The applicant may amend the application for the purpose of limiting the products or services or withdrawing from the whole the element causing the objection, provided that such amendment does not substantially alter the trade mark as it was applied for.

Grant

If the trade mark applied for does not fall within any prohibition and if no opposition has been filed against it, the Spanish Patent and Trademark Office shall grant the trade mark.

Likewise, upon expiry of the term set out for replying to the stay of the proceeding resolved on thorough examination, with or without the applicant replying, the Spanish Patent and Trade Mark Office shall resolve to grant or refuse the registration of the trade mark, succinctly specifying in the latter event the grounds and earlier rights prompting such refusal.

If the trade mark had been granted, its proprietor shall withdraw the certificate of registration of the trade mark and will not be obliged to pay any fee, until the renewal date thereof (10 years from the application date).

Term of protection

A trademark is granted for 10 years and it can be renewed for further 10 year periods without limitation.

Scope of protection

A trade mark registration shall confer on the proprietor exclusive rights to use the trade mark in the course of trade.

The proprietor of a registered trade mark may prevent third parties not having his consent from using in the course of trade:

a) Any sign which is identical with the trade mark in relation to goods or services which are identical with those for which the trade mark is registered.

b) Any sign where, because of its identity with or similarity to the trade mark and the identity or similarity of the goods or services, there exists a likelihood of confusion on the part of the public; the likelihood of confusion includes the likelihood of association between the sign and trade mark.

Spain

c) Any sign which is identical or similar in relation to goods or services which are not similar to those for which the trade mark is registered, where the latter is well known or has a reputation in Spain and where use of that sign without due cause may indicate a connection between those goods or services and the proprietor of the trade mark or, in general, where such use can take unfair advantage of, or be detrimental to, the distinctive character or the reputation of such registered trade mark.

When the requirements listed in the preceding paragraph are satisfied, the following may in particular be restricted:

a) Affixing the sign to the goods or their packaging.
b) Offering the goods, putting them on the market or stocking them for these purposes under that sign, or offering or supplying services thereunder.
c) Importing or exporting the goods under the sign.
d) Using the sign on business papers and in advertising.
e) Using the sign in interconnected communications networks and as a domain name.
f) Affixing the sign to wrapping, packaging, labels or other means identifying or decorating the goods or service, processing or providing the same, or manufacturing, making, offering, putting on the market, importing, exporting or stocking any of those means including the sign, where there is a likelihood that those means may be used to do any of the things that would be restricted under the above-mentioned subparagraphs.

The proprietor of a registered trade mark may prevent traders or distributors from removing that trade mark without his express consent, although he may not prevent their separately adding their own trade marks or distinctive signs, provided that this is not detrimental to the distinctive character of the main trade mark.

The above shall apply to an unregistered trade mark that is "well known" in Spain, within the meaning of article 6bis of the Paris Convention.

The rights conferred by a trade mark registration shall not entitle the proprietor to prohibit its use by third parties for goods which have been put on the market in the European Economic Area under that trade mark by the proprietor or with his consent, except where there exist legitimate reasons for the proprietor to oppose further commercialization of the goods, especially where the condition of the goods is changed or altered after they have been put on the market.

The rights conferred by a trade mark shall not entitle the proprietor to prohibit third parties from using in the course of trade, provided that such a use takes place in accordance with honest practices in industrial or commercial matters:

a) his own name or address;
b) indications concerning the kind, quality, quantity, intended purpose, value, geographical origin, the time of production of the goods or of rendering of the service, or other characteristics of the goods or service;
c) the trade mark, where it is necessary to indicate the intended purpose of a product or service, in particular as accessories or spare parts.

The rights conferred by the registration of a trade mark may only be enforced on third parties after the registration is published. However, the application for trade mark registration confers on the proprietor, from the date of publication, provisional protection consisting of the right to claim a fair and reasonable compensation if a third party should have undertaken, between that date and the date of publication of registration, a use of the trade mark which would be prohibited after that period.

That same provisional protection will apply even before application is published vis-a-vis a person who was notified of the filing and contents of such application.

The provisional protection may only be claimed after the publication of the registration of the trade mark.

The rights conferred by a trade mark registration shall not entitle the proprietor to prohibit its use by third parties for goods which have been put on the market in the European Economic Area under that trade mark by the proprietor or with his consent.

Copyright and Related Rights

Legislation

Intellectual property rights are regulated by Law 1/1996 of April 12, on Intellectual Property, which has consolidated into a single Law the following previous intellectual property laws.

Scope and subject matter of protection

In relation to the classification of the subject matter of copyright, Law 1/1996 includes a broad statement dealing with the description of the subject matter of protection, as well as some particular provisions specifying the categories of protected works.

Generally speaking, the subject matter of protection is all original literary, artistic or scientific works expressed through any tangible or intangible means, including the following categories of works:

(a) Books, booklets, speeches, lectures, reports, pamphlets and any other works of the same kind;
(b) Musical works, with or without words;

Spain

(c) Dramatic and musical dramatic works, choreography, pantomimes and in general dramatic works;

(d) Cinematographic works and any other audiovisual works;

(e) Sculptures, paintings, drawings, engravings, lithographies, comic strips, etc;

(f) Projects, plans, models and designs of architectonic and engineering works;

(g) Graphics, maps and designs related to topography, geography and science;

(h) Photographic works and works expressed by any mean similar to photography;

(i) Computer programs;

(j) Databases and compilations;

(k) The title of a work if it is original shall be protected as part of the underlying work.

Law 1/1996 recognises certain material which is protected under a different arrangement from that afforded to original literary, artistic and scientific works.

Consequently, the law regulates separately from the rights of authors of literary, artistic and scientific works, the rights of phonogram and sound recordings producers, broadcasting entities and performers (Book II of Spanish Law 1/1996 under the title: "Other Intellectual Property Rights").

Authors' exclusive rights

Exclusive rights granted to copyright owners are grouped within the three classic categories: the right of reproduction, the right of distribution and the right of communication to the public of the work.

The author of a work shall have the exclusive right to exercise the exploitation rights over his work and particularly, the rights of reproduction, distribution, public communication and transformation.

Law 1/1996 includes as exploitation rights certain rights such as the Resale Royalty Right/Droit d'suite and the Right of Reconsideration or Right of Withdrawal.

Authors of plastic art works (with the exclusion of works of applied art) shall have the right to receive from the seller a participation in any resale thereof made by public auction, in a commercial office or with the intervention of a commercial trader or agent.

The author is granted the right to withdraw the work from trade after assignment of the relevant exploitation rights, subject to two conditions: (i) that he indemnify the assignee for the prejudices caused by exercise of this right and (ii) that if subsequently the author decides to exploit the work again, he shall offer the relevant exploitation rights to the original assignee at the time of exercising the right of withdrawal and under reasonably similar terms.

Author of protected works and beneficiary of the exclusive rights

Only the natural persons who create works may be deemed to be authors and therefore first beneficiaries of the relevant rights and legal persons or entities may hold copyright as subsequent beneficiaries thereof only by virtue of express conveyance by the author/authors.

However, there are exceptions to this principle, such as in the case of "collective works" whose rights are vested initially to the "natural or legal entity under whose name the work has been disclosed" pursuant to Section 8 of the Spanish Law. Another exception to the aforementioned general principle applies in the case of software programs made by an employee, in which case Spanish Law states that unless otherwise agreed by the parties, the economic rights of a software program created by an employee—in furtherance of his duties or following the instructions of the employer—shall vest to the employer.

Moral rights

Spanish Law affords authors moral rights, including the right of paternity and the right to object to any distortion, mutilation or other derogatory treatment of the work. These rights constitute the traditional moral rights of paternity and integrity, which are declared to be perpetual, inalienable and imprescriptible as opposed to the economic rights.

In accordance with the above, Spanish Law recognizes the existence of two kinds of rights attached to copyrighted works: rights of an economic and personal character.

Additionally, the author shall enjoy certain inalienable rights. These rights include the traditional moral rights of paternity and integrity and others such as the right to decide whether or not the work shall be published and how, the right to withdraw the work from the public due to a change of his intellectual or moral convictions or the right of access to the sole or rare copy of the work for the purpose of exercising his right of disclosure.

Footnotes

[1] Without prejudice to the patentability of inventions concerning a microbiological or other technical process or a product obtained by means of such processes.

[2] However, an element isolated from the human body or otherwise obtained by means of a technical process, including the sequence or partial sequence of a gene, may constitute a patentable invention, even if the structure of that element is identical with that of a natural element.

Spain

Useful Industry Contacts

Oficina de Harmonización del Mercado Interior (OAMI)
Office for Harmonisation in the Internal Market (OAMI)
Avenida de Europa, 4
03008 Alicante
Tel. : (+34) 965-139-100
Fax: (+34) 965-139-173

Ministerio de Educación y Cultura (Registro de Propiedad Intelectual)
Ministry of Education and Culture (Copyright Registry)
C/ Zurbarán, 1
28010 Madrid
Tel.:(+34) 91-593-08.70
Fax : (+34) 91-447-72-41

Oficina Española de Patentes y Marcas (OEPM)
Spanish Patent and Trade Mark Office (OEPM)
C/ Panamá 1
28071 Madrid
Tel.:(+34) 91-349-53-00
Fax : (+34) 91-457-22-80

Instituto Nacional de Investigación y Tecnología Agraria y Alimentaría (INIA)
Spanish Plant Variety Right Protection
Carretera Coruña Km, 7'5
28040 Madrid
Tel. : (+34) 913-47-66-00
Fax : (+34) 915-94-27-68

Sociedad General de Autores y Editores (SGAE)
General Society of Authors and Editors of Spain (SGAE)
Fernando VI, 4
28004 Madrid
Tel. : (+34) 913-499-550 /913-499-500

Centro Español de Derechos Reprográficos (CEDRO)
Spanish Centre of Reprographic Rights (CEDRO)
C/ Monte Esquinza nº 14, 3º dcha,
28010 Madrid.
Tel. : (+34) 91-308-63-30

Asociación de Gestión de Derechos Intelectuales (AGEDI)
Association of Management of Intellectual Property Rights (AGEDI)
C/ Pintor Juan Gris, nº 4, 2 p. Izda,
28016 Madrid.
Tel. : (+34) 91-555-81-96

Artistas Intérpretes o Ejecutantes, Sociedad de Gestión de España (AIE)
Artists and Performers Spanish Collecting Society (AIE)
C/ Prìncipe de Vergara, nº 9, bajo dcha,
28001 Madrid.
Tel. : (+34) 91-781-98-50

Spain

Visual, Entidad de Gestión de Artistas Plásticos (VEGAP)
Plastic Artists Collecting Society (VEGAP)
C/ Gran Vía n° 16, 5° dcha,
28013 Madrid.
Tel. : (+34) 91-532-66-32

Entidad de Gestión de Derechos de los Productores Audiovisuales (EGEDA)
Audiovisual Producers Collecting Society (EGEDA)
Ciudad de la Imagen, Luis Buñuel 2 - 3°
28223 Pozuelo de Alarcón (Madrid).
Tel. : (+34) 91-512-16-10

Artistas Intérpretes, Sociedad de Gestión (AISGE)
Artists and Actors Collecting Society (AISGE)
C/ Gran Vía, n° 22 duplicado 5° dcha,
28013 Madrid.
Tel. : (+34) 91-521-04-12

Asociación Derechos de Autor de Medios Audiovisuales (DAMA)
Association of Audiovisual Media Rights (DAMA)
C/ Fernanflor n° 8, 2° C
28014 Madrid.

Tel. : (+34) 91-420-08-88/ 91-369-43-19

Chapter 27: Sweden

Sweden

By Bengt Eliasson and Helena Östblom
(Zacco Sweden AB)

Introduction
Present status of intellectual property

In Sweden, as in the rest of the European Union, intellectual property is gaining more attention and becoming ever more important. One reason is that many companies have started to realize the economic value of intellectual property and also the importance of protecting their rights. The areas where intellectual property plays an important role varies from art and literature to the fields of biotechnology and information technology.

The law regarding intellectual property is changing and growing and thus today there are several projects at the Justice department dealing with a wide range of laws such as a new design law, trademark law and copyright law.

Legislation

The main Acts on Intellectual Property in Sweden are the Patents Act (1967:837), the Designs Act of 1970, amended as of July 1, 2002 due to the Directive 98/71/EC on the legal protection of designs, the Trade Marks Act (1960:644), which implements the Directive 89/104/EEC to approximate the laws of the member states relating to trade marks and the Copyrights Act (1960:729).

Patents
Legislation

Patents in Sweden are regulated under the Patents Act (1967:837).

The application procedure

A patent can be obtained either as a Swedish patent or as a European Patent validated in Sweden, in both situations either by filing directly with the Swedish Patent Office or the EPO as appropriate, or by entering into the national phase of a PCT application.

Bengt Eliasson and Helena Östblom are attorneys with Zacco Sweden AB in Stockholm. Zacco Sweden AB is one of Europe's leading firms of patent and trademark attorneys with six offices throughout Denmark, Norway and Sweden. The firm provides a full range of IP services, including representation of overseas clients towards the EPO and OHIM, and litigation through its correspondent law firm, Zacco Legal.

Sweden

A Swedish patent is obtained by application to the Swedish Patent Office in accordance with the Patents Act and its implementing regulations. The Swedish Patent Office carries out a full formal and material examination. If granted, the patent will be published, giving third parties a nine month period to oppose. The decision of the Swedish Patent Office in the opposition proceedings can be appealed to the Patent Court of Appeal and in certain cases to the Supreme Administrative court.

If a European Patent is granted, the patent becomes valid in Sweden only if a full Swedish translation of the patent is filed with the Swedish Patent Office together with the publication fee no later than three months from the date of grant.

How long does a patent last?

Patents are granted for a period of 20 years from the filing date of the application, subject to the payment of annuities starting at the 3rd year after filing. It is possible to obtain SPC's as discussed in the European Community chapter.

To whom can a patent be granted?

The right to apply for a patent belongs to the inventor(s) or his or her assignees. If a patent application is filed by a person or entity other than the inventor, the name of the inventor must be stated in the application.

If an employee has made an invention during the course of his or her normal duties, and the invention relates to the activities of the employer or to a specific assignment given by the employer to the employee, the employer is entitled to have the invention assigned to itself—under certain circumstances against payment of compensation to the employee.

It is possible to make different arrangements under individual employment contracts, but the employee's right to compensation is mandatory.

The right to inventions made by employees at universities, public research institutions, hospitals, etc. is governed under a separate act, which shall not be dealt with here.

Once granted, is the patent safe?

A patent may be declared invalid, in whole or in part, by a decision of the courts. The validity of a patent can be challenged throughout the life of the patent, and even after the patent has expired or ceased.

What rights does a patent give?

Once a patent has been granted, the patentee is entitled to prevent others from exploiting any invention which falls within the scope of the patent.

Sweden

Infringement proceedings

In Sweden, a patent is enforced by applying for an injunction to the competent District court or by applying for a preliminary injunction to the same court if the conditions to obtain a preliminary injunction are fulfilled.

Designs

Legislation

Designs are regulated under the Designs Act of 1970, amended as of July 1, 2002, due to the Directive 98/71/EC on the legal protection of designs. A Swedish design registration covers Sweden.

What is a design?

The definition of a design is as discussed in the European Community Chapter. In Sweden, the distinction between trade marks and designs is blurred as discussed in the UK chapter.

It is possible to obtain a design registration for spare parts, but only for 15 years, as opposed to other designs where the design registration lasts for 25 years provided renewal fees are paid every five years.

Design registrations have an overlap with copyrights, but it is expressly provided for in the Copyright Act that a copyright does not exclude the owner from also obtaining a design registration.

The application procedure

A design registration is obtained by application to the Swedish Patent Office in accordance with the Designs Act and its implementing regulations, and the application procedure is substantially as discussed regarding registered community designs in the European Community chapter. It is also possible to obtain protection in Sweden through a community design registration

The Swedish Patent Office carries out a formal examination, but no material examination in particular of whether the design is new and has individual character.

On the request of the applicant and the payment of an additional official fee, the Swedish Patent Office conducts a limited search of other facts of which the Swedish Patent Office has knowledge. The search report is provided for the guidance of the applicant only.

A straightforward design application should be registered within 3-6 months of filing.

The design registration is published, but it is possible to defer publication for a period of 6 months from the date of application or the date of priority, if priority is claimed.

Opposition may be filed after the design has been registered and published. The opposition period is two months as of the publication date.

Prior disclosure - 12 month grace period
In Sweden, registered designs also benefit from the 12-month grace period in respect of the applicants prior disclosure as discussed regarding registered community designs in the European Community Chapter.

The employment relationship
There is no provision in the Designs Act similar to that in the Community Design Regulation that designs created in an employment relationship belong to the employer, but it is generally acknowledged that designs created in an employment relationship are assigned to the employer also without an express provision to this effect in the employment contract. This does not include a possible copyright in the work created by the employee and it is therefore recommended to include an express provision to this effect in the employment contract.

Infringement
The owner of a design right has the exclusive right as discussed regarding registered community designs in the European Community Chapter.

There is no precedence under the Designs Act, but in the doctrine it is expected that design registrations will have a rather narrow scope of protection.

Trade Marks

Legislation
Trade marks in Sweden are regulated under the Trade Marks Act (1960:644), which implements the Directive 89/104/EEC to approximate the laws of the member states relating to trade marks. Trade mark rights can be established by registration or by use.

Registered trade marks
A registered trade mark right is established by application to the Swedish Patent Office for the goods and services covered by the registration. It is also possible to obtain protection in Sweden through a community trademark registration or an international registration designating Sweden.

Registrability and the application procedure
The types of marks that can be registered are substantially as discussed in the European Community chapter.

Sweden

The Swedish Patent Office conducts an ex officio examination including prior rights which includes not only national Swedish trademarks, CTMs and International trade marks designating Sweden, but also company names and family names.

If the mark is accepted, it will be registered and advertised, thereby giving third parties a two-month period to oppose the registration. The decision of the Swedish Patent Office in the opposition proceedings can be appealed to the Patent Court of Appeal and in certain cases further to the Supreme Administrative court.

A straightforward trade mark application without office actions should be registered within 6-8 months of filing.

How long does a trade mark registration last?

A trade mark registration is valid for 10 years from the date of registration, but is renewable in perpetuity for further 10-year periods upon payment of renewal fees.

The registration can be cancelled, in full or in part, by a decision of the courts brought by a third party for substantially the same reasons as discussed in the European Community chapter.

Unregistered trade marks

An unregistered trade mark is established by use of the trade mark in Sweden, and covers the goods and services for which the trade mark is used and continues to be used. An unregistered trade mark is furthermore only protected in the area where it is used. The trade mark right thus expires, if and to the extent the trade mark is not used.

In principle, an unregistered trade mark enjoys the same protection as a registered trade mark.

Advantages of registration

A trade mark registration constitutes prima facie evidence of a trade mark right, which makes it substantially easier to enforce, assign and license registered trade marks. Further, a registered trade mark can be enforced for five years after the trade mark was last used, and if the use is resumed (without the trade mark registration having been cancelled), the registered trade mark preserves its priority date.

While trade marks do not need to be registered, it is recommended not to rely on an unregistered trade mark right at least for important marks.

What rights does a trade mark give?

A trade mark gives the owner exclusive rights to prevent others from:
1. using a sign identical to the mark in relation to identical goods or services, or

Sweden

2. using a sign identical or similar to the mark in relation to identical or similar goods or services, if there is a likelihood of confusion, including a risk of association, on part of the public, and
3. irrespective the limitation in 2. to identical or similar goods or services, also in relation to dissimilar goods or services, if the mark has a reputation in Sweden and the use takes unfair advantage of or is detrimental to the reputation of the mark.

Domain names and brand protection on the internet

The right to use a .se domain name is derived from a contract between the registrant and the company Nic-se who is administering the .se top level domain. The registration of a domain name does not give the registrant any exclusive rights by law.

Since April 2003, Sweden has a new dispute solution called Alternative Dispute Resolution (ATF). The dispute solution is intended to solve disputes where the holder of the domain name does not have any legal right or legitimate interest in the name used as a domain name and the domain name has been registered or used in bad faith.

Copyright and Related Rights

Legislation

In Sweden, copyright is regulated under the Copyrights Act of (1960:729).

Do I need to register copyright?

It is not possible to register copyright in Sweden.

Copyright notice

It is not necessary, but common to attach a copyright notice to the work, e.g. setting out the © symbol followed by the copyright owner's name and date of publication. There is no precedence as to its value in infringement proceedings.

Term

The term of copyright in Sweden is as discussed in the European Community chapter.

Related rights

Rights similar to but distinct from copyright also apply in Sweden to protect:
- the work of performing artists (such as musicians, actors and dancers) in respect of recording and distributing copies of their performances;
- sound and movie recordings in respect of copying or making such recordings available to the public;

- radio and TV broadcasts in respect of their broadcast or otherwise being made available to the public;
- photographs in respect of their copying or being made available to the public;
- titles by prohibiting the publication of literary and artistic works under a title, which may cause confusion with the title of a prior work or its author; and
- catalogues or databases, where there has been a substantial investment of financial, human or technical resources in obtaining, verifying or presenting the material constituting the database.

Further, the author has moral rights in his or her copyright works. They prevent, among other things, 'derogatory treatment' of works and can require the author's name to appear with the work.

Status of latest European Community directive on copyright
The Info-soc directive has not yet been implemented in Sweden.

Confidential Information

Confidential information is protected most efficiently by identifying the information as confidential and carefully managing the disclosure process.

Disclosure should be made on a "need to know" basis only, and only subject to the recipient (whether an employee, a consultant or other business partner) undertaking an express obligation to secrecy.

If the recipient has not undertaken an express obligation to secrecy, he or she will in most situations (in particular in an employment relationship) be under an implied obligation to secrecy which follows from a general obligation of confidence in the contractual relationship between the parties. Obviously, such implied obligation to secrecy is generally more limited that an express contractual obligation.

Trade Secrets are protected under the Act of trade secrets (1990:409). Thus the act is only applicable if anyone has obtained unauthorized access to the trade secrets of that business. Violation of the Trade secret Act is a criminal offense and subject to a fine and imprisonment of up to two years.

Competition

In Sweden, the European Community competition law applies directly together with the national competition law as regulated under the Swedish Competition Act (1993:20).

Sweden

The Swedish competition law has largely been harmonized with the European competition law.

Generally, the Swedish Competition Authorities deal with matters that only or primarily affect Sweden, irrespective of the fact that they may affect trade between member states, whereas the Commission deals with matters that affect more member states and thus has Community dimension.

Action against unfair competition is regulated through the Swedish Marketing Act.

Useful Industry Contacts

The Swedish Patent Office ("Patent och registreringsverket") grants patents, designs and trade marks in Sweden: www.prv.se

Swedish Competition Authority ("Konkurrensverket") administers the Swedish competition act: www.kkv.se

Nic-se administers the .se top level domain: www.nic-se.se

Confederation of Swedish Enterprise ("Svenskt Näringsliv") The Confederation of Swedish Enterprise represents small and medium-sized member companies. www.svensktnaringsliv.se

Stockholms Handelskammare is the Stockholm Chamber of Commerce: www.chamber.se

Svensk Form. Svensk Form is a design centre with exhibitions, café, library, periodicals room, picture archive and shop. It also offers a program of seminars and lectures: www.svenskform.se

The Swedish Anti Counterfeit group (SACG) The organization is engaged in activities against counterfeiting within Europe: www.sacg.org

Sweden

Chapter 28:
United Kingdom

United Kingdom

By Angus Phang and Alexandra Wenderoth
(Willoughby & Partners in association with Rouse & Co. International)

Introduction

Current issues affecting intellectual property

Intellectual property in the United Kingdom plays an important role in an increasingly broad range of areas, ranging from the Internet to health care to nearly all aspects of science, technology, literature and the arts. Currently, intellectual property law in the United Kingdom is evolving to accommodate developments in the fields of biotechnology, nanotechnology and pharmaceuticals. The law is also growing in the areas of personality rights and data protection to secure the privacy of individuals. Further, many industries are grappling with the parallel importation issues discussed in the European Community chapter. The expansion of trade competition in recent years has brought about strong and often conflicting demands in the United Kingdom for wider intellectual property protection which the law is striving to meet.

Legislation

The key statutes on intellectual property in the United Kingdom include the Patents Act 1977, the Copyright, Designs and Patents Act 1988 and the Trade Marks Act 1994. Additional measures are introduced constantly, most commonly arising from European Community directives.

Patents

What is the application procedure?

Patent law in the United Kingdom is regulated by the Patents Act 1977. The process of applying for a patent is complex and can be time consuming. The application for a patent must include a detailed description of the invention and a

---

Angus Phang and Alexandra Wenderoth are attorneys at Willougby & Partners in London and Oxford, the local legal practice of Rouse & Co. International. Rouse & Co. is an intellectual property consultancy, providing a full range of IP services. Mr. Phang specialises in all aspects of IP and IT law, with a particular emphasis on brand protection, technology transfer, e-commerce law and data protection, and intellectual asset management. Ms. Wenderoth specialises in non-contentious IP, including IPR registration and portfolio management, brand and product clearance, licensing and commercial agreements, IPR acquisition and due diligence.

United Kingdom

set of claims stating the parts of the invention for which protection is required. The drafting of the specification and claims is a very precise discipline and the degree of protection achieved depends on how well such claims are drafted. Often it proves necessary to discuss the drafting of claims with the Patent Office. It is therefore advisable for prospective applicants to consult patent agents and/or their solicitors before filing an application.

It is critical that details of an invention which is to be patented are not disclosed prior to the filing of an application. Such disclosure includes the products themselves as well as any literature relating to the products. If they are disclosed, then this may only be in circumstances of confidence, and so a confidentiality agreement should be used. It is possible to file an initial 'priority document' and rely on the date of that document provided a formal application is filed within one year.

Before filing a patent application and incurring the associated fees, it is advisable to search what is known as the 'prior art'. This means a search to determine if a similar patent has been granted in the past for the invention or parts of the invention. A patent cannot be granted for an invention which is not new. Most patent agents will have access to search facilities or alternatively potential applicants can procure their own search through a specialist provider such as The Science Reference and Information Service.

Once the application has been filed, the Patent Office will carry out a preliminary examination to ensure that all relevant formalities have been completed. Unless a 'fast-track' approach has been adopted, it will take approximately 18 months from the filing date of the initial application before the patent specification and claims are published by the Patent Office. Third parties are thereby put on notice that the application is pending.

The Patent Office then conducts a substantive examination to see if the invention is new and non-obvious. Then, if all goes well, the patent will be granted on payment of the appropriate fee, with notice of such grant appearing in the Official Journal. Following publication of the notice, the patentee, as he or she is now known, will receive a certificate of grant.

How long does a patent last?

Patents are granted for a period of 20 years from the filing date of the application, subject to the payment of annual renewal fees in respect of the fifth and subsequent years of the life of the patent. Therefore, for the first four years there is no requirement to renew. For each year after the fourth year a renewal fee must be paid.

United Kingdom

To whom can a patent be granted?

A patent will only be granted to the inventor or anyone else who is legally entitled to ownership. An example of someone else being legally entitled to ownership is where the inventor is an employee who creates the invention during the course of normal duties under his or her contract of employment. In these circumstances the right of ownership of the patent vests in the employer. (It should be noted in passing that employee inventors in the United Kingdom may be entitled to compensation from their employer under the Patents Act 1977.)

Once granted, is the patent safe?

A patent may be attacked during its life for a variety of reasons, including that the invention was not new, was obvious or did not have industrial applicability (in which case the patent will be rendered invalid). Another ground is that the patent was not granted to the correct person (in which case the patent will be revoked).

What rights does a patent give?

Once a patent has been granted, the patentee is entitled to protect its legal monopoly and prevent others from exploiting any invention which falls within the scope of the patent.

Exploitation

It is possible to protect patent rights as from the date the application is made. The application can be protected directly by the applicant or assigned or licensed to a third party. An applicant may choose to license or assign the right if, for example, the application of the product, method or process falls outside the scope of the applicant's normal business activities or if the applicant lacks the financial, staff or technological resources to fully exploit such rights.

Infringement

Patent infringement actions in the United Kingdom have traditionally been brought in the Patents Court, part of the Chancery Division of the High Court. However, due to the complex rules and the associated costs, patent-related litigation can be long and expensive. Since 1988, however, it has also been possible to bring small and less complicated patent disputes before the Patents County Court. This has provided a cheaper and more informal alternative to the High Court.

Streamlined Court procedure

The Patents Court Guide, which came into effect on April 1, 2003, has now introduced a streamlined procedure in which (subject to any other Order) all fac-

United Kingdom

tual and expert evidence must be in writing; there are no discovery or experiments; cross examination is limited; and the total duration of the trial will normally be no more than a day. The trial date, to be fixed when the Order for streamlined procedure is made, will normally be about six months thereafter. An Order for streamlined procedure will be made by agreement or, in the absence of agreement, by the Court where application of the 'overriding objective' indicates it is appropriate. Application for the streamlined procedure may be made at any time after commencement of the action, but should be made at the earliest time reasonably possible.

A party wishing to adopt the streamlined procedure should first invite the other party to agree. If it does, the Court will normally make the Order. If it does not, application must be made to the Court, supported by a witness statement addressing the 'overriding objective' criteria. The Court will determine the matter provisionally on the basis of the written statements of both parties and, unless either side seeks an oral hearing, the provisional Order will come into effect seven days after its service on the parties.

Designs

Registered Designs
Legislation
Registered designs in the United Kingdom are regulated by the Registered Designs Act 1949. United Kingdom registered design law applies in England, Scotland, Wales, Northern Ireland, the Isle of Man, Brunei, Fiji, Gibraltrar, Truks and Caicos Islands, Tuvalu and Vanuatu.

What is a design?
The definition of a design (see Chapter 2) is the same for both United Kingdom and European Community forms of protection.

Registered designs and trade marks compared
Recent changes to the design legislation appear to blur the distinction between trade marks (particularly logo/3D trade marks) and registered designs. Registered design protection may now offer owners an alternative form of protection for trade marks which may be susceptible to objection until sufficient use is made to help qualify for trade mark registration.

Registration process
To apply for a registered design, you must complete an official application form and submit it to the United Kingdom Designs Registry (part of the United

Kingdom Patent Office). The application must be accompanied by two sets of diagrams or photographs of various labelled views of the product (both head on and perspective) which clearly illustrate the features you wish to register. The Registry conducts a simple examination of the application and if it meets the formal requirements for registration it will generally qualify for registration. A straightforward registered design will generally be protected in the United Kingdom within two months of being filed. As with European Community designs, a registered design remains in force for a maximum of 25 years, provided renewal fees are paid every five years.

Prior disclosure - 12 month grace period
United Kingdom registered designs also benefit from the 12-month grace period in respect of prior disclosure discussed in the Registered Design Right section of Chapter 3.

Commissioned designs
A commissioned design is defined as a design 'created in pursuance of a commission for money or money's worth'. Unlike in the European Community, in the United Kingdom a person who commissions a design is treated as the owner of the design.

Infringement
The owner of a registered design has the exclusive right to 'use any design which does not produce on the informed user a different overall impression'. The design owner has the right to restrain third parties from using similar designs, including making, selling, stocking, importing or exporting goods made to those designs.

Acts involving use of a design (or a similar design) which would otherwise infringe the design owner's rights will not necessarily be found to infringe if they are done for non-commercial, educational or experimental purposes.

Unregistered Design Right
What is unregistered design right?
Unregistered 'design right' is an intellectual property right which applies to original, non-commonplace designs of the shape or configuration of products. You do not have to apply to register design right. It is similar to copyright in that the protection arises automatically when the design is recorded in a design document or incorporated in an article.

United Kingdom

History

Design right was introduced in the United Kingdom to bring an end to artistic copyright protection for industrial designs. It was considered that copyright protection was too broad and long-lasting to apply to prosaic industrial articles. The United Kingdom unregistered design right is quite different from the Unregistered Community Design Right. It is regulated under the Copyright, Design and Patents Act 1998.

What can be protected?

The design must be for the shape or configuration of a three-dimensional product. Two-dimensional designs will not qualify (although these are likely to qualify for copyright and possibly registered design protection). The design need not be novel, but it must be original (meaning 'not copied') and must not be commonplace in the design field in question at the time of its creation. The more similarities there are between the article and others in the same design field, the greater the chance the design is commonplace.

Exclusions

Design right does not subsist in:

- surface decoration;
- methods or principles of construction;
- features of an article which enable it to fit or match another article (known as the 'must fit' and 'must match' exceptions); or
- spare parts used for repair purposes (for example in cars).

Qualification

Generally, only designs created or commissioned by nationals, residents or companies of the European Community, and nationals of New Zealand and the United Kingdom colonies, are protected by design right. While other countries may also qualify, the United States is not among them. In certain circumstances, protection may also be achieved if the article is first marketed in the United Kingdom.

Commissioned designs

A person who commissions an unregistered design is treated as the owner of the design.

What rights does it give?

Design right is not a monopoly right but a right to prevent copying. It lasts for 10 years from first marketing products made to the design, subject to an overall limit of 15 years from creation of the design.

United Kingdom

Design right is an 'exclusive right' for five years after first marketing and, as such, is infringed by unauthorised dealing in such products. Design right then becomes subject to licenses of right for the remaining five years of its term, during which time anyone is entitled to a license on fair terms to produce and trade products copying the design. However, the rights owner will not be required to make its know-how available to that person. A design right is property that may be bought, sold, licensed or used as security.

Infringement

The test for infringement is slightly different than for that under copyright law in that mere proof of copying is insufficient. The plaintiff must also show that the article produced by the defendant is identical or substantially similar to the original article which incorporates the design. Infringement also occurs if the defendant:

- imports the infringing article into the United Kingdom for commercial purposes;
- has possession of the infringing article for commercial purposes; or
- sells, lets for hire, offers or exposes for sale or hire in the course of a business the infringing article, where the defendant knows or has reason to believe the article is an infringing article.

Trade Marks

Registered trade marks

Trade marks in the United Kingdom are regulated under the Trade Marks Act 1994.

Registrability and the application procedure

The types of marks that can be registered in the United Kingdom are as discussed in the European Community chapter. In the United Kingdom, the applicant must be using or intending to use the mark on the goods or services applied for.

The United Kingdom Trade Marks Registry will examine each application and, broadly, will reject any mark which:

- is not sufficiently distinctive or is merely descriptive (e.g. Lavender Soap for lavender scented soap), unless the applicant can adduce sufficient evidence to show that the mark has acquired distinctiveness through extensive use; or
- is contrary to public policy or likely to deceive or confuse the public.

Intellectual Property Law in the European Community

United Kingdom

The Trade Marks Registry will also search the Register for any conflicting prior applications or registrations and will object to the application if it considers any of the earlier marks to be too similar. This objection can be overcome if the applicant can show that the owner of the earlier mark consents to concurrent use by the applicant of its similar or identical mark.

If the mark is accepted it will be advertised in the "Trade Marks Journal" thereby giving third parties the opportunity to oppose the application on relative or absolute grounds before registration is finally granted.

A straightforward trade mark application should be registered within nine months of filing.

How long does trade mark registration last?

Trade marks can currently be registered for an initial period of 10 years and are renewable thereafter in perpetuity for further 10-year periods upon payment of renewal fees. Trade mark registrations can however be revoked, in full or in part, if the mark has not been used for a continuous period of five years. It is up to a third party to bring such a challenge.

What rights does it give?

A registered trade mark gives the registrant exclusive rights to prevent others from:

1. using a mark identical to the registrant's mark in relation to identical goods or services;
2. using a mark:
   (a) identical to the registrant's mark in relation to similar goods or services; or
   (b) similar to the registrant's mark in relation to identical or similar goods or services, where there is a likelihood of confusion on the part of the public; and
3. using a mark identical or similar to the registrant's mark in relation to identical, similar or dissimilar goods or services if its use takes unfair advantage of or is detrimental to the registrant's mark's reputation in the United Kingdom.

Advantages of registration

While trade marks do not need to be registered to enjoy some degree of legal protection, if a trade mark has been registered it is much easier to bring an action for trade mark infringement as, generally, the claimant is not required to produce evidence of established goodwill or show that damage has been suffered each time an action is brought.

United Kingdom

Unregistered trade marks

Trade marks do not need to be registered to confer rights to legal protection on their owners. This is because the law of passing off enables a trader to protect his or her business from unfair competition by allowing him or her to restrain another from trading in such a way as to cause the public to confuse the traders or their products. There are three basic requirements which a claimant must fulfill if it is to bring a successful action in passing off:

(i) that the claimant has used the mark in such a way as to establish a reputation or goodwill in respect of the claimant's goods or services;

(ii) that the defendant, in the course of his trade or business, has made a misrepresentation as to the origin of goods or services; and

(iii) that, as a result, the claimant has suffered, or is likely to suffer, actual damage to its business or reputation.

However, due to practical difficulties and costs involved in obtaining the necessary evidence to sustain an action for passing off (proving reputation and goodwill is notoriously difficult) many traders prefer to register their names, marks and logos at the Trade Marks Registry.

Domain names and brand protection on the internet

Nominet UK is the registry for all .uk domain names (www.nic.uk).

It is worth noting a number of issues that have arisen in the context of brand protection on the internet.

Disputes often arise where parties wish to register a name for the purposes of selling it to somebody else rather than using it themselves ('cybersquatting').

A dispute may also arise where a party uses its competititor's trade mark in the metatag for a page of its own website so that users using a search engine to find information about the competitor will be directed to that party's site instead.

Similarly, gateway sites are available which allow people to type in a well-known company name as a keyword to find relevant information about that company. If the directory then points to information about an unrelated company, this may be caused by private search engines selling "keywords" to businesses so that when users search for a particular name or trade mark, the payer's information or banner advertisement appears, instead of or in addition to information about the actual brandowner whose name is in the keyword.

The above activities may amount to trade mark infringement.

Resolution of such claims will involve taking legal action or making use of the available dispute resolution procedures.

United Kingdom

Copyright and Related Rights

What is copyright?

The law of copyright protects a wide variety of original works including those embodied in books, photographs, paintings, sculpture, music, drama, records, films, CDs, videos, architecture, computer software, broadcasts, and the typographical arrangements of published works. It also protects literary, dramatic, musical or artistic works which are computer generated (the author of which will be the person who undertakes the arrangements necessary for creation of the work).

Copyright in the United Kingdom is regulated by the Copyright, Design and Patents Act 1998.

Do I need to register copyright?

It is not necessary or possible to register Copyright in the United Kingdom. However, because of this, proving ownership of copyright can be difficult unless proper written records are kept.

Copyright notice

It is advisable to attach a copyright notice to the work, setting out the © symbol followed by the copyright owner's name and date of publication. Although this is not essential in the United Kingdom to prove ownership, it can help in infringement proceedings. It may be needed to show copyright in certain foreign jurisdictions, and can therefore serve as a warning notice to others against copying.

What rights does copyright give?

Copyright does not protect against independent development of the same ideas, only against the actual copying of another's work. It can also however prevent unauthorised use of copies of a work, such as preventing lending, rental, issuing, distributing copies to the public, showing, broadcasting, performing or adapting the copyright material, or putting the copyright material on the internet.

Term

The term of copyright in the United Kingdom is in accordance with the European Community directive discussed in the European Community chapter.

What else does copyright protect?

Rights similar to but distinct from copyright also apply in the United Kingdom to protect:

- the work of performers (such as musicians, actors and dancers) in respect of recording and distributing copies of their performances; and

United Kingdom

- databases, where there has been a substantial investment of financial, human or technical resources in obtaining, verifying or presenting the material constituting the database.

Moral rights, an additional category of similar but distinct rights, also exist. These rights vest in many, but not all, copyright works. They prevent, among other things, 'derogatory treatment' of works and can require the author's name to appear with the work.

Recent European Community directive on copyright

On October 31, 2003 the United Kingdom implemented regulations to bring into force the European Community copyright directive on new economic rights discussed in the European Community chapter[1].

The Regulations will grant all copyright owners new economic rights, including:

- the right to control any communication to the public of their works by electronic transmission, including in such a way that members of the public may access them from a place and at a time individually chosen by them (for example, by downloading works from the internet). This is wider than the old concepts of 'broadcasting' and 'cable programmes'); and
- a new exclusive right given to performers to control the making of recordings of their performances available to the public (previously performers were only given rights to reimbursement in such cases).

The Regulations also protect against devices and services which illegally circumvent the technical measures used by copyright owners to protect their works against unauthorized reproduction and other infringement.

Confidential Information

Confidential information, such as industrial and commercial secrets and know-how, are by their very nature highly sensitive. In some cases confidential information can be one of the most valuable assets of businesses—witness the formula for Coca-Cola. Copyright generally only protects the expression of an idea and not the idea itself. To be protected at law, business information must be kept secret and confidential and it must be identifiable and of some potential commercial interest.

'Trade secrets' and 'know-how' compared

There is a distinction between 'trade secrets', which an honest person of reasonable intelligence would recognize as such, and the general knowledge, acquired skill and 'know-how' of a company's employees. While trade secrets are likely to enjoy protection under the general obligation of confidence, general know-how

United Kingdom

will probably only attract protection under an express contractual provision.

Protection of confidential information

Businesses with such assets (and those investing in them) must recognize the importance of protecting their confidential information—for example, by ensuring staff do not disclose any information to persons who do not 'need to know' whether inside or outside the workplace; imposing non-disclosure covenants for a period after employees leave the business; or requiring possible business partners to sign confidentiality agreements prior to disclosure.

Obligations of confidentiality may be implied in the absence of a contract, where information is imparted in circumstances importing an obligation of confidence. To attract protection, the confidential information must have the quality of confidence and must not be trivial.

However, where possible, businesses should not seek to rely on implied confidentiality but should buttress confidential information with the kind of contractual obligations outlined above, as contractual damages are often higher than those awarded for 'breach of confidence' which is much more difficult to prove.

There is no legal remedy for disclosure of a trade secret which was discovered independently by a third party and subsequently made known to the public.

Patents and designs

Contractual protection of confidential information is critical in the area of patents and designs, which can be rendered invalid if it is proved that they were disclosed to third parties before their filing date with the particular registry other than under obligations of strict confidentiality.

Exploitation

Assuming they are protected, trade secrets are a valuable asset to a business and can be exploited like any other. Frequently patents and associated know-how are licensed to third parties together, as a bundle of rights, helping to develop the business and providing royalty income to the proprietor.

Employer/employee relationship

In the employment context, a distinction is drawn between the extensive duty of confidence owed by employees during the term of their employment and the more limited duty owed after termination of their employment. After an employee has left an employer, the main interests the ex-employer can protect are goodwill in its customers and its trade secrets.

United Kingdom

Modern contracts often go further than this and impose restrictions on former employees setting up in competition, as it is easier to prove that a former employee has set up a rival business than that he or she has used confidential information.

Remedies

Remedies for breach of confidence include injunctions (important if the plaintiff hopes to contain the confidential information before its release), account of profits, delivery up or destruction under oath, and damages.

Competition

In the United Kingdom, competition law is subject to the regime outlined in the European Community chapter.

This regime co-exists with the national Competition Act 1998, which prohibits anti-competitive agreements (agreements which have the effect of preventing, restricting or distorting competition) unless they have received an individual exemption from the Director General of Fair Trading, or are the subject of a block exemption which exempts whole categories of agreements.

Practical Tips for Protection of Intellectual Property

Awareness

Many companies do not recognize the valuable intellectual property that exists in their assets: not only in their products but also in packaging and advertising material. Companies are well advised to run brand awareness campaigns and training in basic intellectual property concepts across their business.

Audit

A key determinant of how well intellectual property will be protected against deliberate or unwitting imitation by competitors is whether title to the original intellectual property can be proved.

Meticulous written records of the development of intellectual property should always be maintained and kept in a secure environment. For example, an industrial design team should keep log books of its prototypes and all other data relating to the conception of its designs. All drafts should be labeled, dated and signed. Confidential information should, to the extent possible, be kept separate from other documents, and documents containing confidential information should be prominently marked 'Strictly Private and Confidential'.

United Kingdom

Data security

Data should be secured by way of both physical and electronic safeguards such as restricted access, passwords and encryption software. Data should only be provided on an 'as needs' basis to employees, and should never be disclosed to third parties except under obligations of strict confidence and where a rigorous confidentiality agreement has been put in place. This is particularly important where the validity of the intellectual property in question can be undermined by its disclosure to third parties, for example in the case of patents and designs.

Clean rooms

The use of a 'clean room' environment (a situation in which intellectual property is developed without reference to the pre-existing intellectual property in the relevant field, or 'prior art') can lend strength to an argument that the intellectual property so conceived does not infringe the intellectual property rights of others. This will be most appropriate in very competitive fields where there is extensive prior art on the types of intellectual property being created.

Contractual protection

Many companies also fail to implement adequate contractual protection for their intellectual property. For example, when commissioning the creation of anything from advertising copy to industrial designs, a document should be put in place assigning the intellectual property rights in the creation from the creator to the company. Otherwise, the creator may assign the rights in the creation to a competitor.

Professional advice

Finally, sound professional advice should always be sought on the legal and commercial strategies for protecting intellectual property to ensure that valuable ideas, in which so much creative endeavour has been invested, are not lost forever.

Footnotes

[1] 2001/29/EC of the European Parliament and of the Council of May 22, 2001 on the harmonisation of certain aspects of copyright and related rights in the information society.

Useful Industry Contracts

The United Kingdom Patent Office is responsible for copyright, designs, patents and trade marks in the United Kingdom
www.intellectual-property.gov.uk

United Kingdom

PACT (the Producers Alliance for Cinema and Television) is a United Kingdom trade association representing independent television, feature film, animation and interactive media production companies. Membership benefits include access to standard form contracts. www.pact.co.uk

The Publishers Association (PA) is the main representative organisation for book, journal and electronic publishers in the UK. Its website contains guidance notes for contracts between publishers and authors. www.publishers.org.uk

British Computer Society (BCS) is the leading professional and learned Society in the field of computers and information systems. www.bcs.org.uk

The National Computing Centre (NCC) is an independent membership and research organisation whose mission is to promote the more effective use of information technology. www.ncc.co.uk

Other contacts
See also the links at:
www.intellectual-property.gov.uk/std/resources/ip_organisations/index.htm

Chapter 29: Afterword

Afterword

By Angus Phang and Alexandra Wenderoth
(Willoughby & Partners in association with Rouse & Co. International)

Protecting Intellectual Property

The greatest strength of intellectual property rights lies in the protection they bring to the product or brand in question in the key market territories. But their strength is not automatic. Intellectual property rights need to be well protected and looked after, both at the stage of any initial registration requirement and later on. Although business prudence may suggest that it is not cost-effective to protect intellectual property rights in territories where the sales do not justify the cost, in an increasingly global market, the rights holder now has to consider the risk of products flooding into major sales territories from unprotected markets.

Exploiting Intellectual Property

Intellectual property as an asset

Intellectual property rights are assets which can be owned, licensed or assigned. Intellectual property rights can also be mortgaged or used as security. Indeed, a company that has a standard bank overdraft secured by a debenture may well already use its intellectual property in that way, often without being fully aware of the fact. In having done so, it may no longer be free to deal with or license that intellectual property without the bank's permission.

A company can offer its intellectual property alone as security, rather than as part of a mortgage of its entire property and undertaking. However, intellectual property has an obvious disadvantage as the basis of security in that it is of uncertain realisable value and life-expectancy. In this regard not all intellectual property is equal.

Angus Phang and Alexandra Wenderoth are attorneys at Willougby & Partners in London and Oxford, the local legal practice of Rouse & Co. International. Rouse & Co. is an intellectual property consultancy, providing a full range of IP services. Mr. Phang specialises in all aspects of IP and IT law, with a particular emphasis on brand protection, technology transfer, e-commerce law and data protection, and intellectual asset management. Ms. Wenderoth specialises in non-contentious IP, including IPR registration and portfolio management, and licensing and commercial agreements.

Afterword

The value of intellectual property assets

A well-established brand clearly has an ascertainable value, but because of the different methods of valuing brands, expert valuers might legitimately arrive at significantly different figures.

Problems are also likely to arise in seeking to value, for instance, leading-edge patents, where the value is to a large degree speculative, or fashion-led products, such as computer games, where the market is extremely fickle.

It is worth entering a word of caution here about the commercial value of intellectual property rights in themselves. Although a good, strong intellectual property portfolio is, as we have discussed, undoubtedly a valuable commercial asset, it does not in itself guarantee business success. It is the end-product that will succeed or fail in the marketplace, but only after considerable time, effort and expense has already been expended in marketing and sales. It is worth remembering that only about 10% of patents actually recoup the expense incurred in obtaining them, and only about 1% produce the profit levels that are generally imagined to derive from the legal monopoly of a new invention. Ultimately, in valuing intellectual property, it is difficult to separate the market value of the underlying intellectual property rights from the quality of the goods or services to which they are attached and the marketing skills used in their exploitation.

Intellectual Property in the European Community

The existence of a mosaic of different legal regimes regulating the intellectual property rights from country to country throughout the European Community can make the prospect of protecting and exploiting intellectual property rights in Europe seem formidable.

But with the integration of Europe through the European Community, although it is a gradual and piecemeal process, comes ever greater harmony among the laws of its Member States.

And the standard of professional advice on the world-wide protection, development, marketing and accounting for intellectual property has never been higher. The well-advised business should take away from its professional advisers not only a clear view of the process involved in protecting its intellectual property rights, but also a sound view on the commerciality of doing so.

Afterword